Manufacturing Political Trust

Performance measurement and targets have been widely criticised as distorting policy and engendering gaming – yet they continue to be widely used in government. This book offers an original new account explaining the persistent appeal of performance measurement. It argues that targets have been adopted to address a crisis of trust in politics, through creating more robust mechanisms of accountability and monitoring.

The book shows that such tools rarely have their intended effect. Through an indepth analysis of UK targets on immigration and asylum since 2000, it shows that far from shoring up trust, targets have engendered cynicism and distrust in government. Moreover, they have encouraged intrusive forms of monitoring and reform in public administration, with damaging consequences for trust between politicians and civil servants.

Despite these problems, performance measurement has now become embedded in techniques of public management. It has also become normalised as a way of framing policy problems and responses. Thus despite their acknowledge problems, targets are likely to retain their allure as techniques of political communication and governance.

CHRISTINA BOSWELL is Professor of Politics at the University of Edinburgh. She is author of '*The Political Uses of Expert Knowledge: Immigration Policy and Social Research*' (Cambridge, 2009). Christina is currently leading a major ESRC project entitled '*Seeing Illegal Immigrants: State Monitoring and Political Rationality*', which explores how public authorities in France, Germany and the UK have constructed and monitored irregular migrants since the 1960s.

Manufacturing Political Trust

Targets and Performance Measurement in Public Policy

CHRISTINA BOSWELL
University of Edinburgh

CAMBRIDGE
UNIVERSITY PRESS

CAMBRIDGE
UNIVERSITY PRESS

University Printing House, Cambridge CB2 8BS, United Kingdom

One Liberty Plaza, 20th Floor, New York, NY 10006, USA

477 Williamstown Road, Port Melbourne, VIC 3207, Australia

314–321, 3rd Floor, Plot 3, Splendor Forum, Jasola District Centre, New Delhi – 110025, India

79 Anson Road, #06–04/06, Singapore 079906

Cambridge University Press is part of the University of Cambridge.

It furthers the University's mission by disseminating knowledge in the pursuit of education, learning, and research at the highest international levels of excellence.

www.cambridge.org
Information on this title: www.cambridge.org/9781108421201
DOI: 10.1017/9781108367554

First published 2018

Printed in the United Kingdom by Clays, St Ives plc

A catalogue record for this publication is available from the British Library.

ISBN 978-1-108-42120-1 Hardback

Cambridge University Press has no responsibility for the persistence or accuracy of URLs for external or third-party internet websites referred to in this publication and does not guarantee that any content on such websites is, or will remain, accurate or appropriate.

Contents

Preface

This book is essentially about the relationship between information and governance. It engages with a long-standing interest of mine in how governments and international organisations produce and deploy different forms of knowledge to ground their legitimacy. In this sense, it is a sequel to my 2009 book *The Political Uses of Expert Knowledge: Immigration Policy and Social Research* (Cambridge University Press). But while that book focused on the (largely symbolic) uses of research, this one explores the deployment of more technocratic public management tools in the form of targets and performance measurement. My central argument is that we need to understand performance measurement not just as a tool for enhancing government capacity and accountability, but more broadly as a response to a crisis in political trust – at both the level of public trust in politics and of trust relations between politics and public administration. Performance measurement represents an attempt to reground trust through establishing precise and authoritative modes of signalling and monitoring government performance.

This book thus focuses on how governments – and the UK Government in particular – has used tools of performance measurement to produce or manufacture political trust. The verb 'to manufacture' has two meanings: to make something on a large scale using machinery, and to invent or fabricate. The classic contributions by Walter Lippmann, Edward Herman and Noam Chomsky on 'manufacturing consent' clearly build on elements of the second meaning: consent is secured through propaganda and manipulation.[1] My usage of the word is intended to be somewhat closer to the first meaning. I understand performance measurement as an attempt to

---

[1] Walter Lippmann, *Public Opinion* (New York: Harcourt); Edward S. Herman and Noam Chomsky, *Manufacturing Consent: The Political Economic of the Mass Media* (New York: Pantheon Books).

produce trust through the use of a complex array of management tools. But of course, we can also read such attempts as instances of duplicity or spin, so the second meaning is not irrelevant. One of the main insights of this book, however, is that governments are rarely successful in securing the trust they aim to enlist. Thus, the form of the present participle 'manufacturing' implies a work in progress: an attempt that does not generally result in success, but that nonetheless is something for which governments continually strive.

By focusing on the question of political trust, this book engages with a wider set of issues around political disaffection and mistrust of politics in democratic countries – questions that have become especially critical over the course of writing this book in 2015–17. I struggled with the question of how to deal with this development: does the rise of populism imply the need to radically rethink the role of performance measurement, or is this a temporary blip in patterns of political mobilisation that will settle down in the coming years? The compromise I settled on was to briefly explore a number of different scenarios linked to the rise of populist movements in part of the final chapter; but I am aware of the risks in forecasting political trends, and hope future readers do not judge me too severely on this.

The core of this book is the product of a three-year project on 'The Politics of Monitoring: Information, Indicators and Targets in Climate Change, Defence and Immigration Policy', generously funded by the UK Economic and Social Research Council. The idea of focusing on targets initially emerged from discussions with my Edinburgh University colleagues working in Science, Technology and Innovation Studies – Eugénia Rodrigues, Graham Spinardi and Steve Yearley. Through our collaboration on the project, these three colleagues helped me develop and clarify many of these ideas in this book. Hilary Cornish, Colin Fleming, Laura Martin and Ewen McIntosh provided valuable research assistance at different stages of the project. Colin Fleming in particular made an important contribution to the analysis in Chapter 4 of this book. Hilary Cornish carried out a number of the interviews. Ewen McIntosh assisted with the quantitative analysis of press coverage. And Laura Martin provided valuable assistance with editing the final draft.

Other colleagues at Edinburgh have been a fantastic source of feedback and support. Within Politics and International Relations, Philip Cook, Marc Geddes, Iain Hardie, James Mitchell and Mathias

Thaler offered very valuable suggestions on parts of this book. And I am especially lucky to have had the support of colleagues in the Centre for Science, Knowledge and Policy (SKAPE), which Steve Yearley and I set up in 2014. Many of my SKAPE colleagues – including Richard Freeman, Sotiria Grek, Fadhila Mazanderani, Martyn Pickersgill, Katherine Smith and Steve Sturdy – have offered excellent insights along the way. To Sotiria I owe a particular debt of gratitude: she has been a continual source of inspiration, ideas and support throughout the project, and I am privileged to have her as a colleague and friend.

Beyond Edinburgh, many colleagues and friends commented on various iterations of chapters, provided valuable feedback at seminars or paper presentations, or talked through the concepts. My thanks in particular to Frank Baumgartner, Clare Dunlop, Jennifer Elrick, Kijan Espahangizi, Wendy Espeland, Matthew Flinders, Shaun Gallagher, James Hampshire, Marc Mölders, Annabelle Littoz-Monnet, PerOla Oberg, Regine Paul, Claudio Radaelli, Jill Rutter, Rudolf Stichweh, Colin Talbot and Jan-Peter Voss. Matt Cavanagh was enormously helpful in sharing insights into the Ministry of Defence and Home Office, and in helping broker interviews. As ever, my sister Julia Gallagher offered excellent comments and encouragement throughout.

Most of all, thank you to my children, Imogen and Ben, for tolerating a mother who is too often distracted in the service of projects whose worth remains obscure. And to Alex, for bearing with me in so many ways.

1 | *Performance Measurement and the Production of Trust*

The use of performance measurement as a tool of governance is now ubiquitous across economically developed countries. Governments, public service agencies and international organisations have employed an array of such tools to monitor and evaluate performance. Indicators, targets and balanced scorecards have been used to guide and measure performance in organisations; rankings and league tables have been deployed to compare outcomes among groups of organisations or countries, while benchmarking and quality standards have been used to evaluate performance against specified standards. What these techniques have in common is a reliance on quantitative measures to monitor and assess the 'outcomes' or 'delivery' of organisations or services. Originally developed in the private sector, these techniques for monitoring and evaluating performance have been steadily rolled out across different public sector organisations since the early 1980s.

Advocates of performance measurement see such tools as bringing clarity and precision to public service goals. They enable citizens and consumers to monitor performance, thereby increasing transparency and informing choice. By monitoring the conduct and performance of public services, such tools create new mechanisms for holding governments and public sector organisations to account. And they provide incentives for those making and implementing policy to improve their performance, thus producing better governance (Boyne and Chen 2007).

Yet after more than three decades of performance measurement in public policy, most commentators agree that they have yielded few benefits, and many adverse effects. The use of such techniques is criticised from a range of perspectives. Tools of performance measurement are seen as focusing on a limited range of quantitative targets or indicators, thereby narrowing down the focus of policy-making and political debate to a small and often unrepresentative aspect of policy (Bevan and Hood 2006; Boyne and Law 2005; Diefenbach 2009; Pidd

1

2005). The information they produce is not effectively used or applied in decision-making (Talbot 2010; Taylor 2009; Walshe, Harvey and Jas 2010). They can create perverse incentives and encourage 'gaming' on the part of those setting and implementing them (Hood 2006; Hood and Peters 2004; James 2004; Smith 1995). The imposition of top-down and often simplistic quantitative targets and indicators can sap morale in organisations and erode trust (Diefenbach 2009; Hoggett 1996; Micheli and Neely 2010). Not least, such tools frequently fail as a means of demonstrating improvements in public services (Hood and Dixon 2010; James and John 2007; Pollitt 2006a). So they are not even trusted by the publics they are designed to persuade.

Not surprisingly, these acknowledged problems have produced some scepticism about performance measurement in policy circles. In the UK, for example, the Labour administration of 1997–2010 had been enamoured of performance measurement in its first few years of government, developing an elaborate system of targets across departments and at different levels of governance. But No. 10 appeared to cool off the use of targets towards the late 2000s, influenced by a growing perception that they were too clunky and centralised, and a realisation that the information they provided was not widely trusted as authoritative. The Conservative–Liberal Democrat administration that came to power in 2010 vowed to eschew targets as a technique for steering public administration. But analysis of departments in British government suggests that targets are far from dead or moribund. They may have been rebranded as 'strategic objectives', but as a recent study concluded, 'an informal culture of targets across Whitehall is thriving' (Richards, Talbot and Munro 2015). A similar tendency has been apparent in Australian government, where a commitment to simplifying performance measurement has produced little change in practice (Woelert 2015). The use of quantified, output-oriented tools for measuring performance appears to be as widespread as ever. Indeed, in some organisations, such as the Home Office, the Department of Education or the Department of Health, they have taken root to an unprecedented degree.

So what explains the appeal and tenacity of performance measurement? Existing accounts tend to see such tools as a technique of control. They are valued by 'principals' – whether elected politicians or senior managers of organisations – as a means of steering the performance of agents. This form of control, it is argued, is particularly important given the 'hollowing out' of the state (Rhodes 1994). Since the 1980s, many government functions have been outsourced to private and third sector organisations, or to quasi-autonomous agencies, or 'quangos'. The outsourcing of many areas of government activity has deprived the state of direct hierarchical oversight and control over the elaboration and implementation of policy. Governments have therefore turned to techniques of performance measurement to replace more traditional modes of command and control (Hood 1991; Pollitt 1990). As we shall see later in the chapter, this account is plausible as far as it goes. But it fails to explain why such techniques prove so tenacious, given their persistent and acknowledged shortcomings.

The first aim of this book is to provide an alternative account of the appeal of performance measurement. I want to understand the conditions that lead political actors to deploy such tools, both as a mode of political communication and as a means by which to steer the performance of public administration. I explore how political and organisational dynamics create a recurrent demand for tools that can vouchsafe performance and reduce uncertainty. My account builds on the work of Michael Power and others, who have understood such techniques as playing a symbolic role: they are valued as a means of signalling order and control. In his work on audits, Power argues that audits operate as 'rituals of verification', providing assurances where there are low levels of trust (Power 1997, 2003).

This book further develops this account in two ways. First, it elaborates the concept of *trust* as a basis for theorising the role of performance measurement. Performance measurement can be understood as a response to a wider problem of political trust: a reluctance to invest authority or resources in others to act on our behalf. The problem of trust manifests itself in two sets of relationships. The first concerns the relationship between politicians and their publics. Traditional resources for establishing relations of trust between politicians and voters – in the form of familiarity or symbolic sources of authority – have been eroded. Instead, political leaders need to fall back on alternative modes of producing trust. One important device is to create new mechanisms of accountability, by establishing forms of performance measurement. Targets – which will be the focus of this book – have emerged as a particularly appealing tool for producing trust. Politicians frequently deploy targets to signal their commitment to values and goals, and to establish credibility with sceptical and disillusioned voters.

The problem of trust is also evident in a second relationship: that between political leaders and their civil servants and public services providers. The relationship between political leaders and the organisations implementing policy has become increasingly fragmented and indirect, as policy-making and implementation have become more specialised and the arrangements for delivering services more complex (Rhodes 1997). These developments have heightened the problem of trust between politics and public administration. Performance measurement becomes a means of reassuring political leaders that they can monitor and steer the behaviour of organisations delivering on targets. Such tools create an aura of clarity and control, establishing precise goals, producing detailed information about organisational practices, and ostensibly providing senior managers and politicians with levers for influencing behaviour. Performance measurement offers a form of comfort for those grappling with complexity and uncertainty, a ritual that assuages anxiety where there are deficits of trust. Such techniques of monitoring can also send a signal to observers and critics that political leaders are effectively in control, that they are applying credible and robust tools of public management.

Indeed, tools of performance measurement possess a singular appeal and authority as a mode of producing trust. Their focus on outputs or outcomes promises an especially robust mode of verifying performance, one that claims to measure how policies impact people's lives. Thus they appear to offer an unrivalled tool of accountability. At the same time, their use of quantitative techniques invokes deep-seated notions of rationality, objectivity and precision. Once performance or goals have been translated into these standardised measurements, it becomes difficult to revert to the vaguer formulations that preceded them. Moreover, once adopted, performance measures can be appropriated to mop up a range of other political and organisational problems (Orlikowski 1992). Different actors in politics, the administration and the media can become invested in them for varying reasons. Targets, performance indicators, rankings and league tables can be taken up by those critiquing or scrutinising government in order to expose their transgressions. And they can be deployed within organisations to justify particular courses of action or to solve a range of internal problems.

This book focuses on one particularly favoured tool of performance measurement: the use of targets. Targets are especially adept at addressing the dual problems of trust described earlier in this chapter. They appear to offer a robust tool for steering public administration, through codifying clear and specific goals, and providing a tool for monitoring performance towards these goals. At the same time, they can be deployed as a tool of political communication, signalling a firm commitment to goals and establishing a mechanism for publics to hold their governments to account. The use of targets therefore offers an excellent case for exploring the appeal of performance measurement, both as a technique of control and as a signalling device.

But do targets and other tools of performance measurement succeed in this task of producing trust? The second aim of this book is to explore some of the tensions and paradoxes created by performance measurement, and targets in particular. One of these is what I term the chain of dependence. The adoption of ambitious, public-facing targets can be highly risky for politicians, placing them under heightened political scrutiny and pressure. Since targets tend to codify outputs or outcomes, this pressure is passed on to the public administration involved in delivering the promised outcomes. This can trigger intrusive forms of political intervention or engender persistent decoupling of formal compliance and informal practice in organisations. So targets can disrupt the already fragile settlement between political leaders and their civil servants. This in turn exacerbates problems of trust, creating a need for *more* tools for monitoring performance.

A further tension concerns the way in which targets are interpreted and applied in public administration. Despite their acknowledged defects, a variety of actors appropriate targets for different ends, and such tools become normalised, an expected part of bureaucratic management. But their deployment coexists with cynicism about their utility and with constant attempts to evade, reinterpret or subvert them. Targets are communicated and deployed by different actors, even as they hold them in disdain. This irony will be familiar to anyone working in a large organisation (universities are a prime example). The governance of organisations is heavily influenced by key performance indicators, rankings and league tables; employees with different roles become committed to targets and indicators, often perceiving themselves as 'playing the game'. And yet these indicators and rankings become highly influential, establishing a new plane of reality (Rose 1991), which influences reputation and resource allocation.

We can identify a similar anomaly in the way publics and other audiences perceive targets. While these quantitative tools carry authority in certain settings, they are also frequently treated with scepticism or seen as irrelevant. Publics and the media may expect and demand clear signals of intent, but they are also profoundly wary of such promises. Some targets are ignored; others attract huge attention, but much of it negative. And yet political aspirants feel the need to lock themselves in to such pledges, and their opponents have strong incentives to invoke them in order to expose government failings. Thus targets can create a dysfunctional dynamic. They are marshalled to address a problem of trust. Yet they engender forms of scepticism that create the need to mobilise yet more resources to shore up trust (Shapiro 1987). So despite scepticism about the premises behind targets or the methods involved in calculating them, targets frequently become normalised as a way of describing policy problems and assessing outcomes. Indeed, we can characterise this as a form of irony: the widespread acceptance and use of modes of appraisal that are known to be deeply flawed.

This book will explore these tensions and paradoxes in the use of performance measurement. It will examine how targets emerge as an attempt to produce trust; what sorts of responses and adjustments they evoke from politicians, civil servants, the media and voters; and the range of effects they have on policy-making and political debate. The analysis shows clearly that targets have not succeeded in producing political trust, either on the part of voters or between political leaders and their bureaucracies. But the real interest of the analysis lies in investigating why targets should retain their appeal, despite these evident failings, and in exploring the range of often inadvertent effects that targets have on politics, administration and political trust.

In the pages that follow, I will set the scene for this analysis. I start by exploring the use of performance measurement in public policy, and review theories seeking to explain the trend. I sketch the contours of a different approach, building on theories of trust, as well as borrowing insights from organisational studies. I then introduce the focus of the study, the use of targets in UK government since 1998.

Performance Measurement in Public Administration

The past three decades has seen a huge expansion in performance monitoring across the globe (Talbot 1999: 15; Torres 2004). To be sure, the application of such tools has varied across countries, with Anglo-Saxon and Scandinavian countries, as well as the Netherlands, among the most enthusiastic (Torres 2004). But many other countries, including in continental Europe, Africa, Asia and Latin America, have introduced some form of performance measurement, whether at central or local government levels (Heinrich 2012; Pollitt and Bouckaert 2011; Van Dooren, Bouckaert and Halligan 2015). Government departments and public service providers are expected to gather data on multiple aspects of their activities, and to make this information publicly available for scrutiny. International organisations and NGOs have been keen to get in on the act. The OECD, European Commission, UN agencies and various third sector organisations have been avidly promoting targets, performance indicators, rankings and league tables for comparing and evaluating the performance of governments.

Much of this attention has been focused on monitoring *processes*. Since the 1980s, many governments have rolled out systems for monitoring efficiency and value for money in public sector management (Talbot 1999). Indeed, scholars such as Power (1997, 2000, 2003) and Strathern (2000) have explored how public management is subject to increasingly wide-ranging and complex systems of verification, revolving around the scrutiny of organisational processes and procedures. Many of these practices involve monitoring financial and administrative conduct and procedures through forms of audit.

Arguably even more striking, however, is the rise in tools for measuring outputs and especially *outcomes*, or 'delivery'. Outputs are typically understood as the 'immediate results' produced by governments and their agencies (Treasury 2000); while outcomes are understood as their 'ultimate results' (Treasury 2000): the 'consequences, results, effects of impact of service provision' (Boyne and Law 2005: 254). In practice, they are often difficult to distinguish. Indeed, the demarcation between outputs and outcomes is largely contingent on how one defines policy goals. For this reason, in this book I refer to both types of performance measure as 'outcome' measures. Governments have made increasing use of instruments measuring outcomes, whether through quality standards, league tables, benchmarking, targets or performance indicators (Heinrich 2002).

This focus is valued as a way of correcting some of the biases of procedural monitoring, notably the potential for treating processes as an end in themselves, decoupled from their results. The measurement of outcomes homes in on how far particular approaches or actions contribute to achieving the desired policy or organisational goals. The focus on outcomes also has an important political dimension: the monitoring of outcomes is more likely to form the basis for how voters appraise a government's record or achievements. The relationship between policy outcomes and desired goals such as equality, fairness, prosperity or security is more direct. In this sense, the measurement of 'delivery' can be a tool for mobilising public support for government.

There has been extensive literature in the field of public administration seeking to explain the growth of such tools of monitoring. Performance measurement is typically understood as being part of the 'New Public Management' (NPM) (Hood 1991) or 'managerialism' (Pollitt 1990) that emerged in the 1980s. Christopher Hood suggests that NPM is characterised by seven doctrines, two of which are directly relevant to performance measurement. The first is NPM's penchant for 'explicit standards and measures of performance', in the form of quantified goals, targets and indicators. The second is its emphasis on performance 'outcomes', a preference for measuring 'results' rather than procedures (Hood 1991: 4–5). The use of performance measurement is thus seen as a central feature of NPM.

So what explains the emergence of NPM? One dominant account sees NPM as a means of asserting control over otherwise difficult-to-steer actors or processes. As we saw, in the 1980s many traditional state functions were outsourced to the private and third sectors, as well as to government agencies (Moran 2001; Rhodes 1994). The creation of a large number of quangos created new challenges for central government steering of many areas of public service delivery. Faced with a loss of control over these entities, governments developed new tools to retain indirect control (Christensen and Lægreid 2006; Hoggett 1996). Techniques such as performance review, staff appraisal systems, performance-related pay, quality audits, customer feedback mechanisms, league tables, chartermarks, quality standards and targets were developed to enable control at a distance (Hoggett 1996). Hoggett sees such tools as part of a new 'evaluative state', which was concerned to extend central government control over decentralised operations (23). Rose and Miller (1992: 187) similarly understand such techniques as a means of 'governing at a distance': governments 'enrol' the compliance of difficult-to-control organisations through inscribing certain technologies of data collection and evaluation.

These accounts share the thesis that performance measurement is a technique for retaining government control. Yet as I suggested earlier, there is extensive research suggesting that such techniques are failing to produce the desired effects. Targets have engendered various forms of distortions and gaming (Hood 2006; Hood and Peters 2004; James 2004; Smith 1995); led to a narrowing down of priorities and resources to the exclusion of other (less measurable) areas of policy (Bevan and Hood 2006; Boyne and Law 2005; Diefenbach 2009; Pidd 2005); produced confusion and inconsistency within and between organisations (Micheli and Neely 2010). These problems have also been widely acknowledged among policy-makers. Indeed, in the UK they generated increasing disillusionment with formal monitoring tools from the mid-2000s onwards. Given these obvious problems, what explains their persistent appeal?

One way of understanding the tenacity of targets is to explore their symbolic functions. Targets can have at least two types of symbolic use. The first relates to their potential to provide a form of psychosocial certainty for those setting them. Governments and core executives are clearly anxious about their capacity to control the individuals and organisations involved in public service delivery. They face serious impediments in their attempts to steer these processes, as has been long identified in literature on principal–agent relations (Shapiro 2005). 'Principals', understood in this case as political leaders, and their 'agents', the civil servants they are trying to steer, often have divergent preferences. And civil servants tend to have access to privileged information about the intricacies of organisational practices and policy implementation. Information asymmetries and divergent preferences mean that those elaborating and implementing policy often have substantial scope to reinterpret or even subvert political goals. This anxiety can be usefully respecified as a problem of trust: a reluctance on the part of political leaders or the core executive to endow civil servants with responsibility for acting on their behalf. Bestowing trust would imply making a leap of faith, under conditions of uncertainty.

Niklas Luhmann suggests that politicians attempt to address this asymmetry through creating 'symbols of trustworthiness': indicators or thresholds, the transgression of which may result in the withdrawal of trust (Luhmann 1979). While political leaders cannot directly control public administration, they can control the extent to which they are prepared to trust these bodies. Establishing such conditions or thresholds helps reassure the truster that 'he is not trusting unconditionally, but rather within the limits and in proportion to specific, rational expectations. It is himself he must curb and control when he puts his trust in someone or something' (Luhmann 1979: 129). Understood in this sense, targets are a symbolic tool, established to provide psychological reassurance to those taking the risky step of endowing others with responsibility to act on their behalf.

Targets and performance indicators give the 'principal' a sense of control, even if this control relates more to her decision about when and why to bestow trust than to her actual control over the 'agent'. Of course, this is a very pessimistic account of steering, suggesting that the capacity of political leaders to steer public administration is highly circumscribed. But whether or not we accept Luhmann's scepticism about the possibility of steering (Luhmann 1997), it is a useful perspective for understanding the symbolic appeal of performance measurement. It suggests that targets retain their lure, even in cases where such tools prove inadequate or ineffective.

A second symbolic function of targets concerns their capacity to bestow credibility on political leaders and organisations. New, hyper-rationalist techniques imported from the private sector are seen as more legitimate governance techniques, especially in the face of uncertainty and risk (Power 1997, 2000). As with techniques of audit, such tools provide 'signals of order' (Power 2000: 118) or 'rituals of verification' (Power 1997), designed to restore faith in public administration. This implies that tools of new public management are not valued and appraised based on any objective or rational analysis of their effects. Rather, their appeal lies in their symbolic value, their usefulness as a means of signalling rationality and order (Power 1996: 92). They perform a cultural function, meeting expectations about appropriate and credible modes of steering.

This idea of ritual finds support in neo-institutionalist theories of organisations (DiMaggio and Powell 1983; March and Olsen 1976, 1983; Meyer and Rowan 1991). Rationalist techniques of control are adopted not so much as a means of controlling organisations, but to signal the soundness of procedures and practices (Feldman and March 1981). Organisations are under pressure to conform to expectations about legitimate structures, and they adopt what they consider to be modish and credible management principles and techniques. The appeal of such approaches as a way of legitimising the organisation can often trump considerations of performance. Such techniques may produce 'an image of tidiness and clarity', but this is 'unrelated to the work unit's actual performance' (Gupta, Dirsmith and Fogarty 1994: 269). Indeed, the use of such techniques is often at the expense of efficient or rational decision-making (Strang and Meyer 1993).

Performance Measurement and Political Trust

The notion of targets as a ritual or signalling device is helpful in understanding their cultural traction, and also their psychosocial appeal as a way of allaying anxiety under conditions of uncertainty. Yet this book suggests that in order to fully account for the allure of targets, we need to understand the political importance of these tools. Literature on public administration and organisational sociology tends to analyse performance measurement as a tool political leaders and core executives deploy to steer public administration. But as we saw, performance measurement – and targets in particular – also have an important outward-facing function. They are adopted to demonstrate to the public that the government is introducing improvements to public services, and delivering on its pledges. Targets create a tool of public accountability.

This outward-facing function of targets needs to be understood in the context of problems of public trust in politics and politicians. As many scholars have shown, citizens across democratic countries are experiencing declining confidence in government and in the system of politics. This is typically manifested in the form of political disenchantment, resulting in a disengagement from politics (Flinders 2009; Hay 2007; Stoker 2006). Voters appear profoundly disappointed with the performance of government, feel frustrated at the perceived lack of possibilities to influence politics and are increasingly cynical about politicians' motivations and conduct. One way in which politicians have attempted to respond to public scepticism is to signal their commitment to certain goals. They employ monitoring techniques to bind themselves to specific objectives and to vouchsafe these are being achieved. Improving public service performance and a focus on 'delivery' are common mantras deployed to establish political trust. They represent an attempt to produce public trust through locking governments in to clear pledges that resonate with voters' concerns.

Yet the emphasis on delivery creates a number of risks. By staking their credibility on tangible outcomes, political leaders are effectively creating a new mechanism through which they can be held to account. And it is one that focuses on outcomes rather than rhetoric and symbolic measures. Targets are designed to encourage voters to judge political leaders on what they do, not what they say. We would expect such a shift to make it harder for politicians then to fall back on rhetoric or cosmetic adjustments. Politicians will need to demonstrate that they are redeeming their pledges, and the performance measurement regime will typically provide tools to monitor such 'delivery' on a regular basis.

This emphasis on delivery raises important questions about the relationship between politics and the administration, and it is worth saying a few words about these two levels of policy-making. The distinction between politics and the administration has a long tradition in political science, and there are many ways of characterising the relationship between the two – in terms of actors, institutions, roles or tasks. The approach taken in this book is to draw the distinction in functional terms. In other words, the systems of politics and administration are identified with distinct tasks and logics of action, rather than with sets of actors or institutions. Following the work of Gianfranco Poggi, we can understand the political system as preoccupied with the competitive mobilisation of electoral support. Political parties mobilise support by framing rival demands for state action (Poggi 1990: 138). These demands are communicated through speeches, parliamentary debate, party manifestos and mass media coverage. Such communication tends to take the form of largely symbolic, declaratory politics, designed to resonate with public beliefs and values (Edelman 1999). These rituals of declaratory politics provide the broad – and often very approximate – framework for more detailed policy. It is at this level of symbolic politics that we can understand the use of targets as a tool of political communication. Targets are deployed to signal the commitment of political leaders to particular goals, as a means of shoring up public trust. They are thus largely symbolic interventions, aimed at mobilising support for particular policies and bolstering the credibility of political leaders.

However, by framing such commitments in terms of quantitative targets, politicians commit themselves to delivering a number of policy outcomes. And these need to be implemented by actors in the public

administration. Public administration refers to the government departments involved in translating broad political programmes into more
detailed collectively binding decisions, and overseeing the implementation of such decisions. Actors in the public administration are motivated by a rather different set of concerns to those driving the political
system. While organisations in the public administration are tasked
with elaborating the broad policies emanating from the political system, they are also preoccupied with responding to a range of other
pressures. As large organisations with complex tasks to achieve, they
need to generate loyalty and motivate their members (DiMaggio and
Powell 1991; Scott 1995). They also need to meet expectations from
key constituents in their environment about legitimate norms, goals
and structures. For example, they often need to conform to prevailing
ideas in their environment about appropriate management structures
or styles, or decision-making procedures (March and Olsen 1976), or
the use of expertise and evidence (Boswell 2009).

As Nils Brunsson and other organisational sociologists have argued,
these pressures often pull administrative departments in different direc-
tions (Brunsson 2002; Brunsson and Olsen 1993). And it is by no means
certain that organisations will passively conform to the wishes of their
political leadership. Organisations are adept at bypassing, diluting or
subverting attempts at political steering (Brunsson and Olsen 1993).
This is clearly the case with the implementation of tools of performance
measurement. Targets and indicators may conflict with a range of organisational values, beliefs and practices, creating conflicts and tensions for
the organisation. And this may engender forms of resistance or 'gaming'
as a response to externally imposed performance measurement.

One way organisations deal with these tensions is to detach their formal
rhetoric and structures from their informal structures. Formal rhetoric
and structures refer to the outward-facing image and communications of
the organisation, or what Luhmann calls the organisation's 'semantic'
(Luhmann 1964). Informal structures, meanwhile, refer to the norms,
beliefs and practices that guide the day-to-day actions of the organisation's members (Meyer and Rowan 1991). Meyer and Rowan term this
divergence 'institutional decoupling', a strategy for helping organisations
reconcile conflicting demands from their environments. As Brunsson and
Olsen point out (1993), such decoupling may also be a means of resisting
attempts at top-down reform of an organisation. Where politically driven
reforms do not accord with the organisation's informal structures, they

are likely to prove extremely difficult to implement. Resistance may not be simply due to organisational inefficiency or inertia. Rather, the attempts at change conflict with prevalent values, roles and routines within the organisation, and the maintenance of these informal structures and procedures may be critical to retaining the loyalty and motivation of members, and to enabling effective action. Thus rather than blithely implement targets or other forms of performance measurement, the organisation may combine a rhetorical commitment to change with merely cosmetic changes to its informal structures.

But the intriguing aspect of performance measurement is that it threatens to constrain this form of decoupling. Targets and indicators measure performance through precise criteria and robust monitoring techniques. And this may impede the organisation's attempts to decouple formal adjustments from informal practice. The imposition of specific, measurable performance indicators based on organisational outputs or outcomes can delimit the potential for deviant behaviour. Thus, strict performance measurement tools may lead to a 'tight coupling' or 'recoupling' of formal and informal practices (Espeland 1998; Hallett 2010). By exploring how organisations have responded to targets, we can therefore contribute to a more nuanced understanding of decoupling as an organisational response to top-down reform.

A second interesting aspect of performance measurement and organisational change concerns the often unanticipated effects of such tools. Even where targets are adopted in a cosmetic way – where organisations merely adjust formal structures without reforming their informal practices – such tools can still have a range of impacts on organisational behaviour. They can alter incentive structures and behaviour in unexpected ways; create tensions between different parts of the organisation; damage organisational morale; threaten or enhance the organisation's reputation or resources; and disrupt relations with its political leadership. Targets may not succeed in their goal of steering public administration, but they can still have major effects. By conceptualising politicians and the administration as distinct but interrelated spheres, we can help elucidate these effects. We can examine how targets emerge as a tool of symbolic politics; and how they go on to affect both relations of political trust between politicians and voters, and the relationship between politics and public administration.

In summary, the use of targets can engender important shifts in the relationship between politics and the administration. It creates a chain of dependency. Political leaders become more reliant on their civil service and other public service providers to deliver on their promises. Politics and the administration become even more tightly bound together by expectations about performance. And this in turn heightens the pressure on the administration to 'deliver' or 'perform', and exacerbates politicians' frustrations at their inability to steer government departments in the way they would like. The shift towards monitoringoutcomes or delivery implies a greater dependence on public administration to implement policy successfully.

Targets and Indicators in UK Policy

We can find an exemplary case of a shift towards performance measurement in UK policy from the 1980s onwards. UK governments have been particularly energetic in using performance indicators to steer the performance of public administration (Pollitt 2006a). This partly reflects a culture of government that is more 'managerial' than many of its European counterparts (Richardson 1982). It is also linked to party political ideologies: pro-business governments since 1979 – of both Conservative and Labour persuasion – have been keen to borrow lessons from the private sector. The influence of performance measurement can also be attributed to the strength of UK governments in rolling out radically new approaches. UK governments typically enjoy strong parliamentary majorities, and very few veto points in introducing administrative reform. Executive power is highly centralised in the 'core executive' (Dunleavy and Rhodes 1990: 3): the institutions, networks and practices surrounding the Prime Minister and his or her cabinet. This means that once new management philosophies and practices have been adopted by the core executive, they 'can be spread quickly and forcefully throughout the public sector' (Pollitt 2006a: 38).

The first significant use of performance measurement in UK government can be traced to the establishment of performance indicators in the early 1980s. In 1982, Margaret Thatcher's Conservative administration established a code of practice for the publication of local authority annual reports. These reports were designed to enhance accountability through providing information on 'performance and efficiency', including 'comparative statistics' (Smith 1990: 57). The publication of the data would place local authorities under pressure to improve their performance, by enabling a comparison of their performance and efficiency with those of other authorities. The use of indicators was further developed in relation to the National Health Service, with a series of 123 performance indicators for local health authorities published in 1983, most of these covering financial information. In this case, the value of indicators lay in their potential to improve the efficiency of health services and central government oversight (Smith 1990: 59). At the same time, the government was keen to instil general principles of performance measurement across the civil service. The Financial Management Initiative of 1983 suggested that it was essential for managers at all levels of government to develop 'performance indicators and output measures which can be used to assess success in achieving objectives' (cited in Carter 1991: 86). Neil Carter notes that the number of performance indicators in the Public Expenditure White Paper multiplied from 500 in 1985 to more than 2,000 by 1988 (Carter 1988).

In the early 1990s, performance indicators were given renewed emphasis as a tool for overseeing newly created executive agencies. Each new agency was required to publish performance targets in a Framework Agreement, and the Treasury was active in helping departments and agencies to 'develop a suitable "portfolio" of output and performance measures' (cited in Carter 1991: 87). As Carter wrote at the time of the initiative, performance measurement was seen as a way of delivering 'hands-off managerial control and democratic accountability: central departments, particularly the Treasury, need PIs to exercise control without breathing down the necks of the new chief executives; Parliament and the public need PIs to ensure that agencies are delivering the desired services efficiently and effectively' (Carter 1991: 87). Already, we can see a dual rationale emerging: targets were being valued as a means of enhancing performance, and as a tool for citizens to hold public authorities to account. The considerations underlying the use of performance indicators over this period were nicely distilled by Carter and his colleagues, writing at the end of Margaret Thatcher's period in office:

If there is to be value of money, then the activities and outputs of government have to be measured; if there is to be more accountability, then there has to be an accepted currency of evaluation; if there is to be decentralisation, and blocks of work are to be hived off without loss of control, then there has to be a way of assessing performance. (Carter, Day and Klein 1992: 1–2)

The project started under the Conservatives was taken to new heights under the leadership of Prime Minister Tony Blair and Chancellor Gordon Brown. Blair presided over three consecutive Labour administrations from 1997 to 2007, and was succeeded by his Labour Party colleague Gordon Brown in 2007–10. This period saw huge growth in the prominence and use of targets and performance indicators as tools of public administration. In 1998 the government conducted a Comprehensive Spending Review, which introduced performance requirements for government departments. Each department was instructed to introduce a series of improvements and reforms to the way it delivered its services, in order to justify more generous funding allocations. These targets were updated in 2000 with a comprehensive set of Public Service Agreements (PSAs), which were more outcome oriented. The new PSAs set out for each major government department 'its aim, objectives and the targets against which success will be measured' (Treasury 2000).

A key component was the measurement and monitoring of delivery of these targets, through annual departmental reports. Each objective should have at least one target which was 'SMART': specific, measurable, achievable, relevant and timed. PSAs were accompanied by Service Delivery Agreements, concluded between the Treasury (the UK's ministry of finance) and each department, which set out more specific, lower-level targets and milestones to support delivery of the PSA performance targets. In contrast to the previous Conservative government's more cautious approach to targets (Flinders 2001), these new PSA targets were intended to drive tangible improvements in the delivery of public services. Many of the targets were therefore set as 'stretch' targets, designed to engender a radical improvement in government. The ambition of these targets reflected the hubris of the Blair administration. As Michael Barber put it, 'given the political risks of not meeting targets . . ., this was a bold and risk-laden innovation' (Barber 2007: 50). But the government – at least in this initial phase – was confident it could deliver. Again, in Barber's words, 'nothing is inevitable: "rising tides" can be turned' (193).

Most commentators agree that the PSA targets represented an attempt by the core executive to steer organisations involved in public service delivery (James 2004: 387). The Labour government was keen to use targets to incentivise improved performance in government, and the Treasury in particular wanted to see a return on increased investment in public services. This ambition become more pronounced towards the end of the Labour Party's first term in government. From early 2001, the talk became all about 'delivery'. Blair was famously frustrated at what he saw as the civil service's inertia and resistance to reform (Blair 2010). He was determined to step up his agenda for improving public services in his second term. A former senior official in the Department of Health describes the palpable shift in government focus.

There was a really strong narrative around that election of the story now is delivery. Delivery as a word became a thing ... It was all about, so we've come in, we've had our reviews and we've started talking about the money. So now it's about delivery. How are we going to make stuff happen ... We are now going to have to show that we are genuinely making a difference on these areas and that we know what we're doing and that we can, we can do it. And as always, that we can do it quickly. (Interview, August 2014)

The focus on delivery prompted Blair to set up a new Delivery Unit in No. 10, led by Michael Barber. Established in 2001, the Prime Minister's Delivery Unit, as it came to be known, would 'design a system to ensure that departments really did turn the money into outcomes' (Barber 2007: 57). The commitment to targets was also clearly linked to political considerations. The government was keen to demonstrate to the public that it had brought about tangible improvements to public services. By setting publicly monitored targets, the public would be able to track the quality of their public services, and – it was hoped – reward the government for generating these improvements. As a former Cabinet minister put it, the assumption was that if you could show to the British public through meeting targets that you were managing the issue effectively, 'then the public would say, "that's fine the system is now managed and we're happy with that"' (Interview, June 2014).

UK government, and especially the Labour administration from 2000 to 2010, therefore offers an excellent case for examining the emergence and persistence of targets, as well as exploring their effects on policy-making and political debate. Labour's targets can be seen as an attempt at addressing problems of trust at two levels. They had an outward-facing function of reassuring the public of government commitment to improve performance; and they offered a means of monitoring the performance and thus steering the behaviour of public administration. They therefore provide an ideal site for exploring the relationship between performance measurement and political trust, and for examining the effects of targets on public administration and political trust.

Most of the empirical analysis (Chapters 3 to 7) focuses on the Labour administration targets on immigration and asylum over this period. Chapter 6 also analyses the Conservative Party's use of targets on immigration after 2010. Immigration and asylum constitutes a broad area of policy, covering legislation and programmes to manage the asylum system, regulate the entry and stay of different categories of immigrants, and control irregular migration. It has been a highly politicised area of policy since the late 1990s. Under the Labour government, considerable political and media attention was devoted to rising numbers of asylum applications, as well as problems of controlling irregular flows of migrants into the UK. These concerns generated a number of PSA targets, designed to improve the efficiency of asylum procedures in the Home Office. The government also used targets as a tool of political communication, the most notable examples being Blair's high-profile 2003 target to halve the number of asylum applications, and Home Secretary John Reid's 2005 targets on eliminating the 'backlog' of asylum applications.

By the late 2000s, asylum numbers had declined, and political attention had shifted to focus on the scale and impacts of labour migration to the UK. In a context of growing concern about rising levels of economic immigration, it was now the turn of the Conservative Party to set a target. In January 2010, Conservative Party leader David Cameron introduced a controversial pledge to reduce net migration, a target which was to become Home Office policy later that year under a Conservative-led coalition government. Targets on immigration and asylum have therefore been used as a means of signalling government commitment to manage migration flows, thereby creating public trust. And they have been employed to steer the executive organisations involved in elaborating and implementing policy, the Home Office and its UK Border Agency. The policy area therefore offers a clear case of the use of such techniques to both signal commitment to voters and steer what is seen as a dysfunctional civil service.

Two other features make immigration and asylum policy especially interesting. One is the fact that many important immigration and asylum goals were *not* codified as targets. Most notably, goals on irregular migration were never specified as targets. I will explore this omission later on in this book (Chapter 5). A second interesting aspect is the controversial nature of the targets adopted. Blair's asylum target and Cameron's net migration target were both widely criticised for simplifying policy goals and distorting priorities. Meanwhile, targets on the removal of failed asylum seekers and the net migration target both proved impossible to meet. This raises interesting questions about the effects of unfeasible and unsuccessful targets on political trust. It also offers an excellent case for exploring how targets influence political debate. As we shall see, even unpopular and unsuccessful targets can have a significant effect on the way policy problems are framed and debated.

While the analysis focuses on targets on immigration and asylum in UK government, the discussion has ramifications beyond this case. The arguments I develop about performance measurement and political trust apply to many other policy areas. And this book's discussion of the appeal and effects of targets is also pertinent to other tools of performance measurement. This book therefore hopes to contribute to wider debates about the use of performance measurement as a tool of governance. I hope to make the case for why we need to understand this impulse towards performance measurement – this hyper-rationalist approach to policy-making – as an attempt to produce political trust.

Methods

The analysis in this book draws on three main sources. The first and most important source of data was a series of semi-structured interviews with officials, special advisors, ministers and politicians. These interviews were designed to provide detailed information about the objectives and rationales motivating the use of targets, from the perspective of both political leaders and politicians, and officials and advisors working in government. They also provided insights into the procedures and practices involved in the elaboration, implementation and monitoring of targets. And they helped explain the effects of targets on policy-making, and especially on different parts of the organisations involved in implementing them.

We conducted sixty-two interviews between 2013 and 2015, as part of the *Politics of Monitoring* project. These were supplemented with a further three interviews conducted as part of an earlier project on the use of knowledge in the Home Office. All of the respondents had previously been or were currently engaged in developing, implementing or scrutinising targets. Twenty-six of the interviews were with policy actors working on immigration and asylum policy, including many who were involved in setting and implementing Labour government targets. A number of interviews were conducted with politicians engaged in key House of Commons select committees (Public Administration, Public Accounts, Treasury and Home Affairs). Other interviews were with officials and advisors working on climate change targets in the Department for Energy and Climate Change and the Department for Farming and Rural Affairs; the Ministry of Defence; the Department for Work and Pensions; and the Department of Health. These interviews were important for understanding and illustrating more general points about the use of targets in UK government. They also underpin the analysis of defence acquisition targets in Chapter 4.

The second main source was document analysis. We consulted an extensive range of documents, including core executive and departmental reports (Treasury documents on targets, comprehensive spending reviews and PSAs, Home Office and UKBA annual reports and annual reporting on targets); reports of the Prime Minister's Delivery Unit; select committee evidence and reports (notably Select Committees on Public Administration, Public Accounts, Home Affairs); National Audit Office documents; and reports of the Independent Chief Inspector of Borders and Immigration. I also consulted political biographies and autobiographies of politicians and advisors most closely involved in targets over the period (Michael Barber, Tony Blair, David Blunkett, Alistair Campbell, Jack Straw).

Thirdly, we conducted quantitative and qualitative analysis of newspaper coverage, House of Commons debates and transcripts of select committee evidence. We conducted quantitative content analysis of media reporting and parliamentary debate on targets on immigration, climate change and defence, as well as analysing IPSOS-Mori opinion polls on the three areas. This provided us with an initial sense of the scale of public interest in the three policy areas over time. I then proceeded to conduct a more fine-grained analysis of select committee hearings on foreign national prisoners and removals, to inform the analysis for Chapter 5 on information and trust. For Chapter 6 on targets and public trust, I analysed media coverage of targets on immigration and asylum. I analysed reporting in eleven widely read daily and Sunday newspapers, including both tabloids and broadsheets, and across the ideological spectrum. For Chapter 7 on the net migration target, I also analysed discussion of targets in Home Office questions between 2010 and 2015. The data sources and analysis are described in more detail in relevant chapters.

I am uncomfortable with the concept of 'triangulation', with its connotation that different data allow us to view the same phenomena from different perspectives. I prefer the less ambitious notion of 'complementary articulation': different sources of data allow us to develop plausible narratives about distinct aspects of the processes or practices we are seeking to understand. Interviews may provide us with an understanding of how those involved in policy-making interpreted the pressures and constraints they were under, and may help us make sense of their motivations and actions. Of course, interviews often encourage a retrospective 'sense-making' or rationalisation of previous actions or decisions. Content analysis can help overcome this problem of retrospective reconstruction. Qualitative analysis of media coverage over time offers a valuable resource for tracing evolving understandings of policy and politics, provided we are aware of the particular selection criteria and reporting style of different media outlets. Analysing parliamentary debate offers an excellent source for reconstructing the political strategies of politicians, and enables us to explore how the establishment of targets can affect the framing of issues. Select committee evidence allows us to understand accountability relations between Parliament and public administration, through analysing more sustained and focused dialogue between Members of Parliament and civil servants. Each of these sources of data thus has its own strengths and weaknesses, and their combined use can help elucidate different aspects of the appeal, deployment and effects of targets in public policy.

Outline of This Book

The next chapter of this book (Chapter 2) begins by developing a theory of targets as a response to the problem of political trust. It does this in three main steps. First, the chapter introduces the problem of political alienation and disenchantment, and argues that this can be best respecified as a problem of political trust: a reluctance to endow people or institutions with responsibility for acting on one's behalf. Second, following the work of Luhmann and Giddens, it examines how trust deficits have arisen in contemporary societies, characterised by increasing functional differentiation, and a corresponding erosion of traditional bases for grounding trust. It explores how this problem of trust has manifested itself in politics, and some of the responses politicians have adopted to attempt to rectify the problem. The chapter goes on to examine how trust deficits arise in relations between politicians and their public administrations.

The third part of the chapter explores the particular appeal of targets as a means of producing trust. Certain features of targets make them well qualified to address problems of public and administrative trust: namely their focus on measuring outputs and outcomes, and the authority derived from their quantitative methods. However, the chapter concludes by suggesting some of the problems that might arise from deploying performance measurement to solve problems of trust. Following Luhmann, we would expect targets to produce trust through providing descriptions that approximate to truth, or through stabilising expectations about the motivations of political actors. In fact, both modes of producing trust are highly precarious, and indeed may have counterproductive effects on trust relations.

Chapter 3 is the first of six empirical chapters which explore and develop the ideas set out in Chapter 2, through looking at the use and effects of particular targets. This chapter focuses on the dual function of targets. Under the Labour administration of 1997–2010, targets were adopted to simultaneously address two problems of trust: they were designed to shore up public confidence in public services by setting clear targets; and they were intended to rectify problems of trust between politicians and the civil service by motivating improved performance. This dual role corresponds to the two modes through which targets might produce trust, outlined in Chapter 2: targets as authoritative truth claims establishing trust in government, and targets as ways of disciplining behaviour. However, this dual role of targets can create a number of organisational and political challenges. The establishment of ambitious performance targets makes politicians far more reliant on their civil servants to deliver on their public-facing pledges. Moreover, targets adopted as a tool of political communication may not translate smoothly into operative goals that can be feasibly implemented within an organisation. Both problems can further antagonise the already difficult relationship between politics and the administration.

The chapter illustrates these problems through analysing the dual role of targets on asylum in the Home Office between 2000 and 2010. It finds evidence of both sets of problems. The adoption of high-profile 'stretch' targets exposed the government to political risk, and in turn created immense pressure on the Home Office to deliver on what were seen as unfeasible goals. This heightened existing tensions between government ministers and No. 10 and officials in the Home Office. The chapter goes on to consider what these findings imply for the capacity of targets to produce trust. It suggests that the targets were unable to produce authoritative descriptions of government performance, so failed in their signalling function (I explore this further in Chapter 5). Nor were they able to align political and administrative preferences: to the contrary, they exposed and even sharpened existing divergences (as discussed further in Chapter 4).

Chapter 4 explores how organisations in the public administration respond to targets. Much of the literature on performance measurement examines the various forms of gaming and other distortions produced by targets. Civil servants are depicted as canny tacticians, keen to evade targets through gaming. This chapter aims to situate these responses in a richer account of how organisations respond to top-down political pressure. It draws in particular on the organisational sociology concept of decoupling: the separation of formal compliance with external requirements, with informal deviation (or in Nils Brunsson's terminology (2002), the separation of 'talk' and 'action'). Studies of organisations suggest that decoupling is a typical way for organisations to evade unwanted top-down reform. Yet we might expect the imposition of specific, monitored targets to constrain the scope for this form of decoupling, especially where such targets are backed by strong political pressure. Under these conditions, we might expect tight coupling or 'recoupling' of talk and action.

The chapter explores these expectations by examining organisational responses to targets in defence procurement and asylum. It finds that even where targets are specific, measured and closely monitored, they do not restrict decoupling. Both the Ministry of Defence and the Home Office were able to sustain widespread decoupling over this period. In the case of the Home Office, however, intrusive political intervention by the core executive from 2006 onwards did achieve some recoupling, but with heavy costs for organisational morale and trust between civil servants and their political leadership. The chapter concludes by considering the implications of the analysis for relations of trust between politics and the administration.

Governments do not always want to draw attention to policy problems, especially where they are aware they can do little to address them. Chapter 5 looks at a case in which government failed to effectively monitor an aspect of immigration enforcement: the scandal over foreign national prisoners who should have been considered for removal. This area was not subject to targets, and in the early 2000s had not been an operational or political priority for the Home Office. However, in late 2005 a scandal erupted which exposed Home Office deficiencies in monitoring foreign nationals who, it was considered, posed a threat to the British public and should have been monitored and screened for deportation.

The divergent reactions of politics and the administration to the crisis illustrate an awkward tension between a political imperative of signalling clarity and control, and an administrative awareness of complexity and chaos. This divergence in turn partly accounts for the problem of public trust in government: a continual disappointment in the capacity of government to redeem political expectations about regulation and control. The analysis also shows how dependent select committees are on information in order to ground relations of trust with public administration. Where such information is seen as incomplete or inaccurate, this can seriously impede parliamentary confidence in its ability to hold the executive to account.

The next two chapters focus on targets as a tool of political communication. In Chapter 6, I explore how targets are adopted to demonstrate to the public that the government is delivering on promises. Yet existing literature suggests that politicians are rarely rewarded for meeting targets. This chapter explores political responses to targets through analysing public and political debate on two targets: the 2003 asylum target, and the 2010 net migration target. This allows us to compare a target that was achieved with one that proved unfeasible. It also enables us to look at the political and media coverage of targets across two different administrations: the first governed by Labour (until 2010), the second a Conservative–Liberal Democrat coalition (followed by a Conservative administration from 2015). The analysis draws on coverage in eleven popular daily and Sunday newspapers, parliamentary debate in monthly Home Office questions and monthly IPSOS-Mori opinion polls over the period.

The analysis produces a striking finding. It is not so much the feasibility – or even the achievement – of targets that influences the media's willingness to trust politicians. Far more important seems to be the perceived authenticity of those setting targets: how far they are seen as 'truly' committed to the target. Where there is a strong belief in the integrity and credibility of those setting targets, then a failure to deliver may be notched up to external constraints. By contrast, where there is scepticism about the integrity or motives of political leaders, even a successful target may be portrayed as dubious and dishonest. The implication is that targets may have limited traction in securing public trust. Media coverage appears to be more susceptible to symbolic signals of commitment and integrity than to information on outcomes. The chapter considers the implications for the use of targets as a tool of political communication.

While targets may not win trust, they do have a range of other effects. Chapter 7 looks at how targets can influence political attention and issue definition in often unintended ways. Even the most unpopular and controversial targets can have profound effects on how we construct problems and responses. The chapter focuses in particular on two effects associated with quantitative descriptions. First, a classification effect, whereby the target recategorises entities in order to create equivalent units to be counted. This can affect which entities or groups receive political attention, and of what kind. Second, a measurement effect, which normalises quantification as an authoritative mode of describing target populations and policy goals. This influences the types of techniques, actors and venues considered appropriate in defining and assessing social problems.

The chapter explores these two effects through an analysis of the net migration target. While the target was deemed to have failed on almost all measures, it nonetheless shifted the way immigration policy issues were framed in political debate. Through analysing newspaper coverage and parliamentary debate, the chapter explores the two effects outlined previously. First, it finds that the classifications implied by the target served to reframe various aspects of immigration. Notably, it rendered previously unobserved or unproblematic groups the object of political attention, and it forged or consolidated new issues linkages, especially with EU membership. Secondly, the target normalised the use of certain statistics as modes of describing and assessing immigration policy. Even opponents of the target bought into this mode of statistical description as a tool for holding government to account, thereby implicitly reinforcing its legitimacy.

The implication is that even where targets are unsuccessful in producing trust, they can have a profound influence on what we consider normal and appropriate ways of describing and evaluating policy. Even controversial and unpopular targets may have a self-perpetuating effect, normalising this mode of political communication.

The final chapter further develops the central argument of this book. Why do tools of performance measurement appear to sustain their appeal, in spite of their many adverse effects? I approach this question by focusing on the concept of inference: the willingness of voters to extrapolate from previous experience, or from their knowledge of the motivational structures of politicians. Inference is crucial to establishing relations of trust. I revisit the theories of political disaffection outlined in Chapter 2, showing how they can be interpreted in terms of a breakdown of inference. Politicians have attempted to underpin such inference through personalising politics, or through more robust accountability mechanisms, including performance measurement.

The chapter goes on to consider whether these pre-eminently technocratic, evidence-based tools of accountability will retain their relevance given the rise of populist forms of political claims-making. While such tools are firmly embedded in the management repertoire of government departments and agencies, they may be less favoured by populist movements as a tool of mobilisation. Indeed, the chapter argues that scepticism about performance measurement is likely to generate a growing divide between popular political narratives and more technocratic bureaucratic accounts. I consider how this tension can be handled by politics and public administration, and its implications for the future of performance measurement in public policy.

2 | *The Problem of Political Trust*

Studies of performance measurement tend to focus on the uses of such techniques in business and in public administration. But as I suggested in Chapter 1, these accounts overlook the political context of performance measurement. Rather than understanding the appeal of quantitative monitoring as simply an administrative phenomenon, as a set of tools organisations adopt to improve their operations and image, I want to explore the *political* impulses that have propelled this shift in administrative practice. The embracing of performance measurement is not simply a technocratic process sequestered from the dynamics of party politics and public political contestation. And the proponents of targets and indicators are not confined to a cadre of policy advisors and senior managers. As I argue in this chapter, these techniques are highly appealing for political reasons. They are deployed by political leaders in their efforts to generate the trust of sceptical electorates. This is especially evident in the case of targets, part of whose attraction lies in their utility as a tool of political communication. But it is also true of other forms of performance measurement that seek to improve public service performance and enhance political accountability.

In this chapter I suggest that the political considerations influencing the use of targets can be best understood as deriving from a problem of trust. Performance measurement is embraced by political actors to compensate for the decline in more traditional modes of establishing trust: familiarity based on personal contact or socially constructed types. I start by introducing the problem of political trust. I consider a variety of arguments about the supposed crisis of democracy, conceived as a problem of political disenchantment and disaffection. I argue that these problems can be usefully respecified as a breakdown in a readiness to endow political actors or institutions with authority to act on our behalf. Drawing on the work of Niklas Luhmann and Anthony Giddens, I chart the sources of the decline in

28

conventional bases for trust, and explore some of the political responses that have emerged to address the problem. One prominent response is to embrace various forms of political pledge, accompanied by robust forms of monitoring.

The chapter goes on to show how the problem of political trust and the use of monitoring affects the relationship between politics and the administration. The use of performance measurement as a political signal increases the dependency of politics on the public administration, in turn augmenting the demand for monitoring as a tool for steering the behaviour of civil servants. I suggest that two developments imply that performance measurement is a particularly suitable solution to the problem of trust: its promise of monitoring 'delivery', and its use of quantitative description. In conclusion, I raise some doubts about the capacity of performance measurement to ground relations of trust, themes that will be further explored in subsequent chapters.

Political Disaffection

It has long been argued that liberal democracy is facing a crisis of public confidence. Since the 1970s, various accounts have sought to explain why political institutions and/or politicians in liberal democracies appear to be falling drastically short of public expectations. The public disappointment in politics, it is argued, has in turn led to profound disillusionment, or even a crisis of legitimation. Scholars in political science and sociology have tended to attribute this state of affairs to two sets of factors: the changing nature of the tasks and challenges confronting the state, and the dynamics of party politics and the mass media. In both cases, disenchantment or scepticism appears to affect public confidence not just in particular governments, political parties or politicians – what Easton calls 'specific support' – but it is directed more generally at the political profession and/or the political institutions engaged in policy-making, or 'diffuse support' (Easton, 1965).

We can trace this discussion back to German sociological theories of the late 1960s and 1970s. One of the seminal contributions was Jürgen Habermas' theory of legitimation crisis. Habermas argued that liberal states faced a legitimation crisis stemming from their inability to steer the cyclical economic crises endemic in capitalist economies. In order to compensate for this incapacity, states tend to expand the domains of their political intervention, attempting to regulate previously autonomous spheres of social and cultural life, such as education, family life or recreation. These attempts at regulation created a series of knock-on effects for the sociocultural system, or 'life world'. They undermined existing, more organic sources of motivation, thereby endangering social integration (Habermas 1976: 4). While originating in a failure of economic steering, the crisis therefore manifested itself as an overburdening of state capacity, which created a series of social problems, generating a crisis of state legitimacy.

Claus Offe (1972) built on this account, arguing that democratic party politics exacerbated the problem. The system of competitive elections created a dynamic of competitive claims-making, or the sort of 'bidding war' earlier described by Downs (1957). This served to continually raise public expectations, producing a gap between the 'level of pretension and the level of success' (Offe 1972). Public choice theory advanced a rather different variant of this argument, captured in the 'political overload thesis' (Crozier, Huntingdon and Watanuki 1975; King 1975). According to this account, the competitive electoral system encourages politicians to make ever more expansive promises to voters, resulting in spiralling expectations. The escalating costs of such pledges results in an overload of the state, which in turn creates economic crises of the kinds seen in the 1970s (Hay 1996).

Niklas Luhmann similarly saw modern states as overstretched, but located this problem in a different set of developments. Social systems such as health care, education or the economy have become increasingly complex and functionally differentiated. This creates serious challenges for states in attempting to intervene to steer complex systems. A good recent example of this problem was the banking crisis of 2007, which sharply exposed the impotence of state regulation in steering the behaviour of financial markets. Yet at the same time, similar to Offe's account, Luhmann argued that the competitive dynamics of party politics generates expanding public expectations about what the state can do to protect citizens from risk or to intervene to steer such systems (Luhmann 1981). This implies a frequent gap between what governments can feasibly achieve, and expectations articulated in the mass media and by political opposition. States are expected not only to fulfil their traditional functions of guaranteeing internal order, welfare and economic growth, but they are also required to protect their residents from public health risks, nuclear power accidents, global warming or cybercrime. The upshot is a continual tendency in political debate to seek out and expose supposed transgressions on the part of incumbents: their failure to deliver on an ever-expanding set of expectations.

Literature on the 'risk society' (Beck 1992) offers another way of accounting for the problem of overstretch. A number of sociologists have charted how states are increasingly implicated in regulating areas characterised by risk: uncertainty about the (potentially harmful) impact of political interventions or the impact of a failure to intervene (see also Giddens 1994; Luhmann 1991). Niklas Luhmann usefully contrasts the concept of 'risk' to that of 'danger'. In the past, it was acknowledged that societies faced a range of threats, but these potential dangers were perceived as caused by external factors and treated as largely beyond the control of policy-makers. By contrast, the concept of 'risk' implies that future damages can be generated or mitigated by decisions taken now. The state is expected to intervene in such areas to protect its citizens from future damages. In the risk society, political leaders have assumed responsibility for preventing damage, implying a far greater scope of activity (Bovens and 'tHart 1996). Again, this generates onerous expectations, which the state cannot feasibly meet.

Another group of theories has suggested that globalisation constrains the state's capacity to steer the economy and society. On this account, the mobility of global capital compels states to 'internalise' the preferences of capital, providing conditions conducive to investment. This implies embracing a neoliberal paradigm of low taxation and minimal state regulation – regardless of voters' ideological preferences. At the same time, decision-making on aspects of economic policy and regulation is increasingly located at the regional or international levels, with decisions taken by groups of countries or international organisations. Both trends imply that (meaningful) decisions are no longer taken by national parliaments, but are decided by global capital or international and regional bodies. Colin Hay (2007: 151) suggests that whether this account is accurate or not (and there are reasons to suggest it is overstated), it nonetheless exercises considerable influence on public consciousness. And insofar as the perception exists that national political leaders lack autonomy, it encourages declining confidence in the capacity of politicians to represent the concerns of their electorates. The *idea* that globalisation has eroded national political autonomy challenges voters' confidence in the accountability of politicians, leading to political frustration and disengagement.

Recent contributions from political science build on some of these themes. A number of British political scientists have sought to chart and explain contemporary problems of 'disenchantment' or 'disappointment' with politics, or what has been termed the 'second wave crisis' (Richards 2014). Empirical evidence suggests alarming trends in political engagement, with a steady decline in voting and party membership across liberal democratic countries. At the same time, surveys and polls indicate decreasing levels of trust in the motives and conduct of politicians. Analyses over the past decade have identified the problem as one of unfeasible expectations about what politics can deliver. In this sense they echo arguments advanced by the German sociologists in the 1970s. However, the UK literature has tended to locate this problem in certain features of the political system. It foregrounds the role of party competition and media reporting, rather than the challenges of state control or steering. Meg Russell (2005), for example, traces the sources of political disenchantment to problems of communication. She suggests that politicians and the media are failing to convey that politics is essentially about negotiation and compromise over difficult choices. Competitive party politics – the 'permanent campaign' – and a hostile media discourage politicians from making this clear, and also give them incentives to talk down their profession. So there are strong cultural reasons militating against an honest debate, and thus set up unrealistic expectations. The implication is that politicians and the media fail to broach the 'big choices facing society' (4).

The problem has also been linked to public expectations about choice, and the 'marketisation' of politics. Colin Hay argues that political parties have increasingly relied on marketing tools to appeal to voters: branding, product placement and other devices are carefully tailored to appeal to voter preferences (Hay 2007: 55–7). This in turn encourages voters to perceive electoral competition as a market-type choice between products. This not only reinforces the notion of politicians as preoccupied with maximising their resources or power – thereby appearing to confirm an instrumental theory of politics, which sees politicians as following narrow, self-interested goals. It also sets up unrealisable expectations about the sorts of products that can be delivered. Voters expect political leaders to deliver the outcomes promised. But as Gerry Stoker argues, 'politics is bound to disappoint', producing messy compromises that do not meet these expectations (2006: 10).

Other scholars have traced the problem of disenchantment to features of the *process* of politics. Gerry Stoker and Matthew Flinders suggest that discontent with politics arises because citizens are misunderstanding the political process. They are failing to appreciate that politics involves complex and lengthy processes of negotiation, bargaining and compromise, which often produce messy and disappointing outcomes which are difficult to communicate clearly (Stoker 2006: 10). Flinders argues that this produces an 'expectations gap', evocative of Luhmann's account. The gap is reinforced by the dynamics of party politics, which encourage politics to match 'unrealistic and unattainable' promises about public service delivery (Flinders 2009: 3). Or as Seyd puts it, political systems 'encourage citizens to register multiple, and often conflicting, demands on governments, yet deny politicians many of the tools by which to respond to these demands' (Seyd 2016: 327).

Finally, Pippa Norris has argued that disappointment in democratic government is linked to the growth of more educated and critical citizens in liberal democracies (Norris 1999, 2011). Voters are better informed about issues, and less deferential to authority, including political elites. Such citizens have high demands of what democratic systems should deliver, but find that their expectations are disappointed. They are committed to democracy as the ideal form of government, but 'remain deeply sceptical when evaluating how democracy works in their own country' (Norris 2011: 5). More recently, in her work with Ronald F. Inglehart (2016), Pippa Norris has explored which social groups are most susceptible to this form of disenchantment. Inglehart and Norris suggest that dissatisfaction with mainstream parties is most prevalent among older, male voters who feel alienated by the shift towards cosmopolitan and multicultural values since the 1970s.

Whatever the precise combination of factors, authors tend to agree that one of the main symptoms of the problem is a breakdown in political trust. Notions of disenchantment, disappointment or the 'expectations gap' all point to a lack of confidence and faith in politicians and political institutions. Politicians and political institutions cannot be relied on to meet the required standards of behaviour or to achieve satisfactory outcomes. The problem of trust therefore emerges as an important symptom of political disaffection, disillusionment or disappointment in all of these accounts. But while a number of contributions have mentioned the question of trust in passing, none has systematically explored how theories of trust might help elucidate the problem or help explain how politicians have sought to address it. The concept of trust offers a promising perspective for understanding the nature of the relationship between politicians and their publics. It highlights a particular form of dependence relationship, and also provides clues as to why this relationship has been placed under so much strain over the past decades. And it offers a promising perspective for understanding the types of political strategy adopted to respond to this crisis. So let us now turn to theories of trust and consider what they might contribute to the debate.

The Problem of Trust

In sociological literature, trust is generally defined as a state of favourable expectation regarding other people's intentions and actions (Möllering 2001: 404). Two further dimensions need to be added to this definition. First, this favourable state of expectation provides the basis for action: trust enables actors to invest resources, responsibility or authority in others to act on their behalf (Shapiro 1987: 626). It is this feature – that of providing a basis for action – that distinguishes trust from mere confidence or faith. In a situation of trust, the individual is making a decision about whether or not to invest her trust in others to act on her behalf. In this sense, trust implies some responsibility on the part of the truster in creating this state of dependency on the trustee. Confidence, by contrast, is a state of expectation which is not associated with any particular decision or action. The second important aspect is that trust is bestowed under conditions of uncertainty. Acting on trust implies taking a chance, a gamble or what Georg Simmel (1950: 318) called a type of 'faith', in a context of incomplete knowledge. It requires the suspension of ignorance (Möllering 2001: 415).

The ability to trust others in this way is essential to the functioning of society. As Luhmann argues, trust provides a way of reducing the excessive burden of an overly complex future (1979: 13), allowing social interactions to proceed on a stable and confident basis (Lewis and Weigert 1985: 969). It allows actors to 'prune the future'

(Luhmann 1979) or to 'bracket out' possible events or states that might be cause for alarm (Giddens 1991: 127). Trust enables us to act and to coordinate, by neutralising dangers that would otherwise disrupt action (Luhmann 1979: 26). In this sense, trust stabilises expectations, establishing a form of reliability in the face of contingent outcomes (Luhmann 1979: 33). This does not imply that trust necessarily involves conscious reflection; trust can be 'thoughtless, careless and routinized' (Luhmann 1979: 25). Neither does it always invoke rationality: the conditions generating trust may be triggered by emotive cues as well as, for example, rational inference from previous experience.

The notion of trust provides a useful basis for characterising the problem of political disenchantment discussed earlier. Let us apply our three-part definition of trust, considering each dimension in turn. First, the literature on political disenchantment was premised on the claim that many parts of the public appear to lack favourable expectations about politicians' actions. They are not confident about the intentions or actions of politicians (in the case of specific support for politics) or about the capacity of politicians to deliver on commitments given certain structural problems inherent in the political system (diffuse support). Ample empirical data support this claim, as we saw earlier. Political scientists have linked this lack of confidence to disappointment about the outcomes of democratic politics, or disillusionment with its processes, including scepticism about the motivation of politicians. In either case, it seems reasonable to characterise this state as a lack of favourable expectations about politics and politicians.

Coming to the second dimension of the definition, this state of lacking confidence produces a reluctance on the part of large sections of the public to invest responsibility or authority in politicians to act on their behalf. This is most typically manifested as scepticism about politicians and political institutions, which may also prompt political disengagement and a refusal or lack of motivation to vote. Of course, voters exercise very little autonomy in deciding whether to endow politicians with authority to act. They may withdraw support for particular politicians or parties, but this does not address disenchantment with the wider class of politicians or with political institutions. One or another party needs to be tasked with managing the economy and keeping public services running. Indeed, the concept of multiparty electoral systems is grounded in the presumed public acceptance of these political institutions. The decision to disengage from politics simply delegates the choice to other voters; it does not permit the abstainers to withhold their authorisation of politicians to act on their behalf.

This impotence is evoked in the common complaint that all politicians or parties are equally bad, or that there is not much to choose between them, with the implication that voting is pointless. The upshot is that while multiparty democracies are premised on the principle of voter choice, this choice appears frustratingly limited where the object of voter scepticism is the 'political class' or – in the UK case – the 'Westminster system'. It is not surprising, then, that many voters disillusioned with mainstream politics switch their support to populist parties whose programmes are premised on a rejection of established parties or the ruling elite. Indeed, if the only alternatives in democratic systems are to vote or to abstain, then backing an anti-establishment politician or party may appear to offer the only means of withholding trust from mainstream politics.

And here we come to the third dimension of the concept of trust: the notion that trust implies making a leap of faith under conditions of uncertainty. Herein lies an important but neglected aspect of the problem of political scepticism: the enormous difficulties associated with making inferences about political action. A central tenet of democracy is that political representatives are elected to pursue policies that distribute resources and address social and economic problems in line with electoral preferences. (Of course, in practice they perform a range of other more symbolic functions, but this notion reflects the widespread justification for this system of government.) But publics need to vouchsafe whether politicians are acting to promote these goals, and whether they are successful in their endeavours. As Giddens writes, if we could continually monitor the actions of those acting on our behalf, then the problem of trust would not arise (Giddens 1991: 19).

The problem arises from the increasing difficulties associated with observing and accrediting the impacts of political interventions. This in turn reflects the changing nature of political intervention. As many commentators have argued, political interventions increasingly take the form of attempts to steer complex social systems and to regulate risk. In many sectors of policy, such interventions are technically sophisticated and thus difficult to convey in terms which will be comprehensible to a lay audience, or which are likely to be covered in the mass media. Moreover, the impacts of such interventions on social systems are often difficult to observe. Unlike more classical forms of distributive or redistributive politics, the outcomes of which could be observed and measured through reliable data or personal experience, interventions to regulate complex systems are often highly challenging to monitor. And where outcomes can be tracked, it may be very difficult to ascertain how far they were brought about by particular political interventions. The outcomes may not be easily attributed to government policies.

Given the difficulties in monitoring government performance, voters may need to fall back on other cues to ground trust: confidence in the motivations of politicians or the robustness of political processes. Yet as we have seen, trust in the motivation of politicians has been increasingly eroded, in part through the predominance of public choice theories of political behaviour. Nor can voters invoke political processes as a source of reassurance, given the problems Stoker and Flinders describe: the opacity of political processes which appear to produce messy and unsatisfactory outcomes.

Thus one of the key problems of political trust appears to be the lack of regular and reliable information about what politicians and political institutions actually do, and how effective they are in their interventions. In the absence of satisfactory knowledge about how such decisions were reached, or about the nature and effects of political interventions, the trustworthiness of politicians and political institutions remains opaque.

Producing Political Trust

Respecifying the problem of disillusionment as a question of trust implies reformulating the challenge facing politics. The challenge now becomes that of how best to create conditions that enable people to bestow political authority under conditions of uncertainty. This formulation also helps us to understand why previous bases for trust are no longer available or adequate. One of the resources most typically associated with trust relations is that of familiarity. Familiarity implies repeated exposure to the object (or socially constructed type of object) that is to elicit trust. This enables the truster to infer reliability from previous experience. The extrapolation from evidence does not have to be based on specific prior experience. As Luhmann writes, 'decisions about trust generalize experiences, extend them to other "similar" cases, and stabilize indifference to variation in so far as they stand up to the test' (Luhmann 1979: 26). Familiarity is the most common and reliable mechanism for this process of extrapolation.

In traditional societies, trust was anchored in local modes of organisation, which produced familiar and reliable interactions (Giddens 1990: 101). Kinship systems, localised relations, religion and tradition all provided mechanisms for stabilising expectations about the behaviour of others. Trust was assured by repeated exposure to an environment which was immediately experienced. In such localised communities, the expectation of repeated interaction and mutual dependence encouraged behaviour compliant with prevailing norms. Participants 'know they are bound to encounter one another again, and that they are bound to become dependent on one another in situations which cannot be exactly foreseeable, and which sometimes favour one of them, sometimes the other' (Luhmann 1979: 37).

Yet as societies become more complex and differentiated, it becomes less feasible to ground trust in this form of familiarity. Giddens describes this process as a form of disembedding of the individual from local modes of organisation. In modern societies, the development of new technologies for travel and communication implied the separation of time and space. Under these conditions of 'space-time distanciation' (Giddens 1990), social interactions need to be governed by more abstract mechanisms. And this in turn means that action and coordination require different modes for grounding trust. Indeed, Luhmann suggests that the need for such alternative modes for establishing trust becomes especially acute given the growing complexity and variability of the social order. We need to entrust increasingly specialised systems to ensure our security and welfare, to provide us with the infrastructures and information that will enable us to lead safe, productive and satisfying lives. In the absence of the type of familiarity grounded in localised communities, how can we develop the level of trust necessary for action? On what basis can we bracket off uncertainty in going about our daily lives, interacting with others and taking risky decisions?

We can clearly identify this problem in the sphere of politics. In traditional localised societies, rulers were selected by procedures that derived their legitimacy from religion or tradition, and expectations about the behaviour of such rulers became stabilised through familiarity. The selection of representatives in earlier modern democratic systems was also frequently based on familiarity, or at least what Luhmann refers to as 'socially constructed typicality'. In Britain, Members of Parliament were typically drawn from the landed gentry and by and large enjoyed the deference of their local constituents (Dickinson 1994). The emergence of organised, mass parties distinguished by their ideological leanings also ensured a form of trust grounded in familiarity. Party representatives could be reliably assumed to embody traits identified with particular social classes, educational backgrounds, interests or values.

These certainties have been eroded by the decline in traditional categories of collective identification. Class, education and profession are no longer reliable proxies for grounding trust. The readiness to endow authority to people embodying such features or recognisable 'types' has been undermined by a more general decline in deference to elites (Norris 2011). So we can no longer rely on familiarity with socially constructed typicalities such as class or ideology to gauge the intentions or predict the behaviour of our political elites. Nor are we content to endow them with authority based on their education, class or expertise. At the same time, the ideological spectrum has become blurred, as new forms of contestation and political affiliation disrupt conventional clusters of ideological positions (Hooghe, Marks and Wilson 2002). Parties in most liberal democracies no longer neatly conform to categories of 'left' and 'right' (if they ever did). And voters may struggle to classify and predict party positions on a range of issues, given new and unfamiliar bundles of preferences.

One rather paradoxical symptom of this breakdown in conventional modes of trust is the emergence of personalised politics. As we saw earlier, political parties and individual politicians have increasingly attempted to develop 'brands' focused on the characteristics of leaders: their values, authenticity, resolve and so on. This tendency has been partly driven by the prevalence of TV news as a medium of political communication. TV coverage offers a more 'intimate' mode of engagement, one in which leaders need to 'connect' with viewers (Copeland and Johnson-Cartee 1997: 8). Leaders need to be personally likeable, warm but authoritative, able to convey authenticity and the common touch while evoking decisiveness and resolve. For many voters, politicians are also most compelling when they display tendencies of nonconformity and stand somehow outside of 'the system'. Such maverick figures are popular because they appear to buck the trend of self-serving career politicians. While some of these qualities might be rationally associated with the requirements of effective governance, others are sharply at odds with the traits typically required in modern politics: the ability to negotiate and compromise, a good mastery of political communications and a high level of tactical nous. Indeed, when these political communication skills become too evident, publics become disenchanted and mistrustful. We might even say that the appeal of 'maverick' politicians is precisely their eschewal of those conventional traits associated with political leaders: the social standing, expertise or predictable ideological positioning that previously signalled conformity to familiar and reliable types. This paradoxical tendency appears to be at least in part a reaction against those social or ideological characteristics that previously served as cues for political trust.

The decline of conventional proxies as a basis for political trust – and the problem of trust more generally – has encouraged the emergence of a range of alternative mechanisms to stabilise expectations. One obvious candidate is the range of rules backed by sanctions that seek to render social behaviour more predictable. Legal norms backed up with penalties of various sorts help create expectations about the motivational structures of other agents. Authoritative systems of rules can thus act as a substitute for interpersonal bases of trust, or forms of trust derived from familiar types (Sitkin and Roth 1993; Zucker 1986). Such rules provide one of the most effective remedies for reducing the risk of trust, providing grounds to enter relations of dependency under conditions of uncertainty (Hosmer 1995). The agent can more confidently entrust another to act on her interests if she has entered a legally binding contractual relation with him, violation of which will incur penalties. More informal systems of norms within particular sectors and professions can impose other types of sanctions, whether pecuniary or reputational. Such mechanisms shore up relations of trust in many sectors.

However, legal rules generally provide rather blunt instruments for regulating interactions. Indeed, they can have the effect of disrupting informal processes for establishing confidence between parties. Legalistic measures can generate 'an escalating spiral of formality and distance', creating demands for more rules and thus triggering a self-perpetuating process of rule definition (Sitkin and Roth 1993: 369). Moreover, they are likely to have limited leverage in the sphere of politics. Barring instances of corruption or embezzlement, political transgressions are not generally of the order to elicit legal sanctions. Instead, the performance of politicians is controlled through a more informal set of norms and penalties based on the notion of accountability. Political accountability can be understood as an obligation on the part of public office holders to explain and justify their conduct (Bovens 2007: 450). Accountability typically implies that there is some form of sanction or cost associated with failing to explain or justify one's conduct in a satisfactory way. It therefore represents a 'softer' way of grounding trust relations, one that seems more suitable to politics than the instruments of law.

The most obvious mechanism of accountability in democratic politics is the system of regular elections, which allows voters to reward or punish candidates based on their record or prospective programmes. This practice is underpinned by certain expectations about motivation: we assume that politicians are driven by a desire to win elections and obtain political power, and thus will adjust their behaviour to maximise votes. But elections offer only a very clumsy tool of accountability. They typically occur only every four to five years, and over a cluster of issues that does not allow voters to register their approval or disapproval in relation to specific policies. Moreover, voters often find that they are offered only a very limited choice of alternatives.

Given the obvious inadequacies of elections, other mechanisms of accountability have proliferated. As John Keane charts (2009), the post–World War II era has seen the burgeoning of tools for monitoring government. Traditional institutions responsible for scrutinising government policies – notably parliaments and courts – have now been joined by a huge range of monitoring bodies, ranging from ombudspersons, watchdogs and auditors, to special commissions and enquiries. The media, campaign groups and researchers offer a plethora of informal modes of scrutiny. Keane concludes that we are witnessing a new mode of democracy, what he terms 'monitory democracy', characterised by the 'spread of power-scrutinising mechanisms into areas of social life that were previously untouched by democratic hands' (Keane 2009: 708). These mechanisms imply that we have vast amounts of information at our disposal regarding the conduct or performance of politicians and public services. Public bodies, professional and campaign groups, the traditional media and social media, can identify and expose government transgressions as never before. So might this 'monitory democracy' help engender trust, or even remove the need for trust?

Accountability mechanisms may influence public trust in politics and politicians in two ways. First, such forms of scrutiny may influence the behaviour of politicians and public officials. They are designed to create incentives for policy-makers to respect their promises, act in the public interest, respect appropriate norms of conduct and so on. A failure to act in such a way may incur a range of informal penalties such as loss of reputation, public disapprobation – or even formal penalties such as demotion or divestment of public office. In this sense, accountability may create trust through stabilising expectations about the behaviour of politicians and public officials.

The risk of exposure through such forms of accountability certainly influences political behaviour. But it does not eliminate such transgressions – nor can it. The types of political failings that appear to produce public scepticism cannot easily be fixed by these forms of scrutiny. Indeed, as we saw earlier, public disappointment appears to be generated by a range of factors linked to the (perceived or actual) challenges of political steering, party political and media dynamics, a failure to appreciate political process or the emergence of more critical citizens. These problems cannot be easily addressed through new forms of scrutiny. If anything, critical scrutiny further exposes the very conditions creating disenchantment. The problem is not so much that the individual motivations or conduct of politicians need closer monitoring or adjusted incentive structures. If we follow most accounts of political disappointment, the issue is not so much one of the individual behaviour of politicians; rather, politicians and governments are faced with unrealistic and unmeetable expectations.

New tools of accountability thus appear to offer limited prospects of grounding trust through stabilising expectations about political conduct. But there is a second way in which accountability might help to produce trust. Here we must return to Luhmann's discussion of the conditions under which trust may be bestowed. We saw that Luhmann describes law as a mode of producing trust through creating incentives to conform to expectations about appropriate conduct. However, Luhmann also identifies a number of other media that help stabilise expectations over longer chains. He suggests that money, love, power and trust all act as 'carriers' for reducing complexity: in different ways, each of these media enables us to stabilise intersubjective expectations about the behaviour of others. Of these media, 'truth' is most pertinent to our analysis of democratic politics. The establishment of authoritative truth claims allows us to transmit expectation about compliance over longer chains. We can rely on others to make the same selections, or agree on certain claims. Truth thus establishes a basis for trusting the behaviour of unknown others.

The forms of monitoring outlined earlier could help to create trust, through producing reliable information about the conduct and performance of politicians. In this sense, they might reduce the forms of doubt or uncertainty that make voters reluctant to bestow trust. If certain aspects of the conduct of politicians is rendered transparent through monitoring and critical scrutiny, then there may be better reasons to believe their claims. Monitoring thus produces *truth* about the decisions and effects of political leaders. Of course, no system of monitoring can keep track of all the actions of politicians – indeed, if it could, there would be no need for relations of trust. But by producing truthful observations of a sample of behaviour or outcomes, voters may be reassured about the performance of political leaders and feel able to bestow their trust in instances where behaviour is not being monitored.

The problem with these tools of accountability, however, is that most bodies responsible for holding government to account are essentially critical. Their mandate is to bolster confidence in the democratic system, but not necessarily in particular governments or politicians. So the truth claims they produce tend to imply criticism of their accountees. Very rarely will a watchdog, auditor or special commission produce findings that focus on condoning the performance of incumbents. Indeed, their very raison d'être consists in their identifying weaknesses and suggesting remedies. In the instances where they do praise the conduct of governments or public servants, such assessments will rarely be reported in the mass media, which prefers to focus on critical stories. The existence and activities of such bodies may provide symbolic reassurance by signalling that the government is being held to account. But this form of monitoring is unlikely to inspire specific support for politicians and governments. Instead, such forms of holding to account may merely serve to exacerbate problems of trust. In this sense, systems for scrutinising political behaviour and holding politicians to account are ill-equipped to bolster confidence in politics and politicians. Rather than solving problems of political trust, conventional tools of accountability through scrutiny and public exposure are just as likely to exacerbate the problem. Their attempt to galvanise better conduct or outcomes are clunky and misdirected. Public disaffection is not generated by poor decisions or misconduct that can be fixed by adjusting incentives structures. And the truth claims issued by such bodies are more likely to undermine than strengthen trust in politicians.

If externally imposed systems of accountability are failing to establish trust, what other strategies have politicians developed to restore trust? Political leaders can of course create their own mechanisms of account-ability. Indeed, this is precisely what they do when they establish tools of performance measurement. They produce various forms of binding commitments: pledges, promises, lock-ins. And they create forms of surveillance and reporting that produce clear incentives to meet these promises. By adopting performance measurement tools, political leaders not only commit themselves very publicly to certain goals. They also establish the means through which such commitments can be monitored and appraised. In this sense, performance measurement – and more particularly targets – can be characterised as a self-imposed mechanism of accountability. As we shall see, the very fact that it is self-created can be a source of strength: political leaders can select which aspects of performance they would like to be foregrounded and how they are to be measured. Such mechanisms are designed to showcase achievements, rather than critically scrutinise and expose transgressions. However, this freedom in designing and controlling their own monitoring is also a source of weakness. It undermines the authority of such tools, thus eroding their capacity to inspire political trust.

We shall explore the appeal and problems of self-imposed account-ability tools later in this chapter, and again in more detail in Chapter 5. Before doing so, we first need to link this discussion of political trust to the question of trust in public administration.

Trust in Public Administration

Thus far, this chapter has focused on the problem of political disaffec-tion and trust. But how does this problem manifest itself in public administration? First, it is important to point out that the breakdown of trust in political authority does not necessarily extend to public scepticism regarding civil servants, ministries or government agencies. Indeed, the public does not generally have strong views about the performance of the civil service. To be sure, civil services in many countries evoke negative associations with clunky bureaucracy, red tape and technocracy. But this long-standing image of bureaucracy is somewhat distinct from the type of political disenchantment discussed earlier. Instead, scepticism about politics is much more clearly targeted at elected politicians who head up the ministries in the public admin-istration. The ministries or agencies themselves, by contrast, are typi-cally conceived of as instruments of government or the core executive. Transgressions or deficiencies in the performance of government departments are generally laid at the door of their elected leaders.

However, the problem of political trust affects public administration in another way. It places additional strain on the relations between politicians and their civil servants. This can exacerbate already existing problems of trust between elected representatives and public agencies. Principal-agent theory has long argued that politicians face serious challenges in attempting to control public agencies. Politicians are represented as principals who enter into contracts with their agents, organisations in the public administration, to carry out delegated tasks. However, agents tend to pursue divergent goals from those of their principals, and, moreover, can exploit this because of their superior access to information. They have both the motivation and the oppor-tunity to manipulate processes to their own advantage (Miller and Moe 1983), leading to problems of slack, slippage or bureaucratic drift (Shapiro 2005).

While principal-agent models overly simplify the relationship between politics and the administration (Mitnick 1980; Perrow 1986; Waterman and Meier 1998), their assumptions about goal divergence and information asymmetry and the problems arising from these do provide useful insights into the problem of trust. First, goal divergence may arise because political and administrative actors have different logics or rationalities. Political leaders of administrative organisations emanate from the system of politics, which is preoccupied with framing problems for political intervention in a way that resonates with media and public opinion. In doing so, politicians are generally assumed to be motivated by the goal of power maximisation. This perspective will shape how they approach policy-making and implementation. Political leaders of agencies may also be keen to make a mark on their policy area by introducing policy change or reforming the organisation. By contrast, bureaucratic officials tend to be more risk averse and avoid major reform, preferring incremental change. As we saw in Chapter 1, they are preoccupied not just with meeting the expectations of actors in their environment, but also with sustaining the motivation and loyalty of members of the organisation.

Public officials will also tend to enjoy important information advantages. They will have built up extensive experience, expertise and technical knowledge in their domain. They also benefit from a closer knowledge of the informal workings of their organisation. This information asymmetry undermines the capacity of principals to control the organisation, with the result that politicians often have quite limited authority over policy-making (Poggi 1990: 132). To be sure, principal-agent approaches may exaggerate the extent of information asymmetry: political leaders may also possess information that officials do not hold, such as superior knowledge of political procedures, political negotiations or the positions and strategies of parties and interest groups (Waterman and Meier 1998). The main point is that officials possess *different* knowledge from that of politicians, and this knowledge is relevant to shaping how policy is elaborated and implemented. Officials may be able to impede or slow down reform through various means: marshalling arguments and evidence that oppose change, or resisting implementation through failing to adjust informal structures and operations. Indeed, the organisational literature contains extensive empirical studies of how organisations can 'decouple' formal adherence to change from informal practices (Meyer and Rowan 1991; Orton and Weick 1990).

One well-known strategy for principles to assert control is to monitor the activities or outputs of their officials (Waterman and Wood 1993), and where they deviate from the required tasks, to apply sanctions to bring them into line (Mitnick 1980). Michael Power has suggested that auditing performs this sort of function, providing a form of guarantee for principals entrusting resources to agents under conditions of uncertainty (Power 1997: 134). As we saw in Chapter 1, many authors have argued that monitoring in the form of performance measurement helps politicians to retain control over the organisations involved in elaborating and implementing policy, especially where these activities are outsourced to private actors or quasi-autonomous agencies. Targets and indicators are a form of arm's-length control. By setting specific, measurable goals and monitoring these on a regular basis, principals can continually check up on the activities or outputs of officials. Recent trends in performance measurement have tended to focus on the measurement of output or outcomes. This tends to be the preferred approach where there are difficulties tracking officials' activities (Eisenhardt 1989). As we shall see later in this chapter, outcome or output measurement is also favoured for more political reasons.

I suggested in Chapter 1 that this characterisation of monitoring as a strategy for controlling agencies attributes too much autonomy to the political leaders doing the monitoring. Indeed, if we characterise the (political) principal's problem as one of trust, rather than control, then a slightly different picture emerges. Performance measurement does not involve the assertion of central control, so much as a rather clumsy attempt to compensate for the impotence of political steering. Instead of seeing these 'principals' as dominant and controlling, they emerge as vulnerable and dependent on their implementing 'agents'. Instead of steering behaviour, monitoring is doing little more than setting thresholds for the imposition of sanctions and/or the withdrawal of trust (Luhmann 1979: 29). It offers a form of reassurance for the agent, helping her to decide when to bestow or withhold trust. We shall return to this idea in the next chapter.

We now need to revisit the argument about political trust set out earlier, and consider how the problem of trust in politicians and the political system impacts on the relationship between politics and the administration. The problem of political trust creates particular pressure on the civil service implementing policy. Where politicians use pledges, targets or lock-ins to signal commitment, this creates a corresponding requirement that actors in the public administration put the relevant measures in place. These officials are delegated to implement political promises: they are endowed with the task of creating conditions for political trust. This implies a particularly strong dependency on administration. It shifts responsibility for delivery to public administration. Politicians seek to gain public trust, through demonstrating they can deliver specific outputs or outcomes. This in turn creates pressures on public administration to adjust their structures and operations to realise these targets or pledges. So the use of monitoring as a tool of political communication enhances the already fraught relationship between politics and the administration.

To summarise, literature on public administration has long described the various tensions in the relationship between elected politicians and their bureaucratic administrations. These are often theorised as stemming from problems of goal conflict and information asymmetry. One common strategy for principals to reassert control is to introduce systems to monitor the activities or outputs of their officials. Thus performance measurement has been characterised as an attempt to exercise authority over public administration. I suggested respecifying this move as an attempt to produce trust by stabilising expectations about the behaviour of those on whom the principal depends. Yet the use of performance measurement as a political device places additional pressure on the relationship between politics and the administration, increasing the former's dependence on the latter to deliver the required outcome. As we shall see in the next two chapters, far from solving the problem of trust, this simply creates a series of new problems.

Political Trust and Performance Measurement

Monitoring in the form of performance measurement has emerged as one of the favoured techniques for producing political trust. Such tools appear to exert a particular authority, derived from two features. The first of these is their emphasis on performance, delivery or outputs and outcomes. And the second is the codification of such performance in numerical terms. I shall discuss each feature in turn.

The Delivery 'Turn'

There is a long-running debate about what type of monitoring should be adopted to evaluate the activities of organisations, often characterised as a choice between inputs, processes and outputs (Majone 1989). Inputs are the resources, skills and people engaged in an activity (Majone 1989: 172). Claims about resource investment are often used to signal political commitment to particular goals: a government can show it is prioritising an issue by investing in training more doctors, constructing new roads or injecting money into schools. Input measurement has limited traction as a way of steering administrative behaviour, and tends to be overlooked by principal-agent theorists as a strategy for principals to assert control over agents. Moreover, beyond their function of signalling political commitment, inputs tell us very little about how efficiently resources are being used, or how effective such investments are meeting policy goals. Nonetheless, as Majone points out, input measurement may be the only viable approach where it is difficult to obtain information on either processes or outcomes (172–5).

A second possibility is to focus on processes, the methods used to transform inputs into outputs or outcomes (Majone 1989: 172). This implies monitoring the procedures governing decision-making, financial allocations, personal conduct and so on. This is often described in principal-agent literature as monitoring the *activities* of agents. Process monitoring has been an important technique of accountability in business and public management, as Michael Power charts in his work on the audit society (Power 1996, 1997). Power argues that 'audits are demanded in the context of relations of accountability between two parties and the existence of operational difficulties for one party to monitor the activities of the other' (1997: 134). It is therefore a form of process monitoring that emerges where there is a lack of trust. By contrast, process monitoring is not commonly used in political communication, as information about procedures tends to be too remote from public concerns (unless, of course, organisational procedures have themselves become the object of political attention – we will explore a case of this in Chapter 4).

From the 1980s onwards, however, the form of monitoring most beloved of new public management has been outputs or outcomes, typically defined as the 'consequences, results, effects or impact of service provision' (Boyne and Law 2005: 254). Proponents of outcome measurement often like to distinguish outcomes from outputs, suggesting that outcomes are the longer-term changes effected by outputs, or 'ultimate consequences' of outputs (Boyne and Law 2005: 254). Principal-agent theory posits that output or outcome monitoring can help align the preferences of principals and agents, ensuring that they both work towards the same goals. As such, outcome measurement is seen as a particularly effective way of steering behaviour.

Part of the appeal of output or outcome measures lies in their ability to constrain forms of gaming or manipulation in public administration. Organisational sociologists have long observed that organisations can evade or dilute the effects of top-down change through decoupling their formal structures and rhetoric from informal practice (see discussion in Chapter 1). However, the imposition of precise, measured output or outcome targets that are rigorously monitored is likely to severely constrain the opportunities for such decoupling. Outputs or outcomes have to match political rhetoric, and this correspondence may be closely scrutinised through regular monitoring. Recent contributions have suggested that robust monitoring systems may even engender 'recoupling' of formal and informal operations (Hallett 2010; Sauder and Espeland 2009). We shall explore this question in more depth in Chapter 4.

There are also clear political reasons for favouring output or outcome measurement. The measurement of outcomes homes in on how far the desired policy or organisational goals have been achieved. Measurement of outcomes is thus more likely to form the basis for how voters appraise a government's record. By focusing on the delivery of public services, outcome measures seek to ascertain the ways in which governments are affecting the lives of their citizens. While inputs or processes may have an effect on such delivery, the relation is often indirect and difficult to assess. This notion has been reflected in government slogans such as the UK Labour government's 'what matters is what works' or the Clinton administration's pledge to find out 'what works, and what doesn't work' among existing federal programmes (Heinrich 2002: 713).

Coming back to the concept of trust, we can say that output or outcome measurement helps address uncertainty about the intentions and behaviour of political actors. In the absence of trust grounded in familiarity, appraising the ultimate effects of political interventions may offer a more robust and reliable method than observing processes. These latter may be more susceptible to manipulation, as politicians and officials simply go through the motions of making cosmetic adjustments, rather than introducing substantive changes to achieve the stated goals. The measurement of outputs or outcomes appears to provide the observer with unambiguous evidence of the impact of interventions. Moreover, given the complexity of social steering, most observers will lack sufficient knowledge to track and make sense of the processes whereby inputs are translated into outputs.

Yet complexity also presents challenges to measuring the effects of interventions. How can we say for sure if a reform of teacher training has led to an improvement in exam results? Or if the privatisation of healthcare services has generated a decline in cancer death rates? The relationship between inputs, processes and outcomes is far more complex for policy interventions that seek to steer highly specialised and complex social systems. The implication is that it is often problematic to deploy outcome measurement as a way of assessing performance. Outcomes may not be clearly attributable to policy interventions. Good outcomes may be a product of exogenous factors, while bad outcomes may occur despite governments' best efforts. Where politicians and officials are not confident that their interventions will have clear effects on outcomes, this may limit their incentives to invest in meeting output or outcome targets.

Despite these difficulties, outcome measurement has retained its appeal to policy-makers. Indeed, national and international practices of measuring and comparing performance continue to thrive and expand. Outcome measurements are increasingly deployed to compare or rank different organisations, services or jurisdictions, and such indicators exert a huge influence on policy at both national and international levels.

Trust in Numbers

The performance measurement 'revolution' also needs to be located in a broader trend towards quantification in public life. Quantification – defined broadly as the production and communication of numbers (Espeland and Stevens 2008) – has assumed increasing authority as a means of description and analysis not just in its traditional spheres of economics and business, but also across public services (health care, education, welfare, justice and policing). It has a central role in the techniques associated with new public management, with their penchant for quantified performance indicators and targets, rankings, league tables and scorecards. Chris Pollitt goes so far as to identify a 'logic of escalation' evident in the use of performance measurement (2013: 353).

It is worth drawing on some of the sociological literature on quantification to understand why numbers should exert such strong appeal. Hacking (1990) describes quantification as a 'style of reasoning', characterised by the statistical analysis of regularities in different phenomena. Part of the appeal of this style of reasoning lies in the long-standing association of numbers with rationality and objectivity. Quantitative descriptions are seen as precise, unambiguous and unencumbered by the partial or emotive baggage of qualitative descriptions. Numbers are abstractions that promise to dispense with vagueness and uncertainty. As Hacking famously put it, they represent the 'taming of chance'. One prominent economist nicely captures the appeal of quantitative methods, in a hubristic essay charting the expansion of economics:

The ascension of economics results from the fact that our discipline has a rigorous language that allows complicated concepts to be written in relatively simple, abstract terms. The language permits economists to strip away complexity. Complexity may add to the richness of description, but it also prevents the analyst from seeing what is essential. (Lazear 2000: 99)

The notion of stripping back complex phenomena to their essential features clearly has its roots in a mechanistic understanding of science, whereby behaviour can be understood by breaking down social phenomena into discrete units (or atoms) and identifying the causal mechanisms explaining their interaction. Quantification plays a crucial role in identifying and counting units, and in analysing regularities in the relations between them.

A related appeal of quantification is its production of standardised units that enable generalisability and portability. Counting necessarily requires the classification of units as equivalent, in the process abstracting from the distinctive features of each of the counted entities. This abstraction and the numerical coding of units enables descriptions to be communicated across cultural and geographical space, producing a shared language and method of analysis (Hansen and Porter 2012: 413). Numbers facilitate 'the production of knowledge that transcends and integrates particularities of place, language and custom' (Espeland and Stevens 2008: 432). One way in which numbers bridge difference is in their deployment across the spheres of political debate and public administration. As we shall discuss in Chapter 3, performance indicators and targets can serve as 'boundary objects' which make sense and are deployable across different systems or spheres of activity (Star and Griesemer 1989).

The identification of standardised units also enables more complex manipulation of numbers based on mathematical rules. Here it is useful to introduce Michael Power's (2004) distinction between first-order and second-order measurement. First-order measurement involves the counting of a multiplicity of entities through classification, as described earlier. Second-order measurement involves the production of what Power calls 'measures of measures' (Power 2004: 771), or what has also been termed 'abstractions of abstractions' (Woelert 2015): the generation of complex indices and ratios through the statistical manipulation of first-order measures. These statistical manipulations derive a particular authority from the technical features of formal mathematical methods, which make them appear especially reliable and efficient.

As such calculations become more technical, they imply ever greater abstraction from the concrete entities that they initially referred to. This has the result of buffering them from forms of challenge and critique. On the one hand, their abstraction and technicality forecloses opportunities for scrutiny by non-experts. Only trained researchers can assess the plausibility of their assumptions or evaluate the robustness of their methods. And even those equipped to carry out such assessments have limited time or motivation to question every premise and operation involved in deriving them. On the other hand, the technical authority of such calculations discourages their audience from questioning them. The result is that while first-order measures are often contested, second-order calculations 'forget the circumstances under which they were produced' (Power 2004: 776). Numerical inscriptions render invisible the circumstances of their construction (Latour and Woolgar 2013). The assumptions, techniques and conditions involved in deriving such figures become 'black-boxed'.

In organisations, statistics become institutionalised as techniques for constructing policy problems and framing and evaluating policy responses. Indicators, targets and other techniques of performance measurement become normalised as a mode of knowledge production. They affect organisational behaviour, shifting incentives structures in different and often unanticipated ways, and influencing the organisation's influence and legitimacy. In public political debate, such measurements also become taken for granted as ways of monitoring the performance of governments and public services. This makes it very difficult to dispense with such measurement. Even where performance measurement is recognised as flawed, it can prove very difficult to eschew such techniques (Woelert 2015: 9). The features of measurement described earlier – its precision, generalisability, technical authority and complexity – buffer it from critique. More fundamentally, the very act of classifying objects as countable entities opens up new opportunities for description and analysis, which cannot easily be shut down. As Espeland and Stevens write, 'turning qualities into quantities creates new things and new relations among things' (2008: 412). Measurement produces commensurability between entities, and this profoundly changes the way we see the world (Latour 1993: 118).

This may account for the 'logic of escalation' identified by Pollitt. In his research on the British National Health Service, Pollitt notes that political announcements that performance measurement is having adverse effects 'do not seem to have pushed the system very far back down the escalation curve' (2013: 353). Woelert (2015) sees the same tendency in Australian regulation of universities, where 'repeated promises to relax some of the more heavy-handed performance-based control mechanisms ... have not led to any real de-escalation' (9). Critics may bemoan the simplifying and distorting effects of performance measurement. But quantitative forms of description and evaluation remain as authoritative and compelling as ever. Such statistics are apparently irresistible as a tool of public policy, and once they have been unleashed they prove surprisingly resilient. As a senior civil servant in the UK describes the appeal of quantified targets in her organisation:

I had a meeting with case owners where I asked what you are most proud of doing, and they said, meeting our targets. It was *the* currency for value in the organisation. They were really really passionate about it ... I remember at the beginning for the first few weeks not having a target at all, and it was completely disorienting for everyone, they just didn't know what good looked like. What their rate of productivity should be. And they felt that lots of people were getting away with it and they didn't know how to manage each other without that kind of benchmark. (Interview, August 2014)

Initial Doubts

The analysis of quantification in the previous section can help explain why performance measurement has proved so compelling as a technique of governance. If political disenchantment is respecified as a symptom of declining trust, then it becomes clear why political actors would be on the search for new modes of fostering public confidence in politics. Pledges or targets on policy outcomes emerge as obvious favourites, as they offer a firm, clear signal of political commitment. They suggest that the public does not have to judge politicians by their words, which have lost credibility, but by their actions, which will be carefully monitored. Quantification is the favoured technique for such monitoring, as it is associated with precision, objectivity and generalisability, and endowed with particular technical authority.

Performance measurement does not *replace* relations of trust. It does not eliminate the need for voters to bracket off uncertainty about the motives or conduct of political leaders; at best, it offers them some reassurance that politicians have strong incentives to carry out their pledges, and it offers a way of periodically checking up on their actions. In this sense, it offers alternative *means* of grounding trust, rather than obviating the need for trust. It helps the truster to suppress uncertainty, easing doubts about the risks associated with bestowing confidence. Nor does performance measurement eliminate the need for political leaders to trust their civil servants; again, it can at best provide some assurance about the motivations of officials, and allow political leaders to 'sample' instances of their performance. But these are relatively crude instruments for monitoring behaviour. They allow trusters to *infer* the trustworthiness of their trustees, rather than replacing the need to trust them. So even where performance measurement is doing its job, it is simply offering a form of reassurance that allows people to make the 'leap of faith' involved in trusting.

But does performance measurement really succeed in its mission of generating trust? Following Luhmann and Giddens, I defined trust as a way of pruning the future or managing uncertainty. Given the complexity of our environment, we need to bracket off areas of uncertainty if we are to provide a basis for social action. Trust thus enables us to make decisions and coordinate action under conditions of risk. In what sense do these quantitative techniques of monitoring enable political actors to do this?

Here it is useful to explore how far this mode of producing trust corresponds to the mechanisms identified in sociological literature on trust. As we saw earlier, Luhmann and Giddens have both written about the decline of familiarity as a basis for trust in modern society. We saw how law has emerged as an important mode of grounding trust, through its capacity to stabilise expectations about behaviour. In some ways, the use of performance measurement can have a 'law-like' effect, stabilising expectations through setting out requirements backed by soft sanctions. These soft norms and expectations, and the sanctions for enforcing them, can be understood as mechanisms of accountability. The introduction of indicators or targets is a form of self-imposed accountability political leaders adopt to ground trust. Such tools are likely to produce a myriad of adjustments to the behaviour of politicians, organisations and individual officials whose behaviour will be open to new forms of scrutiny. This is what we termed the 'disciplining' effect of monitoring, i.e. the notion that the introduction of performance measurement will lead to an alignment (or at least an alteration) of preferences and will galvanise changes in behaviour.

As we shall see in the following chapters, these attempts at stabilising expectations through disciplining the behaviour of public administration have mixed results. As has been widely documented, performance indicators and targets can have a range of perverse and unanticipated effects. They can encourage various types of gaming and decoupling. Given the points made earlier about the disruptive effects of formal rules, we might also expect this form of disciplining to destabilise informal bases of trust existing in organisations. This is a theme we return to in Chapters 3 and 4. The discussion will suggest that the failure of monitoring to produce trust between politics and the administration may not lead to the abandonment of performance measurement. Instead, it is just as likely to generate attempts to further specify and adjust such tools.

In the discussion of the authority of quantification, I suggested that performance measurement appeared to exert a particular authority over its audience. This reflected deep-seated beliefs about the validity of quantification as a description of social reality. So while in some contexts numbers may establish trust through discipline and control, the sort of authority described here is more akin to that of truth. Quantitative descriptions may be particularly compelling as truth claims because of the authority of numerical abstractions and techniques of statistical manipulation. Luhmann argues that the establishment of truth enables us to transmit expectations about compliance over long chains. We can rely on others to make the same selections, or agree on certain claims. Truth thus establishes a basis for trusting the behaviour of unknown others. In the same way, we can say that quantitative descriptions, including performance measurement, enable the transmission of truth claims, and thus expectations about behaviour, over long chains. Indeed, trust in such abstract truth claims can become routinised, developed through repeated exposure to claims of a certain type or emanating from a certain source.

The notion of performance measurement as truth therefore represents a second way in which such techniques may help to produce trust. If the first way can be termed the 'disciplining' effect of performance measurement through the setting out of rules and threat of sanctions, the second takes the form of a 'signalling' effect. The rigour and technical authority of targets and indicators signal that they are to be accepted as credible truth claims.

And yet the notion of trust in performance measurement belies the way in which political actors, and the public more generally, engage with such statistics. In practice, such descriptions frequently meet with scepticism, frustration or confusion. Public audiences may take many political claims about performance with a pinch of salt, or even ignore them altogether. Indeed, as we shall see in Chapter 5, performance targets in the UK have often been met by strong scepticism. Similarly, politicians may come to doubt the reliability of data on performance, because they are aware of its limitations or the extent of gaming. Civil servants may become quite jaded about the usefulness of such techniques.

Perhaps even more intriguingly, informal or private scepticism about performance measurement may be decoupled from rhetorical support for such descriptions. Politicians, officials, the media and others engaged in political debate may go through the motions of trusting in particular performance measures, or techniques of performance measurement more generally. It may simply be too costly – in terms of legitimacy, reputation or influence – to challenge such descriptions. Alternatively, there may be tactical reasons to embrace particular measurements, as a means of exposing an opponent, leveraging resources or manipulating the behaviour of others. Whatever the reason, this ritualistic acceptance of performance measurement can ground a form of trust. Despite personal or informally communicated misgivings about the techniques of monitoring, the expectation that others will buy into such descriptions can in itself stabilise expectations. In this sense, performance measurement can create a form of ritualised compliance.

Thus in some cases, performance measurement may produce genuine 'transmission chains' that stabilise expectations across space and time, whether based on systems of rules and sanctions, or based on the expectation that the authority of its descriptions will lead others to adjust their beliefs. But in many cases, such transmission chains produce scepticism and distortion. And in other instances, rather than being grounded in truth, such chains may be built on a circularity of social expectations: a confidence based on expectations that others will play the game. This can indeed produce trust in the sense of bracketing off uncertainty in order to enable action under conditions of uncertainty. But it is a precarious basis for trust, resting as it does on a form of second-guessing the behaviour of others.

3 | *The Double Life of Targets*

As we have seen in the previous two chapters, performance measurement techniques are typically depicted as management tools, designed to improve the performance of public services through what I have referred to as their 'disciplining' function. Targets, performance indicators and other techniques are seen as a means of clarifying and prioritising tasks and of enabling principals to verify whether their agents have adequately performed the required tasks. They are therefore designed to address a problem of trust between principals and agents. Yet we also saw that targets and indicators also have an important public-facing function: they can be adopted by governments to signal commitment to and to underscore achievement of a range of political goals. Indeed, targets, promises and pledges are frequently used as a means of reassuring publics, in an attempt to generate political trust.

These two functions of targets – their use as a tool for disciplining agents and as a means of signalling political commitment – correspond to the two modes of producing trust identified in Chapter 2. On the one hand, performance measurement can establish trust by setting up requirements for action, backed by soft sanctions. Such requirements might be expected to bring about an alignment of preferences between principals and agents, thereby stabilising expectations about behaviour. On the other hand, performance measurement promises to establish trust through producing credible information about policy. Such information can stabilise expectations through establishing truth, in the form of rigorous and authoritative descriptions of policy outputs or outcomes.

This dual role of targets was especially evident under the UK Labour government of 1997–2010. Indeed, the targets set as part of the government's system of Public Service Agreements can be seen as an experiment in attempting to marry two distinct objectives: the goal of galvanising organisational action to implement ambitious reforms and that of securing public support for the Labour administration through demonstrating its ability to deliver improved public services. This chapter explores the tensions between disciplining and signalling through examining the development and implementation of targets in the area of UK asylum policy between 2000 and 2010.

Not surprisingly, the analysis shows that the attempt to combine these functions through the use of targets created a number of organisational and political challenges. The establishment of ambitious performance targets created a heightened dependence on public administration, in turn encouraging intrusive and unwelcome forms of political intervention in organisational action. At the same time, targets adopted to convey a political commitment or to demonstrate performance did not translate smoothly into operative goals that organisations could feasibly implement. The analysis of asylum targets demonstrates well the tensions and paradoxes generated by the dual function of targets.

The Dual Function of Targets in UK Government

The use of targets as a tool of political communication was especially prominent under the Labour administration of 1997–2010. As we saw in Chapter 1, the 1998 Comprehensive Spending Review established a series of performance requirements, which were further fleshed out in the form of the 2000 Public Service Agreements (PSAs). PSAs established a series of specific performance targets for each of the major public service departments, which were designed to clarify priorities and goals and to measure performance to these goals (Treasury 2000).

Right from the outset it was clear that PSA targets had a dual function. On the one hand, the targets were adopted to enhance public sector performance, performing a 'disciplining' function: they were to provide incentives for officials, elected politicians and other actors involved in formulating and implementing policy to improve their performance and ensure value for money. But at the same time, targets were developed for symbolic reasons, to signal commitment to and to underscore achievement of a range of political goals. This dual logic was evident in Treasury documents of the time. The Treasury characterised the PSAs as 'a major agenda to deliver *and demonstrate* change in the commissioning, management and delivery of public services' (Treasury 2002: 13; emphasis added). The targets should be easily understandable by the public – they should not be too technical and should be free of jargon. In the words of the Treasury, 'Departments were given a real incentive to drive up standards in public services and the public was given the opportunity to judge their performance' (12). Or as the House of Commons Home Affairs Committee put it:

First, targets are, in principle, valuable in terms of accountability, not least in assisting Parliament and the public to judge the performance of a Department. Second, PSA targets in particular are intended to set a strategic direction for a Department, ensuring that it has a clear focus and set of priorities. Third, if used properly, targets can be useful as a public management tool, with the potential to improve performance in particular areas, to identify areas of weakness and to motivate staff through incentives for good performance. (Home Affairs Committee, 2004)

Part of the appeal of targets as a tool of monitoring resides in their technical features. Indeed, a number of formal technical criteria guided the selection of targets. For a start, targets needed to be monitored and thus linked to indicators. The potential to measure and monitor targets – and thus the use of performance indicators – was built into the very definition and selection of targets. As we saw in Chapter 2, the use of quantified goals and indicators was seen as a means of making such monitoring more robust and credible and difficult to evade.

Second, targets increasingly became focused on delivery, or outcomes. Outcomes were defined as the 'ultimate results the Government seeks to achieve from its activities, and the activities of those it influences, in order to meet its objectives' (Treasury 2000). These were distinguished from outputs defined as the 'immediate results of the activities of Government and its agencies'; and inputs, defined as 'staff or physical resources required to deliver an output' (Treasury 2000). The House of Commons Treasury Committee, which monitors Treasury policy, reported in 2000 that most of the targets under the 1998 PSA had been process targets (51 per cent) or output targets (27 per cent), with only 11 per cent comprising outcome targets (Treasury Committee 1999). It recommended that the new PSAs established in 2000 focus more on outcomes; and indeed the National Audit Office classified 68 per cent of the targets adopted in 2000 as outcome targets (National Audit Office 2001: 1).

Coupling organisational and political requirements in this way had a number of perceived advantages. For a start, adopting such a public target created intense pressure on departments to deliver. The Blair government was famously very frustrated at the lack of progress in driving through reform within the civil service during its first administration of 1997–2001 (Blair 2010; Campbell 2008; Painter 2012). By setting prominent 'stretch' targets, Blair and his close allies hoped to ratchet up the pressure on the ministers and senior officials involved in public service delivery. This was seen as especially important given the substantial increase in public investment across government over this period. No. 10 and the Treasury were determined to see a tangible return on their investment of resources, especially in the course of their second term in office, from 2001 to 2005.

At the same time, the government was confident – at least in the early days of the PSA targets – that visible improvements in performance would be rewarded by an increase in public confidence in the Labour administration. Targets would galvanise improved performance, while also creating a new way of measuring and publicising such improvement (Panchamia and Thomas 2014). They would be a lever for driving through change in a way that would be monitored by the public.

The task of overseeing delivery of the government's key targets was taken on by the Prime Minister's Delivery Unit, set up in 2001 under the leadership of Michael Barber. The Delivery Unit unremittingly drove forward departmental performance to meet the ten or so key targets that the Prime Minister saw as crucial for demonstrating the impact of Labour reforms to public services. Barber developed an elaborate set of methodologies for setting targets, defining 'trajectories' for meeting goals, identifying the 'drivers' and impediments that would influence performance. Performance was assessed through twice-yearly 'traffic light' reviews and monthly 'stocktakes' with the Prime Minister. Every detail of how to steer behaviour to reach the target was subject to forensic analysis. Participants in these stocktakes recall sitting in meetings where the Prime Minister was poring over the minutiae of obstacles to implementation. A former official from the Department of Health vividly describes the monthly meetings at No. 10:

So the Prime Minister was there; you were supposed to have the Chancellor, but he never turned up. But you did have some Treasury people sort of sneering in the corner. And then you had the Delivery Unit people. You know, the Department [of Health] on the other side, all kind of lined up with the Permanent Secretary and all the kind of senior people. And at this end there would be a big screen with PowerPoint slides. And Michael Barbour dancing at the front telling everybody, 'so here's where we are this month. And if you look at this, there's a downtown, there's an upturn. There's this. And that looks as if that's on track. And that one isn't.' And so there was an amazing, you know, this group of people around the Cabinet table. (Interview, May 2014)

Yet we might expect this double function of targets to create a number of problems for both politics and the administration. Ambitious and high-profile targets create a number of risks for political leaders, placing them under pressure to show they can deliver on their pledges. As we have seen, this can in turn create a heightened dependency on the public administration responsible for implementing targets. At the same time, targets adopted to signal improved performance to the public are likely to be framed in a way that resonates with popular perceptions of policy problems. Targets adopted to address public concerns may not easily cohere with organisational beliefs and practices about policy-making and implementation. We shall explore how these tensions manifested themselves in the case of targets on asylum.

Asylum Targets

Asylum was a highly salient issue in the late 1990s and early 2000s, with concerns about irregular immigration and rising asylum applications receiving extensive media coverage. The Labour government was also keen to demonstrate its credentials as robust in controlling immigration and asylum. This would suggest that targets might play an important signalling role, demonstrating the government was managing the problem. At the same time, the Home Office, the government department with responsibility for immigration and asylum, was widely acknowledged to be overwhelmed by the increased number of applications. Consecutive Home Secretaries struggled to drive through various changes that would improve organisational performance. This might suggest the importance of targets as a tool for disciplining organisational behaviour. Asylum policy therefore provides a good case for exploring how the two functions of targets might be combined, and examining the types of tensions that emerged and how they were handled (or mishandled).

Asylum Applications

Targets on immigration and asylum were originally set as part of the 2000 PSAs between the Treasury and the Home Office. From the outset, two main considerations appeared to guide their development. The first was the spending round agreed with the Treasury. Home Office activities in asylum processing and removals benefited from a substantial injection of resources in the early 2000s, with investment in immigration and asylum control rising from £357 m in 1998–9 to around £1.6 bn in 2001–2 (Home Office 2003: 92) – a sizeable increase, even taking into account the roughly twofold rise in the number of asylum applications over this period. In return, the Home Office was required to demonstrate a corresponding improvement in performance in the area of asylum processing. This improvement was to be measured through meeting two targets: swifter processing of asylum applications, i.e. the determination of whether an applicant was entitled to asylum, and an increase in 'removals' of rejected asylum applicants from the UK. Both targets reflected concerns that the Home Office, and especially its Immigration and Nationality Directorate (IND), were failing to keep on top of rising asylum applications. The target system was somewhat reluctantly embraced by the Home Office, in the words of one official, as 'a necessary evil for doing a deal ... with the Treasury' (Interview, February 2014). Seen from the perspective of Treasury oversight of Home Office expenditure, PSA targets operated as a management tool to drive and monitor organisational performance.

The focus on asylum targets was dictated by a second consideration: the political salience of the asylum problem in the early 2000s. Asylum applications in the UK rose significantly over this period, from fewer than 50,000 in 1997 to more than 90,000 in 2000 and 2001, peaking at 103,000 in 2002. Asylum was the object of what was perceived as relentless negative media coverage. From around 2001, it became one of the top priorities for the Prime Minister's office, or 'No. 10' (Barber 2007). So there were clear political reasons to focus on asylum, as opposed to other areas of immigration. And yet in 2001–2 there was increasing frustration in No. 10 that the PSA target on processing applications was poorly pitched. The target was not seen as sufficiently ambitious, as it focused on internal Home Office procedures, failing to incentivise a range of other measures that might help reduce applications. Nor did it send the right sort of political message about asylum control. As one former special advisor put it, 'If you were worried about public concern about asylum the concern was about numbers. It wasn't about, "oh, they're not being dealt with quickly enough"' (Interview, February 2014). So while it was a sensible management target from the perspective of Home Office reform in the context of increased expenditure, it was not delivering as a political target.

The gradual sidelining of PSA asylum targets was abetted by more personal considerations: the political rivalry between Tony Blair and Gordon Brown, who as Chancellor of the Exchequer oversaw the Treasury's PSA targets. David Blunkett, who was Home Secretary from 2001 to 2004, was a firm ally of Blair's and an influential Labour Party figure with the clout to resist pressure from Brown. This enabled Blunkett to largely bypass the PSA target on asylum processing in his discussions with No. 10 about how to improve performance. Instead, the focus of these discussions was on how to achieve an overall reduction in asylum applications. And there was a determination to use all possible levers – visa policy, border control and various deterrent measures – to achieve this. Meanwhile, the process of reducing asylum numbers was subjected to full Delivery Unit treatment. As a former official described it, 'there was a big pressure in the Home Office from the Barber unit to say, well, what is your delivery plan for these targets?' (Interview, February 2014). As another official put it, the Delivery Unit was 'all over what the IND was doing' (Interview, February 2014).

No. 10 involvement was to become even more intense. By January 2003, with asylum figures still rising, Tony Blair proposed that asylum should be treated as what was termed in Delivery Unit jargon a 'Level 3 emergency' (Barber 2007: 171). This was soon followed by a characteristically personal intervention by the Prime Minister. In February 2003, Blair announced on the flagship BBC television news programme *Newsnight* that the government would halve the number of asylum applications within a year. This so-called *Newsnight* target was set without any prior consultation with the Home Secretary or Home Office officials. Indeed, there was broad scepticism on the part of the Home Secretary, David Blunkett, and the IND board, about whether the target was feasible (Interview, February 2014; Pollard 2004). As one official observed, it would have been nigh impossible to negotiate such a target with the Home Office, so 'the PM just sort of bypassed that whole process' (Interview, February 2014).

The *Newsnight* target was very public and placed the Home Office under even more intense pressure. As one commentator put it, 'Everything became just geared to meeting this objective' (Interview, May 2007). And meet it they did. By 2003, annual asylum applications were back down to 60,000, and the numbers continued to fall year on year to fewer than 40,000 in 2008. By 2005 asylum numbers appeared to be back down to manageable levels. How far this outcome was a product of government intervention remains contested. The Home Office and No. 10 narrative is that a concerted effort to stop entry into the UK – notably through more stringent visa requirements and better offshore border control – was the main driver. Research comparing asylum trends across Europe and the United States has suggested that these measures account for around one third of the reduction, with the main determinant being the incidence of war and armed conflict in asylum-sending countries (Hatton 2009). Asylum numbers were decreasing across most European countries over this period. And indeed, they were already starting to decline at the point Blair made his announcement. As one former Home Office official put it, 'The slight cynic in me knows that Blair knew the number was on its way down anyway because he was getting very regular management information reports on what was happening to asylum applications, which were on the turn by that point' (Interview, February 2014).

Whatever its cause, the fall in asylum applications and the achievement of Blair's *Newsnight* target was not greeted with the public recognition that the government felt it deserved. As we shall see in Chapter 5, media coverage was very sceptical about the way in which the target had been set and about the methods used to measure its achievement. As one former special advisor put it: 'the media never just reports the Government has delivered something, it never does, you know. That's not how it works. And I think that's something that both Blunkett and Blair were very frustrated by' (Interview, February 2014). But it signalled the demotion of asylum from a Level 3 priority and the end of such intensive Delivery Unit involvement. With the number of new applicants down, performance on removals now became the focus of attention, and was widely seen as lamentable. The failure to deport large numbers of rejected asylum seekers exposed the government to accusations that it still did not have a grip on the asylum system.

Removals

As we saw, the first asylum PSA targets had included the goal of increasing the number of removals of failed asylum seekers from the UK. The 2002 Service Delivery Agreement had set the target at 30,000 removals by March 2003. But the Home Office was subsequently forced to admit this target was too ambitious (Home Office 2003: 23). In a scathing critique, the House of Commons Home Affairs Committee, the parliamentary committee responsible for scrutinising Home Office performance, noted that:

We are at a loss to understand the basis for the belief that a target of 30,000 removals a year was achievable, and ministerial pronouncements on the subject are obscure. It is surely not too much to expect that, if it is thought necessary to set targets for removals, they should be rational and achievable. (Home Affairs Committee 2003: 23)

In the new 2004 PSA, this target was adjusted from a specific numerical target back to a 'directional' target, i.e. to remove a greater proportion of failed asylum seekers in 2005–6 compared to 2002–3. The idea was to address concerns that the target was overly ambitious. But the level of removals failed to budge, and by late 2004, even this more modest target looked unachievable. Indeed there was general frustration within the Home Office and No. 10 about lack of progress on removals. Home Office officials felt that they had very limited leverage on the issue, as many cases involved people who could not be removed because they did not have the necessary documentation and were not recognised as nationals by their countries of origin. No. 10, meanwhile, felt that IND officials were making excuses and were not using all possible means to realise the target (Barber 2007). Indeed, there was growing impatience with IND and the Home Office more generally over this period, over its poor management and performance (Painter 2008).

Partly in an attempt to spur the IND to action, No. 10 and the Home Office agreed on a new framing of the removals target in September 2004, the so-called tipping point target. This target proscribed that the number of removals should exceed the number of new asylum applications (Barber 2007: 229). While not introducing any new performance indicator (it was the ratio of applications to removals, both of which were already the object of targets), it was intended to articulate existing goals in a pithier way. Again, it was an example of a politically driven target that was set outside of the PSA process. The tipping point target was reached in early 2006, though as a result of declining applications rather than improved performance in carrying out removals.

In spring 2006, the removals issue hit the media headlines in the context of the so-called foreign national prisoners scandal. Already in autumn 2005 the House of Commons Committee of Public Accounts had begun to question Home Office officials about gaps in data on foreign nationals serving out sentences in UK prisons. This line of enquiry exposed what was seen as the fiasco of hundreds of foreign nationals who had committed crimes in the UK not being deported after their release from prison – a gift to the mass media (see Chapter 5 for a more detailed account of the scandal). And as Committee of Public Accounts member Richard Bacon pointed out, the scandal was 'a microscope through which the wider problem of hundreds of thousands of failed asylum seekers wandering around the UK could be viewed' (Bacon and Hope 2013, 128). Figures produced by the Home Office in spring 2006 estimated the number of 'unresolved cases' – including rejected asylum seekers who had not been deported – as standing at between 400,000 and 450,000.

The scandal prompted the resignation of Home Secretary Charles Clarke, who was replaced by John Reid in May 2006. Reid had a reputation for being disciplined and tough. He was also an astute tactician. On assuming office, he very publicly announced that he was appalled at the poor management and information within the Home Office, which he declared was 'not fit for purpose'. Reid announced radical changes to the Home Office, including the creation of a new Border and Immigration Agency (subsequently renamed the UK Border Agency) to replace the IND. He also declared that he would clear the asylum backlog in five years, by July 2011 – a target which even at the time was widely seen as unrealisable (BBC Online 2006). But it put the new agency under intense pressure. As one official puts it, 'There was a public commitment from John Reid to clear the backlog. That became a very high-profile thing for the business that they had to be seen to deliver on' (Interview, February 2014).

The new 2007 PSA adjusted the asylum-processing target to measure time taken to conclude cases, which implied a focus not just on initial decisions, but on whether rejected applicants were actually removed. Many senior officials welcomed this as a more sensible indicator in terms of driving an increase in removals, though it was set in a complicated and technical way, reducing its political usefulness. The time taken to conclude cases was to be incrementally reduced through a series of temporally staged targets. Thus there was an over-arching target of concluding 90 per cent of cases within six months, by December 2011. And then a series of 'milestones towards this target', with 24 per cent to be concluded within six months, by April 2007, 40 per cent by December 2007 and so on. But most of the targets were not met, nor was the five-year backlog clearance target achieved. A 2009 report by the UKBA Independent Chief Inspector noted that both targets were unfeasible and had been set without adequate consultation or understanding of asylum case processing. Moreover, the completion target had led to widespread gaming, with officials focusing on more easily removable cases to meet phased dead-lines, creating a backlog of intractable cases (UKBA Independent Inspector 2009).

By this time, though, asylum was no longer in the public spotlight. To be sure, parliamentary select committees continued to scrutinise UK Border Agency performance on the issue, and the Treasury retained a concern about Home Office efficiency. But political debate had moved on to concerns about the rising level of labour migration to the UK, and its perceived social and economic impacts. Government objectives in the area of labour migration were not codified as targets. Asylum became far less prominent and contested. The PSA targets on asylum processing and removals remained in place, but from around 2007 onwards they were functioning largely as management tools, used to improve organisational performance rather than to signal government achievements (see Chapter 4 for a fuller discussion).

Indeed, the whole PSA target apparatus was becoming increasingly technical and opaque. The Treasury had instructed departments to reduce the number of targets for the 2007 PSA, but in the case of the Home Office, targets were simply rebranded as 'indicators'. And many of these were subdivided into part (a), (b) and so on. As a former special advisor noted, even select committee members were struggling to make sense of the system: 'we had four and then we contributed to others, and then we had delivery agreements, and we had strategic objectives and everything else. And it became a very complicated architecture.' So while they remained useful for driving organisational behaviour, 'in terms of having a wider audience in public, Parliament, [their use was] pretty non-existent' (Interview, February 2014). By the mid-2000s, 'it had morphed ... into a more technocratic approach', with less public resonance (Interview, February 2014). Thus targets as signalling devices in asylum had their heyday in the early 2000s, but by the second half of the decade, they were being more narrowly deployed by the Labour government as management tools.

Political and Organisational Problems

The targets the Labour government developed in 2000–10 were certainly devised to perform two functions: their purpose was to steer organisational behaviour, while demonstrating improved performance. Yet the fate of asylum and removals targets suggests that even in their prime, targets were never able to couple disciplining and signalling functions in a satisfactory way. The more managerial PSA targets that were designed to improve organisational efficiency proved inadequate as political signalling devices. Meanwhile, top-down political targets to halve asylum applications or eliminate the backlog of legacy cases were not informed by a realistic appraisal of organisational capacity to deliver these goals. Moreover, the use of highly visible and ambitious targets to signal robust action that created political risks was not offset by commensurate political rewards when targets were met. This partly explains the demise in the use of targets as political tools in immigration and asylum policy in the latter part of the decade.

It is worth exploring in more detail the two main sets of problems identified in the analysis. The first problem related to the political risks of adopting ambitious targets. By adopting such prominent stretch targets, the government was effectively shifting the means through which its conduct would be appraised. Governments typically derive legitimacy largely from symbolic politics: rhetoric and cosmetic adjustments rather than the effects of their political interventions on social and economic systems (Edelman 1977; Gusfield 1981; Majone 1989). Yet in setting measurable targets, governments are effectively making assessment of their performance contingent on achieving certain observable outcomes. And in so doing, they are limiting their scope for relying on symbolic adjustments to garner legitimacy. To paraphrase Scott and Meyer, they are shifting from institutional to technical modes of legitimation (Scott and Meyer 1991), in which they derive support from their actions rather than their talk (Brunsson 2002).

There are, of course, potential advantages to moving from a symbolic to an outcome-oriented mode of legitimation. There is an immediate dividend of being seen to be locked into a measurable pledge, which might signal greater commitment than relying on rhetoric alone (although, of course, this is another form of symbolic legitimation based on a promise of action). And clearly, if a government is successful in realising the target, then it might expect to be rewarded by public support. But of course, there is a risk that further down the line the government will be unable to deliver, especially if the target is ambitious.

But the possibility of failure creates clear political risks. Matthew Flinders (2001) describes how just such concerns about feasibility prompted the pre-1997 Conservative administration to be cautious about going against the advice of its senior civil servants in setting targets. As one of Flinders' Home Office interviewees noted, 'It would take a brave minister to enforce a change in targets which the Permanent Secretary said was unrealistic and could have dangerous consequences' (cited in Flinders 2001: 282). Similarly, Michael Barber, the architect of New Labour's methodology for implementing targets, observes how the Australian government avoided stretch targets, instead opting for an 'underpromise and overdeliver' approach (Barber 2007: 81). Not so the Labour administration, which, as we saw, set a number of ambitious and arguably highly politically risky targets. Ambitious stretch targets exposed the administration to the danger of being seen to fail. A former Home Office special advisor expressed the tension in this way:

So I think the, the problem the kind of contemporary politicians face is that ... they have this tension between wanting to be responsive but also to be responsible. And the responsible thing says well you can't promise more than you can deliver, you are constrained by lots of things, you can't overdo things. And the responsive, this puts you entirely in the other direction, you know. (Interview, May 2014)

The Blair government was able to meet the *Newsnight* target – through a certain amount of luck, but also through hugely intrusive steering of the Home Office. (We examine its attempt to steer public administration to achieve this target in more depth in the next chapter.) It had less success in shifting performance on removals and clearing the backlog. Yet even where it was able to meet targets, the government found that it was not politically rewarded. As one former advisor put it:

targets can be useful to help you get there and focus people's attention ... Whether that helps you over here with what you say to the public and whether they actually believe you or not and whether they're going to vote for you again, those are two separate things in my book. I think there's a big distinction, because I think most people think, in politics, well if we show progress with certain things then that's going to translate into those, but it doesn't. (Interview, February 2014)

This asymmetry in the political capital accruing from public targets was one of the reasons Labour retreated from their use as a signalling device. An initial enthusiasm for targets as a tool of legitimation was dampened by the dawning realisation that the media and other political actors were simply not interested in reporting on successes. To be sure, the decline in asylum applications was accompanied by reduced political attention to the problem: a 'thermostat'-like response, as Will Jennings (2009) observed. But the achievement was not explicitly chalked up as a government success. There was no air time for stories about government achievement of targets. This finding supports earlier studies showing that meeting PSA targets did not bring clear dividends in terms of increasing public confidence in public services (Hood and Dixon 2010; James and John 2007).

Targets thus had limited success as an exercise in deriving political legitimacy. They failed to convince the public of improved performance, nor were they widely adopted (in the media or political debate) as a trusted tool for measuring government achievement. They were unable to establish credible, authoritative claims about government performance. Perhaps even more problematic was that even where they did, these claims were not seen as pertinent to assessing the performance of incumbents. This suggests that governments cannot be credible sources of such descriptions: where they attempt to produce tools for self-measurement, these are likely to lack legitimacy. Moreover, they may have limited control over which outcomes are seen as most important. While they may emphasise particular outcomes through setting targets, other outcomes they preferred not to measure or emphasise may emerge as the preferred indicators for assessing performance. We will explore these dynamics further in Chapter 5.

The second set of problems concerned relations between politics and the administration. Where a government is seeking legitimacy through demonstrating outcomes, it will obviously need to achieve a related shift in organisational behaviour. The ministries charged with (overseeing) the delivery of targets will need to introduce a number of reforms to their structures and modes of operating. The use of specific, high-profile targets certainly galvanised a series of adjustments in the Home Office. It placed immense pressure on the organisation, most of it unwelcome. This is hardly surprising. Five decades of studies in organisational sociology have taught us about the problems in attempting top-down reform, especially in public sector organisations. Reform driven by political goals and/or informed by modish ideas about good management frequently conflicts with the internal requirements of effective organisational action (Brunsson 2002; March and Olsen 1976; Meyer and Rowan 1991). Indeed, as Brunsson and Olsen argue, the policy/ ideas and action-oriented parts of organisations tend to be only very loosely connected, and display a limited understanding of one another (1993: 63). A reform plan that makes sense to the (political) management may show a lack of understanding of the structures and processes necessary for effective action.

Our analysis of asylum targets suggested that these tensions were particularly acute where politically driven targets were set in a top-down manner, without due regard to organisational capacity. In line with the literature on decoupling, our study found that politically motivated targets tended to be based on a limited understanding of organisational action; indeed, in some cases they were based on aspiration, at best informed by a superficial reading of macro-trends in the phenomenon. Those setting the targets appeared to assume that the organisation could take on board and implement political targets in a straightforward fashion. While our analysis focused on the case of asylum targets, interviews with senior officials in other departments suggested similar tensions between politically driven targets and what civil servants considered the most effective means of driving change to achieve goals. As a former Department of Health official put it:

Part of the dilemma with that is that if you really asked yourself what would it be that would improve, whether it's service standards in the immigration services or, you know, reduction of errors in immigration claims or whatever ... If you really asked yourself, if we really wanted to get to the best possible position that we could on that, what [is] our best understanding of how you would do that – how you would get there? What's the path that you would take? And then how would you work with this enormous complex system to mobilise all of the efforts and activities to that end? You would come up with an answer but you would not be able to persuade any politician it was desirable ... It wouldn't sound quick enough, firm enough, you know, prescriptive and clear from the top. (Interview, May 2014)

While top-down interventions certainly prompted organisational adjustments, the changes they effected were arguably short term and highly localised and tended to produce a number of distortions. Thus the *Newsnight* target to halve asylum applications did produce a flurry of activity in the Home Office, largely effected through robust Delivery Unit intervention. But as Barber himself concedes, such No. 10-driven interventions did not always have a lasting impact on wider organisational culture (Barber 2007: 192–4). And in this case, the narrow focus on applications did little to address longer-term trends such as the sluggish processing of asylum claims and the rising backlogs of unresolved cases, problems that would subsequently undermine the credibility of the asylum system. In the case of Reid's legacy backlog target, as we saw the target was never close to being met – indeed by October 2013, more than two years on from the original target date, the backlog still stood at almost 34,000 (Home Affairs Committee 2013). The manner in which Reid set the target, combined with his scabrous attack on the organisation, meanwhile left a serious dent in Home Office morale, contributing to problems with retention (Boswell 2009).

Arguably the most successful use of targets was as a more low-profile, technocratic management tool, with just enough transparency to motivate action, but foregoing the political signalling function that initially appeared so promising to the Labour administration. Targets worked best as tools developed within and for the organisation, to clarify priorities and objectives, to provide direction, roles and a sense of achievement. This suggests that there are good reasons to keep political targets at least partially independent of management targets. Targets lack the degree of abstraction and ambiguity that would enable them to operate across the worlds of politics and management. The requirement that the PSA targets be specific, measurable and outcome-oriented rather delimited their flexibility in moving across these spheres.

That said, short-term political rationality may crowd out such considerations. Combining political and organisational goals in the form of high-profile targets can appear to bring immediate political dividends that outweigh the longer-term risks. Despite the multiple problems with combining disciplining and signalling functions, this formula appears to retain its short-term political appeal. The implication is that whatever their shortcomings and political risks, we can expect such politically motivated targets to continue to crop up in policy-making.

Two Modes of Producing Trust

I have suggested that the use of targets as both signalling and disciplining devices created tensions and risks for policy-makers. In this last section of this chapter, I explore some of these tensions by returning to our discussion of theories of trust. The two functions of targets can be analysed in terms of their capacity to produce trust, whether through imposing rules backed by sanctions (disciplining), or through establishing reliable truth claims (signalling). Let us consider each in turn.

First, how far were targets able to produce trust through setting out rules and sanctions that stabilised expectations about behaviour? The targets on asylum established a number of specific, measurable and monitored objectives for public administrators to pursue. They were publicised as part of a high-profile set of PSA objectives, and in some cases as personal political pledges. By attaching such political and organisational importance to these targets, the core executive was introducing a variety of possible sanctions for noncompliance: reputational (the risk that the organisation or senior managers within it be discredited), financial (the threat of the Treasury withholding resources) and power-related (the prospect that the organisation or its senior managers would lose influence or autonomy). In theory, these sanctions were designed to align the interests and behaviour of civil servants to those of their political leaders. Indeed, the expectation was that the targets would create trust through motivating such an alignment.

The analysis of asylum targets suggests that this strategy failed to produce trust between politics and public administration. The imposition of ambitious targets heightened awareness of the divergence between political aspirations and what the organisation considered it could feasibly deliver. Civil servants saw the targets as an imposition, and considered most of them unachievable. The failure of the Home Office to meet the initial targets generated increased frustration on the part of political leaders, which senior management clearly picked up on. Pressure to achieve the targets also engendered various forms of gaming and distortions, as we shall see in the next chapter. So in many ways, the imposition of targets had the reverse effect on trust. Rather than aligning preferences through adjusting incentives, it exposed and even sharpened existing divergences between politics and the administration. Insofar as sanctions had an effect on behaviour, they encouraged officials to show they were meeting targets on paper, while underlying organisational structures remained largely unaltered. These dynamics are considered in more detail in the next chapter.

If targets failed to produce trust through their disciplining function, did they at least produce trust through establishing authoritative truth claims? Again, the answer has to be a resounding no. Targets as a tool of political communication did not appear to generate an increase in political trust in the area of asylum policy. This was most obviously the case for those targets that were not met: those relating to removals and eliminating the backlog of asylum cases. Failure to meet its own high-profile targets exposed the government to critical scrutiny from its political opposition, the House of Commons select committee system, and the media. But even where the government was able to meet targets, targets were not widely accepted as authoritative descriptions of policy performance. This is partly because of the problem of 'air time' mentioned earlier: the media was not interested in covering stories about the government meeting its targets. Thus where targets were met, such as the halving of asylum applications in 2003, they received very limited media coverage. Indeed, when one problem appears to be addressed, the media and political attention are likely to shift to other areas of immigration and asylum policy. Public concern may simply be switched to another, related policy problem. We explore this problem in Chapter 5.

The lack of attention to positive stories about government targets may also reflect a wider problem with the authority of such claims.

The audiences that targets seek to mollify – the public, the mass media – may not accept the credibility of measures developed by the government. They may be sceptical of giving too much credence to modes of assessment devised by governments, which are clearly developed to cast the governments in a favourable light. This suggests that governments may have limited autonomy in controlling the way their interventions are assessed. And, indeed, they may have limited scope for determining which areas they are assessed on. The upshot is that targets are likely to have limited effects on trust in politics. They may have some traction at the point at which they are announced – although repeated declarations followed by disappointment or doubt may also come to be treated with scepticism by a jaded public. Even where such targets are achieved, they appear to have a negligible impact on how publics assess and reward government performance.

4 | Monitoring Public Administration

Deficits of trust occur under conditions of uncertainty: where those dependent on the actions of others – the trusters – are unable to continually observe the actions of those they are endowing with responsibility to act on their behalf. Performance measurement in the form of targets, indicators and related techniques holds the promise of addressing this problem through providing tools for monitoring behaviour.

In organisational theory, this type of monitoring may be expected to limit the scope for organisations to evade or subvert top-down control. As we saw in Chapter 1, organisations frequently respond to reform by separating talk and action, or through what has been termed 'decoupling' (Meyer and Rowan 1991) or 'loose coupling' (Orton and Weick 1990; Weick 1976). In order to reconcile conflicting pressures, organisations commit themselves formally and rhetorically to a reform (or target), but in practice they fail to adjust their informal operations to implement reform. In theory, monitoring through performance measurement should reduce the scope for this form of decoupling (Hallett 2010). Targets in particular might be expected to constrain the scope for decoupling, by virtue of certain formal features: namely, the requirement that targets be quantifiable, specific and involve a robust monitoring system. Performance targets also tend to focus on organisational outputs, or even outcomes – hence limiting the opportunities for organisations to separate talk from action. Outputs or outcomes have to match the rhetoric, and this correspondence is closely monitored through reporting requirements. Thus close scrutiny through indicators and targets should engender tighter coupling or 'recoupling' (Espeland 1998) of organisational rhetoric and practice.

This chapter explores how far performance measurement succeeds in limiting decoupling of this kind. It focuses on the strategies and practices organisations develop to evade or reinterpret performance measurement, and examines how targets have constrained such attempts. While Chapter 3 focused on asylum targets in the Home Office, this chapter compares responses to targets in two organisations: the Home Office and the Ministry of Defence. I focus on a subset of targets developed between 1998 and 2010 specifically designed to improve organisational performance. For the Home Office, this involved targets on asylum processing; for the Ministry of Defence, the targets related to the procurement of defence equipment. In both cases, the targets were specific and measurable, implying limited potential for decoupling and reinterpretation. Both targets were also concerned with delivering outcomes, thus reducing the scope for decoupling.

The two cases vary, however, in terms of the level of political commitment behind meeting the target. Asylum policy was highly politicised over this period, while defence procurement was relatively sequestered from political and public scrutiny. Partly as a result of this, the core executive played an active role in steering targets in the Home Office. By contrast, No. 10 and the Treasury were far more reticent about intervening in Ministry of Defence matters. We would expect higher political salience to produce more rigorous public and political scrutiny and more robust monitoring, thus making tight coupling more likely (Hallett 2010; Sauder and Espeland 2009). As a result, we can expect greater scope for decoupling in the case of defence procurement, with asylum targets by contrast being subject to closer scrutiny, and thus enjoying less leeway for evading unwanted top-down directives.

Targets and Public Sector Performance

As we saw in Chapter 1, the literature on public administration has long observed that targets can have distorting effects on public policy. Much of this literature has focused on the incidence of gaming, examining how organisations seek to bypass the requirements imposed by targets through various forms of manipulation (Bevan and Hood 2006; Heinrich 2002; Hood 2006; James 2004; Pidd 2005; Smith 1990, 1995). These contributions are good at describing and categorising the ways in which organisations can subvert and manipulate targets, and the various distortions produced as a result. However, they have less to say about the sorts of organisational pressures created by top-down targets. Public sector managers emerge from the analysis as canny tacticians, trying to evade unfeasible or ill-thought-through requirements. There is less focus on why these targets are so challenging for organisations, or what sorts of factors shape the choice of organisational response. Moreover, responses are viewed as strategic, whereas much of the literature sees organisational action as shaped by institutional factors that exert often unacknowledged influences on behaviour, and may also shape organisational understandings of appropriate strategy (Greening and Gray 1994; Modell 2001; Oliver 1991; Suchman 1995; Weaver, Trevino and Cochran 1999). In order to understand responses to targets, we therefore need some theory of the factors influencing how organisations respond to imposed change.

The institutionalist school of organisational studies offers useful insights into these questions (Brunsson 1993, 2002; DiMaggio and Powell 1983; March and Olsen 1976, 1983; Meyer and Rowan 1991; Scott 1995). This approach has long suggested that top-down attempts at steering organisational behaviour are likely to be highly problematic (Brunsson 2009; Brunsson and Olsen 1993). Such attempts are based on a rational-instrumental theory of public administration which conceives of bureaucracy as the tool or instrument of politics. In reality, the relationship between politics and the administration is far more complicated. Organisations in the public administration are guided by norms, beliefs and practices which are deeply institutionalised and which offer members a sense of purpose and stability (DiMaggio and Powell 1991: 15). Moreover, these rules and practices are often well attuned to responding to the multiple and contradictory demands typically faced by large and complex political organisations (Brunsson 2002). The top-down imposition of politically driven reform – or in our case targets – can risk disrupting these arrangements, and so is likely to encounter substantial resistance at different levels of the organisation.

How do organisations respond to such top-down imposed reform, given these challenges? As we saw in Chapter 1, one of the most common responses is to engage in some form of 'decoupling' (Meyer and Rowan 1991), or 'loose coupling', in Orton and Weick's terminology (1990). Organisations delink their rhetoric and formal structures (which embrace reform) from their day-to-day informal operations (which resist it). Brunsson (2002) distinguishes between four types of decoupling, of which two are particularly pertinent to our study. First, organisations may decouple talk from action. They may appear to be complying with reform, but without any significant increase or reallocation of resources to meet the target, or change to procedures. A second, related form of decoupling involves maintaining a discrepancy between the organisation's message to its external audience and its internal communication with staff regarding required changes. Different messages are conveyed to different audiences: key actors in the organisation's environment or its political leaders may be reassured that the organisation is committed to making changes to meeting the target, while the operational division of the organisation is largely permitted to retain its existing informal structures and goals.

More recently, Bromley and Powell (2012) have suggested that studies of decoupling have interpreted the practice too narrowly, focusing solely on the separation of formal policy and practice. Such a focus implies that the organisational changes triggered by top-down reform are purely cosmetic, overlooking the ways in which even formal and largely symbolic changes to organisational structures can generate changes to operational practices. Bromley and Powell suggest we should be attentive to how organisations do indeed adapt their practices to implement the requirements imposed on them, but in a way that is decoupled from the core goals or tasks of the organisation. They refer to this as means-ends decoupling, a practice that is especially likely to emerge in a context of increased external monitoring and evaluation of organisational activities. The organisation may interpret and implement requirements in a strict or narrow sense, but in doing so, fail to meet the underlying objectives of the reform. In the case of targets, this would imply formally meeting the target on paper, but neglecting to deal with the broader set of problems the target was designed to address.

Scholars have also explored the conditions under which decoupling is more or less likely to occur. Scott and Meyer (1991) distinguish between two types of institutional sector in which organisations operate: institutional and technical. Institutional organisations tend to rely on symbolic adjustments, such as changes to rhetoric and formal structures, to meet expectations about appropriate behaviour. Technical organisations are more dependent on securing support or resources through the quality of their output, and are thus more likely to align formal and informal structures. Brunsson (2002) introduces a similar distinction between action organisations, which rely on organised action for legitimacy, and political organisations, which need to reflect inconsistent demands by decoupling talk from action. Building on this insight, other authors have suggested that a change in the organisation's environment – for example the introduction of more market-like features or more stringent accountability requirements – could engender a shift from decoupling to tight coupling, a tendency which has recently been coined 'recoupling' (Espeland 1998; Hallett 2010; Sauder and Espeland 2009).

This chapter builds on these contributions, to explore how far targets limit the scope for decoupling. I argue that two main sets of factors are likely to play a role. The first of these relates to formal properties of targets. As a management tool, targets were designed precisely to limit organisational evasion and manipulation. In the language of New Public Management, targets should be SMART: specific, measurable, achievable, relevant and timed. These features impose quite rigid conditions on organisations. For a start, they set out goals in a specific and fairly unambiguous way. Moreover, the achievement of these targets is subject to ongoing monitoring, usually through quantifiable performance indicators. This limits scope for organisations to decouple symbolic adjustments from informal operations (Hallett 2010; Weaver et al. 1999). They are unable to 'buffer' their operations from external scrutiny and inspection (Oliver 1991: 155). The capacity for decoupling is especially constrained where targets are focused on outcomes: i.e. where performance measurement is based on changes the organisation effects on its environment. In this case, the organisation cannot rely on rhetoric or purely formal adjustments to meet targets.

The second factor relates to the political environment of the organisation. Previous contributions have suggested that more powerful external constituents can limit the scope for decoupling (Basu, Dirsmith and Gupta 1999; Oliver 1991). This is in line with resource-dependency theories, which assume that organisations are reliant on key actors in their environment and adjust their behaviour to meet their requirements (Pfeffer and Salancik 1978). We explore more specifically how far political salience affects an organisation's ability to evade targets through decoupling. Political salience refers to the degree of political attention an issue attracts, as indicated by mass media coverage and political debate. Highly salient policy issues are likely to mobilise governments to invest more attention and resources in addressing problems, including through closer monitoring of performance. Political salience may also encourage other organisations such as opposition parties, parliamentary committees, agencies and lobby groups to scrutinise policy-making and organisational performance more closely (Pollitt 2006: 39). Given that political salience can wax and wane over time, organisations may switch between decoupling and recoupling as ways of coping with external pressures. As close political scrutiny gives way to less intrusive monitoring, organisations may find they have more scope for decoupling talk and action, while a shift from low to high political attention may engender recoupling.

This chapter analyses these dynamics by comparing responses to targets in two policy areas subject to differing degrees of political salience: asylum and defence procurement. The analysis is based on thirty-four interviews with senior officials, special advisors, ministers and parliamentary committee members involved in setting, implementing and scrutinising targets in the two organisations over this period. It also draws on departmental reports, parliamentary committee reports and transcripts and reports by the National Audit Office and the Independent Chief Inspector of UKBA.

Asylum and Defence Procurement Targets in UK Government, 1998–2010

Once again, our story starts with the Public Service Agreement (PSA) targets adopted by the Labour government from 1998 onwards. The PSA targets set for defence procurement and asylum had many elements in common. First, both organisations were seen as inefficient, verging on dysfunctional. The Home Office had long had a reputation as a beleaguered and scandal-prone organisation dealing with a range of controversial and intractable problems (Painter 2008). Within the organisation, the Immigration and Nationality Directorate (IND) had responsibility for immigration and asylum policy. The IND had faced especially acute problems from the late 1990s onwards, grappling with a huge rise in the number of asylum applications. It was quite clear by 1999–2000 that it was unable to cope with the task. Several officials and special advisors described it as 'in meltdown' over this period. As one official put it, it 'was this monolithic old school civil service giant that was not able to cope with anything' (Interview,

December 2013). A former special advisor describes the level of chaos in the organisation in the early 2000s.

> But most of the things that were happening – I never actually saw for myself, but I heard, and I believed, that people were just stuffing paperwork in cupboards, with no attempt to just to get it off their desk, just hiding it, with no attempt to keep a record of where it was or what it was. (Interview, August 2014)

Not surprisingly, then, the PSA targets on asylum were therefore very much focused on the efficiency and effectiveness of asylum processing.

Like the Home Office, the Ministry of Defence also had a history of inefficiency. Indeed, the new Labour government of 1997 was faced with a significant overspend in the defence budget, as well as severe delays in equipment entering service (National Audit Office 1997). As defence commentator Philip Stephens put it at the time, 'the defence ministry's capacity to waste money is legendary. Procurement is a dismal story of delays and extortion.'[1] This reflected a long-standing problem with procurement procedures in defence (Gansler 1980; Page 2006). The Ministry of Defence also faced a series of new operational challenges, with 9/11 prompting debates about new security challenges, as well as the controversial and protracted deployment of British forces in Afghanistan (2001) and Iraq (2003).

The key difference between the cases, though, was the level of political salience of asylum and defence procurement. Asylum issues were continually in the media throughout this period, with ongoing negative coverage and party political debate over the government's handling of the issue. By contrast, while British military operations were widely covered in the media, defence procurement remained relatively sequestered from public political debate for most of the period. As one former advisor who worked in both areas commented, in the Ministry of Defence negative media coverage 'was part of a consideration but it never felt, until 2009, it never felt like a systematic campaign. Whereas in immigration it felt like a systematic campaigning issue from, I don't know, 2001, all the way through to 2010' (Interview, August 2014).

---

[1] Philip Stephens, 'Short range target: Tony Blair's defence review has taken the politics out of the issue but has missed the opportunity to think 10 years ahead', *Financial Times*, 25 May 1998.

The Home Office and Targets on Asylum

The initial PSA targets on asylum agreed in 2000 involved two components: the target of processing 75 per cent of applications within two months by 2004, and the target of removing a greater proportion of failed asylum seekers. As we saw in Chapter 3, these targets were set in the context of a massive injection of resources for asylum and immigration control. The Treasury was keen to see a return from this investment, and the targets were an instrument for galvanising improved efficiency. At the same time, the Prime Minister's office (No. 10) was concerned about improving performance in the area of asylum, which had become a highly salient issue in UK politics and the media by the early 2000s. The government wanted to demonstrate that it was managing the problem, and part of this involved being seen to meet the targets.

The targets prompted a number of formal structural changes, including the establishment of new Delivery Teams to help meet the targets, the placement of managers with responsibility for the targets in operational offices and the establishment of an Asylum Decision Service Unit to 'streamline the process further' (Home Office 2001: 102–3). However, in the first years the organisation struggled to achieve the targets or to make substantial improvements to operational performance. This was most patently the case with the removals target, which the IND repeatedly failed to meet in the first half of the decade. On processing, it managed to meet the 75 per cent target from 2002 onwards. But the target turned out to be a misleading indicator, as it disguised wider problems with processing. The government was frustrated at the continued problems with processing and removals, and saw the failure to improve performance as emanating from poor management in the IND and from a resistance to reform. As one former minister commented, 'the policy imperative to change the process and the way that people worked wasn't achieved [by 2004] and it was still dysfunctional' (Interview, June 2014). As the minister saw it, the IND was characterised by 'inertia ... and the unreceptiveness to change' (Interview, June 2014). Home Office officials were keenly aware of this lack of faith. As a former official put it bluntly, 'he thought we were all useless' (Interview, August 2014).

Part of the problem was the Home Office's perception that it lacked influence over many aspects of asylum and removals processing.

As a former advisor told me, 'They [officials in IND] were just looking at this challenge and thinking, why are these guys telling us – either the ministers on the one hand or the press on the other, sort of ganging up – telling us how crap we are, when actually, don't they realise how difficult this is?' (Interview, December 2013). Officials felt that the targets and associated changes were 'being done to them rather than with them' (Interview, August 2014). Yet the sense in IND was that they were dealing with a set of intractable problems. One aspect of this was the consistent underestimation by senior management of the challenges of asylum processing. In the first half of the 2000s asylum processing was treated as a fairly routine organisational task, which did not require extensive training and could be subjected to strictly timed targets. Until 2006, processing of cases would be done by (relatively junior) executive officers who would be responsible for just one stage of the process. As one official described it, the process was 'a series of mini silos' (Interview, August 2014): a financial decision, then an initial decision, then an appeals process, then removal and so on. But in practice, processing frequently involved making decisions based on complex legal considerations, with limited information and a high degree of uncertainty. Sloppy administration or poorly grounded decisions at one stage of the process created delay and higher costs further down the line.

The fragmentation of the process into distinct stages also meant that each team was trying to meet its own targets, linked to just one stage of the process. Thus faced with a target of processing 75 per cent of applications within two months, the temptation was to prioritise more straightforward cases. Moreover, the target only referred to processing of initial decisions – while it was the subsequent phases of the process (appeals, and removals) that tended to be more challenging and time-consuming. Thus while the IND managed to meet its initial decisions target, it saw slippage on final appeal decisions and on the proportion of appealed decisions being upheld (see Home Office 2003: 150 and 2005: 13). The combination of a rather narrowly defined target, and the clear challenges to speeding up processing, led to means-ends decoupling. Staff were meeting the 75 per cent target on paper, but there was a failure to address the broader operational problems that had created the administrative crisis. And the political management became aware of this quite early on: 'we started to worry more and more ... obviously we should have done this earlier, we started to join up the dots between, we've got this massive problem of far too high a rate of challenging, overturning decisions' (Interview, August 2014).

Increasing the rate of removals, meanwhile, proved even more challenging. Removing failed asylum seekers from the UK frequently presented insurmountable obstacles, for example in ascertaining identity, securing documentation, dealing with judicial appeals and eliciting support from the authorities in countries of origin. Officials variously described it as 'a nightmare' (Interview, February 2014) and as 'one of the most intractable problems I came across in government' (Interview, August 2014). This was understood by staff dealing with removals, but, as one official put it, 'the senior managers' response tended to be, yeah, I know it's difficult but you just have to work harder' (Interview, August 2014). So the operational response to the removals target in the early 2000s was to aim at the 'low hanging fruit', with the result that 'a larger and larger share of what's left is beyond your control' (Interview, August 2014). Thus despite various shifts in the way the target was set, removals targets consistently proved impossible to meet. Here we can see an instance of means-ends decoupling.

Poor performance on removals surfaced as a political scandal in late 2005. Under scrutiny by the House of Commons Committee on Public Accounts, the Home Office was forced to concede publicly that there were around 400,000–450,000 unresolved or 'legacy' cases (Committee on Public Accounts, 2006b). This triggered the setting of new, more rigorous targets in 2006 under Home Secretary John Reid. Two targets were especially high profile: clearing the backlog of legacy cases, and processing cases to conclusion, i.e. until an applicant had been granted some kind of leave to remain or had been removed from the country. The Home Office was under more political pressure than ever, with the focus of political attention now shifted to Home Office performance itself, including the organisation's lack of internal coherence and poor communication and data management. John Reid further crystallised the problem around poor organisational performance by famously declaring to Parliament that the Home Office was 'not fit for purpose'.

The parliamentary committee system now swung behind monitoring the new targets. As a former advisor put it, the new targets became 'a big drive in Home Office behaviour' with senior officials 'dragged in front of the Home Affairs Committee every couple of months to talk about the latest numbers' (Interview, February 2014). Indeed, progress on the backlog target was now monitored through six-monthly reports to the Home Affairs Committee. The new targets were also accompanied by more far-reaching organisational reforms, especially in the processing of asylum cases. A New Asylum Model was introduced which put more senior higher executive officers (HEOs) in charge of processing a case through from start to finish. Around forty HEOs – mainly talented fast-stream recruits – were brought in to head up teams, replacing the previous asylum caseload directory. A new senior manager was brought in to run immigration, who was strongly committed to the targets, and 'ran that very severely'. As one former official put it, 'There was no flexibility about those targets' (Interview, August 2014).

The targets were widely considered to be very ambitious. And as before, there were instances of means-ends decoupling, especially around the processing targets. For example, staff might prioritise easier cases to ensure a particular target was met, neglecting more complex or higher-risk cases (Interview, August 2014); more recent applications were prioritised while older ones were stockpiled, in order to meet the target of dealing with cases within six months (UKBA Independent Inspector 2009: 11), and performance would dip in the months after a particular deadline had passed (UKBA Independent Inspector 2009: 11). Yet there clearly was a major improvement in operations, with asylum cases being processed more efficiently and rigorously. Most of the targets were met, and, moreover, there was less decoupling of targets and underlying objectives. The organisational reforms limited the 'silo' tendency that was so prevalent before, while the target of processing to conclusion prevented the tendency of shifting the problem to the next phase of decision-making. By around 2006–7, the Home Office had truly swung behind the targets, both in its rhetoric and in its operations.

Thus from 2006 onwards, a combination of sustained political scrutiny, more carefully designed targets and substantial organisational reform appeared to generate a recoupling of targets and operations. As one former advisor put it, 'So you relentlessly focus on this stuff, and with a combination of some small legislative changes, but a lot of just internal management stuff and throwing resources – throwing people and money at the problem – you could increase them. So it was extremely difficult, but not impossible' (Interview, December 2013). The achievement of targets was also greatly aided by the steady decline in the number of asylum applications from 2003 onwards, implying that the flow of cases through the system was more manageable. 'There was a sense that the intake was going down and that was a huge relief. And that we were pretty much keeping on top of the kind of targets we were aiming at ... And that this sort of basket case had turned into something a bit better ordered' (Interview, August 2014). As a special advisor remarked, 'it felt like a much more orderly process in 2005–9' (Interview, August 2014).

As anticipated in the literature (Hallett 2010), recoupling did take its toll on the organisation. Hundreds of administrative staff were redeployed or made redundant in order to implement the New Asylum Model, many of whom felt aggrieved and poorly treated. And the general lambasting of the Home Office in the media left huge scars. One official describes how harrowing it was to be under such negative media scrutiny:

I think what affects morale worst is constant criticism of the system actually, externally. I think that's the thing that has a really negative impact more than anything. I think the fact that there are backlogs, it's kind of part of the job and people get on top of it ... I mean the debates in public about the operation of the immigration system, there's no other part of government that gets the kind of criticism that the Home Office gets. (Interview, June 2007)

In particular, Reid's very public description of the Home Office as 'not fit for purpose' has had a lasting legacy. As one former special advisor put it, 'in terms of the kind of corporate impact of what he said, it was pretty catastrophic, I think. And I'm not sure the department ever recovered' (Interview, August 2014). Another official commented:

It still feels like that phrase hangs over the whole of immigration, and there are all sorts of behaviours you can see which happened because people were afraid of looking like they'd get it wrong, they were afraid of dropping the ball, they were afraid of making a mistake, which means they take very very few risks. (Interview, August 2014)

A former special advisor describes the breakdown in trust between officials and John Reid.

So, you know, by the end of his tenure, John didn't believe a word that anybody was telling him. And so ... every sentence, every statement he gave to the Commons ... began with 'my officials have advised me that ... ' or ... 'reports say that . . . '. Rather than, you know, I think his confidence in the, in the ability of the department to come up with the right numbers or have the right solutions was, was shot by that point. (Interview, February 2014)

The Ministry of Defence and Procurement Targets

The overall objective for equipment in the first Ministry of Defence PSA was 'to procure equipment which most cost-effectively meets agreed military requirements' (Treasury 1998: 69). Given the problems with procurement processes mentioned earlier, it was logical that the targets would be geared to reining in overspend and overrun. There were three specific performance targets for procurement: 'on average, no in-year increase in major project costs'; 'on average, in-year slippage of In-Service Date of new major projects of less than 10 days'; and 'on average, in-year slippage of In-Service Date of existing major projects of less than 4 weeks' (Treasury 1998: 72). The targets for 2003–6 included a further performance indicator (PI): '97% of customers' key requirements attained and maintained through the PSA period' (Ministry of Defence 2004: 12).

From the outset, officials in the MoD were more reticent about adopting the targets. Indeed, the MoD was one of the government departments most opposed to targets, arguing that it could not control policy outcomes (Interview, June 2014). Nor was the department keen to be subjected to close Treasury scrutiny of its procurement processes. As one former special advisor in the MoD put it, the Treasury 'tried to apply pressure to the MoD to say, look, you need to sit down and decide what you need to cancel, what you need to stop spending money on because this is unaffordable. The MoD refused to do that' (Interview, August 2014). Indeed, the MoD comprehensively failed to adjust its internal procedures in a way that would enable it to meet the targets. A report by the National Audit Office (2009) identified a decline in the Department's performance, with £1 billion worth of cost overruns and delays of 242 months 'across the Department's larger procurement projects'. In 2009 an independent report carried out for the Ministry noted that on average equipment programmes 'cost 40% more than they were originally expected to, and are delivered 80% later than first estimates predicted', implying an average cost increase of £300 million (Gray 2009: 16). There was a clear acknowledgement that the MoD was falling well short of its targets.

These failings were certainly evident to others in government at the time. The Treasury was aware of the problem, but had fairly fraught relations with the MoD and was reluctant to get closely involved in MoD decision-making, seeing its role as limited to exercising external budgetary discipline in the hope that the department would 'sort themselves out' (Interview, August 2014). The Prime Minister, while keenly following military operations in Afghanistan and Iraq, was less interested in defence procurement. Indeed, equipment for ongoing operations was managed through a separate fast-track procurement procedure for 'urgent operational requirements', which tended to be more efficient than the normal MoD route for longer-term procurement (National Audit Office 2004). More generally, the MoD was seen as something of a 'black box', whose decision-making premises and operational culture remained obscure to other parts of public administration. As one interviewee put it, 'Blair genuinely thought that if he'd had the time to be CEO of IND he would have done a better job. I'm not sure that anybody thought that of defence procurement' (Interview, December 2013).

This lack of close Treasury or No. 10 scrutiny appears to have allowed the department to engage in widespread decoupling of talk and action. One of the main features of this was the retention of procedures that created incentives to commission expensive new projects. The procurement process pitted the three services (army, navy, air force) against one another to compete for the same resources to fund acquisitions. Projects had to pass through 'initial gate' and then 'main gate', after which point projects were rarely abandoned. As a former special advisor notes, we 'increased these tougher gateway hurdles to get over but still no project was ever turned down' (Interview, December 2013). Decisions to cancel projects were politically sensitive, as they indicated the MoD had wasted public money, generating a kind of sunk costs fallacy. Thus there were strong incentives not just for the chiefs of service, but also for the MoD and industry to rush projects through main gate, often prematurely, which resulted in overly optimistic costing and time planning (Gray 2009). As one defence analyst described it, the procedure 'almost lends itself to perfect game theory where non-collaborative behaviours are rewarded, and collaborative behaviours are, are not rewarded' (Interview, February 2014). The budget was 'overstuffed with programmes' (Interview, December 2013). Thus the targets were undermined by informal organisational structures that militated strongly against meeting those targets. This state of affairs has been described as a 'conspiracy of optimism' within MoD procurement practices.

Other structural factors also perpetuated the 'conspiracy of optimism'. Senior officials in the MoD were aware of a range of political and economic considerations influencing defence procurement, which are not easily reducible to quantifiable performance targets. There are the security risks associated with purchasing equipment from foreign producers, the need to make decisions that signal certain commitments or priorities to different allies, the financial and strategic value of exporting procured equipment to key allies, the importance of supporting domestic manufacturers to sustain jobs and local economies and the need to retain a healthy level of specialised domestic suppliers. In short, 'there are a whole range of other potential public value type items' that might militate towards commissioning expensive, new and sophisticated equipment, rather than already priced off-the-shelf items (Interview, August 2014). These sorts of considerations were not captured by Treasury formulations, which partly explains the strong impetus to decouple procurement practices from targets. Narrowing down performance criteria to questions of cost and overrun simply did not allow leeway for meeting these other priorities.

MoD officials adopted a number of practices to avoid the resulting overspend showing up in performance indicators. One such practice was to delay delivery of equipment, thereby aligning current budgets but deferring costs to subsequent reporting periods. Thus even in the few instances where targets appeared closer to being met, the department already knew of substantial financial overruns in the acquisition process. The decision to delay delivery would allow the MoD to stick to budget, but it had the result of driving up costs substantially over the long term. A second form of decoupling was to limit 'overheating' of the defence budget by reducing the units ordered, or so-called descoping (Interview, February 2014). One former advisor described it as follows: 'if you have a six-billion-pound project to build twelve type forty five destroyers, you just, you know, as the cost overruns, as the unit cost increases you simply reduce the number. And we ended up ordering six rather than twelve. So, you know, does that count as a cost overrun? I mean that depends on how you define it.' This practice would clearly have been exposed if there had been a unit cost target, which would have indicated 100 per cent price inflation per unit. As the special advisor described it, 'typically the MoD had managed this by pushing, just pushing the data to the right and descoping and reducing numbers' (Interview, August 2014). Thus rather than adjusting their procurement practices to prevent cost inflation, officials allowed such inflation to occur and sought to disguise the fact through reducing the quantity ordered. This is another case of officials seeking to meet targets nominally, while informal practices remained largely unchanged.

By the mid-2000s, many within the MoD and the Treasury were concerned about a looming crisis in MoD procurement. The persistent failure to meet the targets and the awareness that officials were constantly deferring expenditure to the next year – 'pushing the problem to the right' as it was put – suggested that sooner or later the MoD was going to run out of money and would simply be unable to pay staff and contractors. As a former special advisor put it:

What you had was a very long, slow build-up of an intractable problem that the managers dealt with by pushing it to the right, pushing it to the right. Just essentially, do whatever we need to do this year, push the problem further to the right. Even though doing that makes the problem worse. So essentially, you haven't got enough money to manage in a year, so we'll just delay things, even though you know that is going to increase the cost next year. It will make it worse. (Interview, August 2014)

The political leadership of the MoD was aware of this looming crisis.

That was the crisis I feared, and I feared it, and the MoD feared it, but were unable to do anything to pre-empt it. And the sort of political judgement was, when they come to you every year, when you pore over the spreadsheets, are they just sort of scaremongering or is it really going to happen this year? (Interview, August 2014)

In summer 2009, the MoD was indeed hit by a political scandal over equipment. The media picked up on claims that British forces in Iraq were being put at risk because of poor equipment and underfinancing of defence.[2] Although equipment for Iraq was procured through the urgent operational requirements channel, the two issues became conflated in public debate. 'So people connected the two things even though they weren't very closely connected in reality' (Interview,

---

[2] Holly Watt, 'MPs' expenses: Armour was so poor that troops couldn't wear it', *Daily Telegraph*, 29 September 2009.

August 2014). Problems with longer-term defence procurement were exposed, and critics of the government made the argument that British forces were dying because of government underspend on defence.[3] These criticisms hounded Prime Minister Gordon Brown up until the general election of April 2010, in which the Labour government was defeated.

In sum, unlike in the case of the Home Office, in the MoD there was substantial scope for decoupling talk from action. The top-down targets imposed by the Treasury failed to disrupt existing incentive structures within the MoD. As a result, the MoD's informal practices were not significantly affected by the introduction of targets and accompanying reforms. Instead, officials attempted to meet the letter of their target commitments through deferring delivery and descoping commissions, practices which in turn led to further cost escalation and overrun.

Decoupling, Recoupling and Trust

The analysis of Home Office and MoD responses to targets has shown that both organisations faced serious problems in attempting to meet top-down targets. Nonetheless, targets had considerably more traction in the area of asylum than they did in defence. After a shaky start, by around 2006 more concerted political commitment from both senior management in the Home Office and No. 10 resulted in substantial adjustments within the organisation. This did not mean that the targets were always achieved, or that the decoupling of means and ends was eliminated. But it did mean that asylum processing was structured and managed in a way that largely recoupled informal operations with targets.

This might imply that targets succeeded in aligning political and organisational preferences. And indeed, this may be the case in a purely formal sense: senior management perceived the need to adjust organisational practice in a way that would meet political goals. Yet far from producing trust, this convergence – or recoupling – led to a number of problems for the organisation. In particular, the 2006 interventions by John Reid galvanised reform, but they also engendered a climate of anxiety and suspicion. The degree of political pressure and

---

[3] Patrick Wintour, 'Chilcot Iraq war inquiry to grill Gordon Brown over cuts to defence budget at height of war', *Guardian*, 5 March 2010.

intervention required to recouple organisational practice and overarching political goals necessitated extensive redeployment of personnel, and had a hugely destructive effect on morale. This supports recent studies exploring the 'turmoil' created by recoupling (Hallett 2010).

In the case of the MoD, there was much more scope for sustained decoupling. Through most of the 2000s, officials complied with targets on procurement in their rhetoric, but in practice very little changed in terms of defence procurement. There were still strong incentives for officials to commission expensive equipment, and a tendency to defer payment and rescope commissions in a way that led to further cost inflation and overrun. In this case, then, targets made very little difference to relations between the political leadership and officials in the organisation. If anything, the targets confirmed the beliefs of civil servants that their political leaders did not understand the complexities of defence procurement, while they also exposed the impotence of the Treasury and No. 10 in steering the organisation. So targets served to highlight a series of problems in relations between the organisations and their political leaders.

One reason for the difference between the two cases, as expected, was the degree of politicisation and public scrutiny encountered by the two organisations. Asylum targets were the object of intensive political scrutiny and ongoing public debate, generating far more attention from No. 10 and the Treasury. From 2006, this took the form of quite detailed scrutiny of organisational practices. Organisational inefficiency became part of the framing of the problem, with Home Office practices on asylum processing, removals and data management exposed as defective in the media and political debate. Defence procurement, by contrast, was less politicised and less of a priority for No. 10. The implication was that the MoD could get away with much more widespread decoupling. While the Treasury was keen to limit the MoD's overall budget, it largely kept out of internal decision-making. This may partly have reflected the MoD's reputation within government as a largely impenetrable 'black box', which helped it to buffer its workings from external steering. But it was also a function of the lower political salience of defence procurement. Defence procurement remained a largely technical, managerial concern.

The asylum case therefore suggests that political salience in itself does not guarantee political commitment to implementing targets. Rather, the organisation's workings – or malfunctions – have to be part of the political 'story'. The extent to which public administrative practices are drawn into this story depends on prevailing constructions of the problem. If the problem is seen as largely separable from organisational practices, then these latter may be exempt from central government interference. But where organisational inefficiency is seen as directly responsible for the problem, or is even the object of media attention itself, then it is more likely that top-down measures will be backed up with more concerted and rigorous intervention.

These findings have a number of implications for theories of organisational responses to performance measurement. Firstly, I suggested that the introduction of targets might engender tight coupling, reducing the scope for organisational evasion of targets. The example of defence procurement suggests that this is not necessarily the case. Even where targets are clearly specified and rigorously monitored, organisations may engage in widespread decoupling.

Secondly, this chapter anticipated that a high level of political salience might produce more robust scrutiny of the implementation of targets, thus producing tighter coupling. The findings on this are more nuanced. The intense political attention to asylum in the 2000s did prompt a more intrusive and rigorous oversight of targets in the Home Office. But even this effort was not sufficient to produce recoupling. Political salience only seemed to generate recoupling where the organisation itself was the object of political attention. The political problem needed to be framed in a way that implicated organisational practices as culpable, as occurred from 2006 onwards. Thus political salience per se is not a reliable predictor of recoupling or decoupling. Rather, such responses are likely to vary depending on political constructions of the problem. Tight coupling is more likely to occur where organisational performance and behaviour are part of the political narrative of the problem.

The third finding is that where an organisation is under strong political pressure to adjust to external targets, it may shift from policy-practice decoupling to means-ends decoupling. This was the case in the Home Office: even once asylum targets were recoupled with practice from 2006 onwards, the organisation nonetheless continued to engage in means-ends decoupling, through various types of 'gaming'. Again, where these tactics themselves become the object of political attention, we can expect political leaders to devote more resources to clamping down on such decoupling practices. What this suggests is that there is a close and constantly evolving relationship between political problem construction, top-down pressures for organisational reform, and opportunities for organisational decoupling.

Finally, we should consider the implications of the analysis for the problem of trust between politics and the administration. Public administration literature has suggested that targets are designed to create trust, especially in areas where there are obstacles to observing and directly controlling agencies involved in implementation. Principal-agent theory similarly suggests that monitoring can serve to align preferences between political leaders and their implementing agencies. Our analysis of targets in the MoD and Home Office suggested that the imposition of targets in itself has very little impact on the alignment of preferences. Even where targets were high profile, specific, measured and output oriented, both organisations responded by decoupling compliance from informal practices. In many cases this took the form of means-end decoupling, i.e. separating formal compliance with the letter of targets, from adjusting practices to meet the underlying objectives of such targets. The Home Office case suggested that intrusive political intervention was required to recouple practice to political goals.

The implication is that targets certainly did not remove the need for direct intervention and control. They failed to produce trust between political leaders and public administration. Indeed, the contrary was the case. The intrusive imposition of targets served to undermine trust, in two ways. First, targets rendered more visible the divergences between politics and the administration. They exposed divergent beliefs and values operating in the respective spheres, most obviously in terms of policy and organisational objectives, and beliefs about the government's capacity to steer behaviour. Second, where targets elicited intrusive attempts at political steering, such interventions eroded morale within the organisation, further undermining trust in the relations between officials and political leaders.

Nonetheless, targets appear to have retained their appeal as a tool for steering public administration. Senior managers and special advisors repeatedly stress the need for some form of performance measurement, including the use of targets. As one former advisor put it:

Organisations need to know what their basic purposes are. They need to have kind of goals that they're all working to and you need mechanisms in place to make sure that limited public resources are being spent effectively. So some kind of architecture of, you know, if it's not PSA's or delivery targets, all the rest of it but you need, you know, you can't just sort of junk the lessons of the last thirty years entirely. (Interview, February 2014)

To help understand the persistent appeal of these flawed instruments, we now turn to an examination of life without targets. If targets create distortions and undermine trust, what happens where social problems are excluded from this form of performance measurement?

5 | *Information and Trust*

Thus far, the analysis has focused on instances where governments are keen to draw attention to their policy goals or performance. They deploy targets to communicate their commitment to policy objectives and to vouchsafe their performance in achieving them. But what of the issues that are not monitored through performance measurement and the goals that are not codified as targets? Organisations have limited attention and competing priorities and they may neglect or even seek to obfuscate social problems that are not articulated in indicators or targets. However, such neglect always runs the risk of exposure: crises or scandals can unexpectedly surface in political and media debate, revealing social issues that organisations or their political leaders have overlooked. I explore the implications of such omissions – and their exposure – for political trust. In particular, I look at a case where a Home Office failure to monitor and deport foreign nationals was exposed as a political scandal. How did politicians and the Home Office seek to explain and address this oversight, and how did it affect trust between politics and public administration?

This chapter focuses on how the UK government handled a scandal in 2005–6 over the Home Office's failure to deport foreign national prisoners who had completed their sentences. The scandal revealed major deficiencies in Home Office monitoring of unauthorised residents and in its capacity to remove rejected asylum seekers and foreign national offenders. This chapter explores why the Home Office overlooked this social issue, failing to anticipate its political significance. I then examine how the scandal confronted the Home Office with a new set of political demands, and how the organisation adjusted its beliefs and practices to respond to these new pressures, including through developing a new set of targets. In conclusion, I consider the implications of this episode for trust between politics and public administration. The unfolding of the scandal shows how fragile trust relations are between Parliament and public administration. In particular, it reveals the crucial role of information in sustaining relations of trust and accountability. Although the practice of demanding and supplying information through select committee hearings is to some extent ritualistic, the effects of its breakdown are profound. Once the authority or completeness of information is cast in doubt, it can have damaging effects on trust.

The analysis draws on in-depth examination of six sessions of oral evidence given to two committees conducting enquires into the question: the Public Accounts and the Home Affairs select committees. It is also based on Home Office and select committee reports and interviews with Home Office officials and select committee members.

The Home Office before the Scandal

As we saw in Chapter 3, the Home Office has long had a self-perception as a beleaguered organisation constantly hit by political crises. It deals with a range of policy areas prone to political scandal: terrorism, crime, drugs and immigration. As former Home Secretary David Blunkett put it, 'the Home Office was reactive, an absorber of punishment. All home secretaries whom I have ever seen interviewed talked about things coming out of the blue sky and hitting them' (Pollard 2004). One of his predecessors in office, James Callaghan, wrote that the department deals with a range of issues, and 'a remote-controlled bomb is concealed in nearly every one' (Callaghan 1983: 10). The organisation is subject to a constant barrage of critical media coverage and often makes the headlines as a crisis or scandal erupts over some aspect of its remit. Officials convey the impression of a constant struggle to keep on top of their brief. They are continually preoccupied with firefighting, with responding to the latest scandal or focusing event, rather than with forward planning.

Within the Home Office, the division dealing with immigration and asylum – the Immigration and Nationality Directorate (IND) – has been especially prone to critical media coverage since the late 1990s.[1]

---

[1] The Immigration and Nationality Directorate (IND) has been the object of a series of reforms – and name changes – since the 2000s. In 2007, the IND was split into a separate executive agency, the Border and Immigration Agency. The agency was renamed the UK Border Agency (UKBA) in 2008. In 2012, the border control division of the UKBA was separated out as the new Border Force. In 2013, the UKBA was absorbed back into the Home Office, losing its status as

Here, it is useful to introduce a distinction between the IND's operational and political wings (see also Boswell 2009). The operational wing includes the various caseworkers engaged in processing applications for asylum, work permits or citizenship. In the 2000s, most of these are based in Croydon, a forty-minute train journey from the Home Office headquarters in Marsham Street, central London (some services have since been decentralised to regional offices). Interviews with Home Office officials suggest that officials involved in more routine, operational aspects of immigration and asylum policy tended to treat their tasks in a very narrow, compartmentalised way. As one former official put it:

You have whole teams of people whose job it is to take a case from one side of the room to the other, and as long as you take the case from one side of the room to the other in the proper way, meeting your local performance target, then that's where you get your job satisfaction. (Interview, May 2007)

This was also reflected in former Permanent Secretary Sir John Gieve's notion of 'soldiering on', even when confronted with a major problem. As he told the Home Affairs Select Committee: 'If there is one culture in the Civil Service generally, and it is true in the Home Office, it is one of soldiering on. People do soldier on and sometimes we wish they would sort of blow the whistle earlier than they do' (Home Affairs Committee 2006b: Q1137). And it is echoed in what has been repeatedly depicted as a 'silo' culture in the Home Office: a tendency for different units or divisions of the organisation to adopt a narrow and self-referential approach to their role, with limited communication or sense of shared strategic goals across units.

The political wing of the IND, by contrast, interacts more closely with the organisation's political leadership. This wing, based mainly in Marsham Street, comprises more senior officials often in the civil service 'fast stream', who work with the Home Secretary and the Immigration Minister in the Private Office. These officials need to be more politically astute, responding to pressures from the minister or secretary of state, and understanding the expectations and pressures emanating from the core executive, Parliament and the media. Given how politicised many of the Home Office's areas of remit are, these

a separate agency, and renamed UK Visa and Immigration. In this chapter, I refer to this part of the Home Office by its name at the time of the events described, the IND.

officials tend to be strongly influenced by the political cues received from their environment, and especially those communicated by the political leadership and through the parliamentary select committee system. So if the operational wing has a rather narrow, self-referential view of its role, the political wing in central London needs to develop more sensitive political antennae and respond to political pressures on the organisation.

In the early 2000s, the IND was under especially acute pressure. The Directorate was going through an exceptionally stressful period, struggling to deal with a large increase in the number of asylum applications. Rising numbers of asylum seekers since the late 1990s had created turmoil in the organisation, with the Directorate described as in 'meltdown', unable to cope with the problem (see Chapter 4). As we saw in the previous chapters, the political leadership responded by introducing asylum targets, initially focused on processing applications and removing rejected applicants. These targets placed enormous pressure on the IND. Both the Treasury and the Prime Minister's Delivery Unit closely scrutinised the performance of targets.

Not surprisingly, then, performance to targets became the main focus of the organisation's attention. Asylum processing saw a huge injection of resources, with knock-on effects for activities that were not similarly high on the agenda. Among those areas affected were a range of operations on monitoring and enforcement of unauthorised residents. This covered data and information processing on the whereabouts and conduct of illegal immigrants: those who had overstayed their visas or who had entered the UK without authorisation, many of whom were eligible for removal from the UK. Also included in this category were foreign nationals convicted of crimes and recommended for deportation once their prison sentences had been served. These areas of IND activity were not the object of performance targets before 2005–6. The only exception was the removal of rejected asylum seekers, which since 2000 had been codified in a series of targets: initially specific quantified targets (to remove 30,000 rejected asylum seekers by March 2003), and then a directional target (to remove a greater proportion of failed asylum seekers in 2005–6 compared to 2002–3). By late 2004, this had become a 'tipping point' target, aiming to remove more rejected asylum seekers than the number of new applicants entering the system (see Chapter 3). However, rejected asylum seekers represented only one category of illegal residents, and the rationale for this focus was based on the Home Office's preoccupation with deterring potential asylum seekers. Other unauthorised residents did not receive similar attention (see, for example, evidence of David Roberts, Home Affairs Committee 2006a: Q813).

The lack of targets on other aspects of removal and deportation may partly reflect the nature of this policy area. It is notoriously difficult for public authorities to monitor unauthorised residents. Those in an irregular situation seek to remain unobserved by state structures. Moreover, the UK's traditionally laissez-faire approach to population registration (there is no ID card and no centralised system for registering residents) makes it particularly challenging to identify or make checks on irregular residents. To be sure, irregular residents may need to register with a doctor, send their children to school and rent accommodation, and they may even obtain a national insurance number. But these different forms of engagement with sector-specific systems of registration tend to remain fragmented. There is no evidence of any attempt to centralise data collection across different registers, or to cross-check data sets – an exercise which would have proved highly challenging, given the absence of a unique identifier for individual records. Certainly in the early 2000s, there was no concerted attempt to centralise and systematise existing data.

Added to this, there are numerous and often intractable challenges in enforcing policies on illegal immigration. In principle, many unauthorised residents are eligible for removal or deportation. In practice, various legal and administrative obstacles prevent returning foreign nationals to their countries of origin. As we saw in Chapter 4, the removal of asylum seekers can be impeded by a series of legal challenges and by the non-cooperation of countries of origin. Implementing involuntary removals also raises serious practical and ethical issues, and tends to be expensive and complex to arrange. Finally, there are the challenges associated with monitoring the whereabouts of those who are subject to deportation. Detention is expensive and controversial. Other forms of surveillance, for example through swipe registration cards for asylum seekers or electronic tagging of former offenders, or ID cards and unique identifiers, were only beginning to emerge in the early 2000s.

These challenges in monitoring and enforcing immigration control, combined with the clear political priority to focus on asylum, meant that removals received limited attention between 2000 and 2005. They were not the object of targets. A Treasury official explained this in terms of resources. It did not make sense to set a target on illegal migration 'because (a) you don't know how big your problem is, (b) even if you did, we don't have the tools to solve that problem. Or you would have to put so much resource into this it becomes ridiculous' (Interview, February 2014). Moreover, unlike in the case of asylum, there was a lack of available data indicating the scale of the problem, thus keeping it buffered from media and political attention. Since the issue had not (yet) been framed as a prominent or salient policy problem, the government had a clear disincentive to ratchet up public pressure in this already challenging policy area. As one former advisor put it, 'You've got to focus on, on things that are workable and doable and that are within your control in order to demonstrate back to the original point that you're making some progress. So you try and set the terms of the debate' (Interview, February 2014). Neither the Home Office nor the government was keen to set the terms of the debate around problems of illegal immigrants.

Former Permanent Secretary John Gieve describes the situation in his oral evidence to the Home Affairs Committee:

IND has been recovering for some years from a near disaster at the end of the 1990s when we did lose control of the asylum intake ... The intake continued to rise until 2002. It was only in 2003 and 2004 that we managed to bring it right back down again ... I think it was inevitable that we should give top priority to that. Everyone knew that that meant other bits of the organisation were stretched and were not getting the attention they wanted. (Home Affairs Committee 2006c: Q1093)

Similarly, the former director general of the IND described the situation in the late 1990s and early 2000s. He was keen to emphasise that other areas were not wholly neglected, but the clear priority was to manage the asylum crisis.

Clearly, there were priorities ... If one goes back again to those years and understands the pressures then on IND, the balancing act was quite different but it was a balancing act and one that did not allow us to be simply negligent or blind as to what the other issues really were ... we were trying to move forward in a constructive way but reflecting the proper ministerial priority on asylum. (Home Affairs Committee 2006c: Q1093)

Thus in the early 2000s the Home Office, and the IND in particular, could be characterised as a reactive organisation with a tendency to compartmentalisation. The IND's operational wing adopted a generally narrow interpretation of its role, focusing on its immediate operational tasks and on what seemed feasible. At the same time, the organisation was under acute political pressure, with its political wing very much focused on meeting high-profile political targets. Not surprisingly, the implication was that less attention was devoted to the monitoring and control of illegal immigration. This implied that the way in which officials prioritised problems was reactive: it followed political pressures and organisational narratives about steering a narrowly defined set of activities.

The Foreign National Prisoners Scandal

In October 2005, the House of Commons Committee of Public Accounts began to focus its attention on the IND's poor record on removing rejected asylum applicants from the country. Part of its criticism revolved around the lack of Home Office data on rejected asylum seekers who had served prison sentences for crimes committed and then been released without being considered for deportation. The committee asked senior Home Office officials how many failed applicants had been released from prison because their removal could not be arranged. The response was, 'We think around 500' (Mr Clark, Evidence to Committee of Public Accounts; see Committee of Public Accounts 2005: Q79). It emerged in the course of the session that the Home Office did not know the whereabouts of these 500 former inmates or what proportion had served prison sentences for serious criminal offenses. This was quickly picked up as a serious political transgression. As a prominent member of the committee, Conservative MP Richard Bacon, commented:

I find it extraordinary that people can commit a criminal offence against citizens of this country, take advantage of the hospitality that is offered them and then we cannot get rid of them. (Committee of Public Accounts 2005: Q86)

The revelations became more 'extraordinary' still, as it emerged that the Home Office was 'choosing not to keep them in detention' (Committee of Public Accounts 2005: Q87) because of the barriers to removal. Given the limited number of spaces in detention facilities, those former prisoners whose removal appeared more feasible were prioritised for detention. As the permanent secretary explained it, 'we have a limited number of detention spaces so we have to use them for the people for whom we are most likely to get a rapid conclusion' (Committee of Public Accounts 2005: Q89). This prompted general consternation from committee members, who could not grasp why potentially dangerous foreign nationals would not be held in detention, even in cases where the Home Office accepted they should be removed.

Following the session, in November 2005 the Home Office provided a revised and slightly lower figure of 403 foreign national prisoners who were not considered by the Home Office for deportation between 2001 and 2005, on completion of their sentences. At the time, the Home Office did not view this as a crisis: the 400 or so were 'thought not to be serious offenders' (Home Affairs Committee 2006c: Q1100). But over the following few months, the Home Office began to drill down into the question. It set up a unit to investigate the problem, and a further audit revealed that the number was in fact much higher. In April 2006 the Home Office released data suggesting that the total figure for 1999–2006 was 1,023 (including 609 for the period 2001–5). The information was announced in the House by Home Secretary Charles Clarke. This became the leading story in the mass media over several days, with the Home Office and IND's inefficiency the target of scabrous critique. The *Daily Mail* summed up the general tenor of media coverage in its headline of 26 April, 'Home Office blunders left foreign rapists in UK'.[2]

Through the spring and early summer of 2006, senior officials and ministers were interrogated by House of Commons select committees on the unfolding fiasco. One prominent theme to emerge from these committee hearings was the gap between Home Office and parliamentary expectations about how best to deal with foreign national prisoners. The Home Office appeared to be guided by a strikingly different model of risk assessment. Given its resource constraints and steering capacity, it prioritised certain forms of data gathering and intervention. We saw this previously in relation to its approach to detention: the decision to prioritise those whose deportation appeared to be more feasible. The gap is also apparent in the Home Office's assumption

---

[2] *Daily Mail*, 26 April 2006.

that the *foreignness* of former prisoners does not in itself imply greater harm to the public. This became clear in the evidence of the permanent secretary to the Committee of Public Accounts in April 2006. In the course of this session, it emerged that the Home Office was monitoring foreign national prisoners through the same techniques it used for UK nationals. From the Home Office's perspective, foreign nationals posed no heightened risk as compared to UK national offenders.

Chairman: Was a close eye kept on all these murderers or rapists? By definition given the information that has now been given to Parliament, perhaps it was not?

Sir David Normington: They would be under the same arrangements as UK nationals. Effectively the thing that we failed to do was to consider them for deportation. They will be treated as UK nationals would. (Committee of Public Accounts 2006a: Q90)

Clearly, this failed to reflect the *political* outrage associated with the foreign status of the offenders. MP Winnick articulated this well, with his notion of 'public repugnance' for these foreign nationals:

Mr Winnick: What I find difficult to understand is the lack on the part of the Home Office at the most senior levels to realise as far as the public are concerned that foreign nationals should have committed offences and, as you know, in a number of instances very serious offences and be allowed to stay on in this country once their sentence was completed without at least being considered for deportation ... It is this lack of sensitivity which I am putting to you as a question, not to realise the public repugnance that these foreign nationals having been convicted, as I understand it, in some instances of very serious offences were not even considered at any stage for deportation. (Home Affairs Committee 2006c: Q1136)

More generally, Members of Parliament (MPs) accused the Home Office of failing to apprise the political ramifications of the issue. Their consternation is clearly articulated in exchanges in the Home Affairs Committee. As a member of this committee observed:

Mr Clappison: These are people who have been convicted of very serious offences, murder, manslaughter, rape or child sex offences. We were very interested in them and asked questions about this at the last meeting. You surely must have been tracking what has been happening with them, whether they have been brought under control, locked up or whatever? You must know what has happened? (Home Affairs Committee 2006b: Q999)

This leads the chair of the committee to wonder:

What is it about IND that tolerates that level of risk to public safety and nobody in the organisation feels a responsibility to do anything about it? (Q999)

Thus there was a growing realisation that Parliament and the IND had quite different ways of defining and prioritising policy problems.

A similar gap between political and administrative framing of the question emerged over the issue of Home Office data. Both the Home Affairs and the Public Accounts Committees rapidly homed in on the problem of poor information provided in the evidence and in supplementary notes to the committee. Initially, this took the form of select committee requests for more granular data. Parliamentarians wanted the data broken down in various ways: longitudinal data, to track trends, or data disaggregated by category, to clarify the gravity of the problem. An early example is Committee of Public Accounts questioning of Home Office officials in October 2005. Committee members were keen to elicit more information to allow them to track performance over time, and also to disaggregate the data according to the seriousness of the crime. This is one of numerous exchanges in which MPs attempted to press for disaggregated data on foreign national offenders.

MR BACON: These 1,023 over this period ... you have got them divided as between arsonists, rapists, murderers, burglars, kidnappers, drug dealers, paedophiles and so on. Presumably you also have them divided by time, by month ...

SIR DAVID NORMINGTON: I do not have those figures, Mr Bacon. You very kindly gave me the notice and we do not have the breakdown month by month.

MR BACON: But you could create it?

SIR DAVID NORMINGTON: I expect we could create it.

MR BACON: In order to create this 1,023 and you know how many of them are in each category, you must have that information, must you not?

SIR DAVID NORMINGTON: It follows that we must have the information. We have been concentrating on identifying these people and dealing with them and not breaking the figures down any more. (Committee of Public Accounts 2006b: Q59)

The Home Office's apparent inability to produce any reliable figures became one of the main sources of rebuke. Senior civil servants were repeatedly lambasted for their failure to provide the data demanded by the two select committees. Members of the Committee of Public Accounts in particular saw it as part of their duty to demand comprehensive data, including a level of detailed breakdown that echoed popular political and media concerns. The close scrutiny of detailed data was a credible and expected tool through which the executive could be held to account.

But the data the select committee required did not mirror Home Office priorities. Instead, the Home Office was deploying categories and processes for data collection based on what it considered to be its operational needs. Part of this reflected the Home Office's beliefs about what it could steer, and especially the feasibility of deportation. We see repeated attempts on the part of senior officials to try to explain the various barriers to deportation.

Sir John Gieve: It is extremely difficult to remove people who do not want to go to countries which may not want to take them back and who are active in trying to frustrate the process. (Committee of Public Accounts 26 October 2005, Q141)

Some of these problems came out clearly in evidence given to the Home Affairs Committee in May 2016 regarding the removal of illegal residents. In his exchanges with committee members, the director of the Enforcement and Removals Directorate, David Roberts, tried to explain the organisation's approach to enforcement. MPs had been querying Roberts on why he could not provide a figure of the number of rejected asylum seekers still in the UK. His response was that there was no system for checking who had left the country in the form of embarkation controls, and as such, there was no reliable way of knowing how many of those who were not registered as having been removed or participated in voluntary return schemes were still in the country. MPs appeared bemused that the Home Office did not track individual cases. It is worth recording the exchange in full:

MR ROBERTS: . . . I do not think that tracking individual cases at the level that you suggest by your question is an effective enforcement strategy in relation (1) to the resources we currently have available and (2) frankly in the internal controls that the UK operates. We have powers, quite properly, to deal with people who are here unlawfully, and I do not think it is an effective strategy to be pursuing individuals. I think we need something more sophisticated.

MR WINNICK: You have got me there, I must confess. I am a simple person and it seems to me if X has no right to be in the United Kingdom then, inevitably, the question is asked why is not X removed? That is an individual case to my simple mind.

MR ROBERTS: Yes, and there was a time quite a few years ago when I was an immigration officer where we knocked on lots of doors following up lots of individual cases, and it came as no surprise that none of those individuals were at the addresses we had for them. What we need is a far more sophisticated intelligence-led approach to this. If you have overstayed and you are here unlawfully and you are working illegally, then we have quite specific strategies in relation to illegal working operations to find you in that environment. I simply cannot accept tracing people as individuals, unless, of course, the risks they present are so huge that you need to do that, individuals, for example, who might present a threat to national security would reach that level of threshold, and, yes, of course it would be right to use whatever capability you had to trace them at an individual level, but for somebody who has overstayed tracing them at an individual level I do not think is an effective strategy. (Home Affairs Committee 2006a: Q832–3)

This exchange captures some of the discrepancies between political and bureaucratic perspectives. The 'simple' question that the MP asked – why are those illegally in the UK not removed? – clearly reflected an intuitively plausible and politically compelling idea about the role of the state in immigration control. If people are here unlawfully, the state should remove them. What the Home Office official was suggesting was that public authorities did not, and indeed could not, develop an accurate picture of how many illegal residents there were in the UK, where they were located and what their activities were. As Roberts admitted earlier in the session when asked how many illegal residents there were in the UK, the Home Office didn't have 'the faintest idea'. Moreover, given its limited resources, the Home Office needed to be pragmatic and prioritise whom it monitored. As Roberts explained, the organisation prioritised on the basis of the probability of apprehension, which implied focusing on those businesses most likely to be employing illegal residents. Individuals were targeted only if they posed a 'threat to national security', and the bar for meeting this condition appeared to be very high – implying, for example, that most foreign offenders would not be prioritised in this way.

We see a similar discrepancy in political and bureaucratic approaches to prosecution. Later in the session, MP Gwyn Prosser asked Roberts why only around 10 per cent of operations against illegal work resulted in successful prosecutions. Roberts explained:

Prosecution is a very resource-intensive response to a threat, is it not? In order to prosecute an individual it requires a huge investment in the investigation and taking that case to court. I think that, frankly, our ability to prosecute for section 8 offenses, offenses in relation to illegal working, is a sledge hammer to crack a walnut. (Home Affairs Committee 2006a: Q857)

This unusually frank response illustrates the familiar problem of unfeasible political expectations. From the perspective of politics – the sphere engaged in mobilising support for rival claims about political intervention – it seemed self-evident that illegal immigrants should be caught and prosecuted. From the bureaucratic perspective, however, individual prosecutions implied a hugely inefficient use of resources – 'a sledge hammer to crack a walnut'.

The exchanges between politicians and officials in select committee hearings thus expose two quite different ways of 'seeing' social problems. For the Home Office, the preoccupation was to sustain motivation and develop operational practices to steer those social problems that were seen as priorities for organisational action. The organisation needed to pursue certain operational imperatives, to 'get things done', in a way that sustained both internal and external legitimacy. Its perceptual filter had the effect of overlooking vast swathes of information about the scale, location or conduct of unauthorised residents – whether because they were not the object of political attention, or because it was not considered feasible or resource efficient to pursue them.

Explaining Home Office Failings

We have seen that select committee scrutiny revealed striking omissions in Home Office monitoring. We now consider how politics and the administration made sense of these omissions. What sorts of narratives did they develop about the reasons for Home Office ignorance about foreign national prisoners? Much of the questioning in the Home Affairs Committee and the Committee of Public Accounts focused on why senior management had not gauged the scale of the problem earlier.

MR WILLIAMS: . . . Did not alarm bells ring? Did you not think: 'Gosh, we are letting all these murderers out. What are they going to do when they get out?' and so on . . .

SIR JOHN GIEVE: First of all, I did not know exactly what crimes these people were accused of or convicted of. That is the new information that we have provided.

MR WILLIAMS: Would you not have thought that was relevant? Would someone not have clicked that that might be relevant and some of them might be rather nasty people? (Committee of Public Accounts 2005: Q142)

The Home Office narrative is one of a gradual realisation of the scale of the problem, as the organisation began to focus its attention on it. This in part harks back to the earlier point about limited resources. Senior officials pointed out that organisational attention was very much focused on asylum over the preceding period. They also flagged up a more general problem of officials failing to escalate concerns up the chain of command. Director Lin Homer of the IND suggests that it was a problem of system overload: too many cases entering the system which could not be processed by the limited number of staff dealing with them. Thus 'it was a more simple process of not getting through the workload than an applied process of saying, "we won't bother about those ones"' (Home Affairs Committee 2006b: Q990). Former Permanent Secretary Sir John Gieve similarly saw it as an omission related to lack of resource, rather than a form of conscious neglect or 'strategic ignorance' (McGoey 2012). Or as Stephen Boys Smith, the former director of the IND, put it: 'people simply were not fully aware of, if you like, the totality of the problem. They were aware that there were people coming out of prison but nobody had measured the problem in the round in order to have a view of the kind that you are now expressing' (Home Affairs Committee 2006c: Q1096).

The phrase he used – viewing the problem 'in the round' – is telling. Officials were preoccupied with their particular operational goals and requirements. They were not reflecting on how other observers might view the problem, or its potential political ramifications. And this is a natural, even inevitable form of neglect in organisations. Their view is necessarily selective. However, parliamentary select committees clearly found it difficult to accept that it might have seemed sensible or rational for the Home Office not to view the problem 'in the round'. They were repeatedly posed questions about who in the Home Office could or should have known what, at which point in time, based on what information. As one MP suggests:

Mr Browne: It is not that the Home Office could plead that there was no incoming information. It just appears not to have somehow filtered through and percolated into the organisational brain of the Home Office once it arrived there. (Home Affairs Committee 2006c: Q1110)

Former Permanent Secretary Sir John Gieve rebutted, 'you have to understand that there are many reports from HMI every year and about 4,000 recommendations. I do not remember her [Home Secretary Jackie Smith] picking up on this particular point.' This is a good illustration of how an organisation's perceptual filter can fail to register stimuli that challenge its beliefs.

Yet parliamentarians could not fathom how the Home Office could have failed to anticipate the political significance of these omissions. Their interpretation implied a highly dismissive view of the Home Office as largely dysfunctional and inept. In particular, it suggested that the causes of ignorance lay in poor management and blinkered officials, who made a series of errors in information processing. This narrative was given credence by Home Secretary John Reid, who was appointed to replace Charles Clarke in April 2006. Clarke's resignation was a direct consequence of the scandal, and Reid was determined to avoid being implicated in Home Office transgressions. He was quite explicit about his mistrust of the Home Office, continually stressing his scepticism about the data Home Office officials provided. He spoke of having a 'health warning on his chest' when providing data from the department (Home Affairs Committee 2006a: Q874). As he explained to the Home Affairs Committee shortly after taking up office:

Unless we get that fundamental overhaul of a lot of these practices, we will be left in a position where every figure we have given will shift; every fact we have given will be unreliable; and it will be a result of the failure of the systems, the coordination, the communication, the management, the leadership and so on and that is now our task to change. (Home Affairs Committee 2006a: Q878)

It is noteworthy that politicians generally concurred with the view that Home Office omissions were a product of incompetence, rather than duplicity. One finds the odd exception in exchanges between MPs and senior officials. On one occasion, an MP notes media scepticism about Home Office motives in suppressing data on foreign national prisoners.

Bob Russell: [I]t has been alleged in the media ... that the immigration authorities deliberately did not initiate deportation action against foreign national prisoners in case this generated more applications for asylum. Is this true?

Stephen Boys Smith explains that such conduct was 'unbeknown to' him, and would 'constitute massaging of the targets and that was not acceptable conduct to me or my senior colleagues' (Home Affairs Committee 2006c: Q1122). Russell wants to have this statement 'on the record', but MPs appear satisfied with Home Office responses and do not pursue the matter further.

In this respect, we should also bear in mind the generally strong personal trust relations between senior civil servants and politicians. These two professional groups benefit from a form of familiarity based on generally shared social and educational backgrounds, as well as recognisable career trajectories. These provide reassuring signals about motives and conduct, which help ground trust. We can see this in exchanges between the committee and former Permanent Secretary Sir John Gieve, which deal with the question of Gieve's personal trustworthiness given the problems he presided over in the Home Office. Gieve had left his job as permanent secretary at the end of 2005 for an appointment as deputy governor of the Bank of England. After a stream of questions highly critical of his role in the foreign prisoner scandal and other Home Office oversights, the Committee of Public Accounts questioned him on this career move. Richard Bacon, a prominent member of the committee, asked him who appointed him to this role. John Gieve responded: 'Gordon Brown. Well, the Queen but on Gordon Brown's recommendation.' This silenced the usually combative Bacon, who simply replied, 'Okay. Thank you very much' (Committee of Public Accounts 2006a: Q88). Later on in the session, another MP returned to the question of personal trust (Q128).

Greg Clark: ... This is a personal question and I am sensitive about asking it but we have a duty as a Committee to be objective ... You are now Deputy

Governor of the Bank of England with specific responsibility for the Bank's financial stability. This is hugely important. How can you reassure the public that you are the man for that job?

Gieve responded by explaining the procedure for the appointment, including his scrutiny before the Treasury Select Committee, which concluded that he 'was qualified for the job'. Again, this seemed to satisfy the questioner.

Importantly, Gieve and his colleagues were ready to demonstrate the requisite amount of contrition. By the end of the session, the committee appeared satisfied that it had extracted the necessary apologies and explanations from those being interrogated. The chairman concluded in a conciliatory fashion, obviously keen to smooth over the more fraught exchanges that had preceded:

I am grateful to you, Sir David. I am particularly grateful to you, Sir John, for coming this afternoon. Despite my frank correspondence with the Cabinet Secretary about your presence here, Sir John, you have been very helpful. Thank you very much. (Committee of Public Accounts 2006a: Q172)

Gieve was absolved of suspicion as to his personal trustworthiness or fitness for public office. MPs were satisfied that the causes of Home Office transgression lay in a complex series of organisational errors and ineptitude, rather than the conscious duplicity or overt omissions of any particular individual. The predominant political narrative, and indeed the Home Office's own public account, was one of collective organisational failings.

The Home Office Responds

It remains to consider how the Home Office responded to the scandal. In what ways did it adjust its practices to accommodate concerns about information management and processing? In other words, how did the organisation seek to correct its omissions?

The scandal certainly evinced a very robust response from the organisation's political leadership. On taking up office, John Reid announced in the House of Commons that the organisation was 'dysfunctional' and 'not fit for purpose'. Within three months of taking office, he launched an 'ambitious set of reforms' to the Home Office. The reform plan, *Fair, Effective, Transparent and*

Trusted: Rebuilding Confidence in Our Immigration System, conceded that:

IND has been forced to work around outmoded systems and make piecemeal improvements. Recent events have shown that this approach can lead to major problems – such as the failure to consider for deportation foreign national prisoners. IND needs to change radically to meet the increasing challenges ahead, deliver the Home Secretary's vision for the future and regain public trust. (Home Office 2006: 4)

The plans included converting the IND into an 'arm's-length' agency, the Border and Immigration Agency (subsequently remained the UK Border Agency). It established the New Asylum Model, discussed in Chapter 4. And it set out plans for a biometric ID card for foreign nationals.

Many of these reforms had already been in the offing – Reid's plan providing an opportunity to expedite or showcase them. But the foreign national prisoners scandal directly triggered a number of measures, and also exposed more general flaws in the monitoring and removal of illegal residents. One of the key goals set out in the plan was 'expanding detention throughout and tagging or monitoring all asylum claimants'. This was reflected in political demands for more comprehensive monitoring. There were also plans to 'remove barriers to deportation and removal', with the priority on removing those posing the greatest risk, including foreign national offenders. In this respect, the Home Office was to usher in 'a new cross-cutting approach by the criminal justice agencies to identifying and case-managing foreign national prisoners', and 'amend the law to make deportation the presumption for foreign national prisoners'.

New targets were introduced on removals. One priority was the removal of foreign national offenders. The Border and Immigration Agency Business Plan for 2007–8 set out a target to remove 340 foreign national offenders per month until November 2007, from which point it would then rise to 400 per month. A new target was introduced for the removal of illegal residents – with the target to remove 1,400 'immigration offenders per month' supplementing the existing target on removal of rejected asylum applicants. And the Border and Immigration Agency pledged to publish removal figures nationally and by region by April 2008. The targets were reiterated as 'Indicators' in the Agency's 2008 Business Plan: Indicator 3 was to

'Increase the number of removals year on year', while Indicator 4 was to 'Increase the removal of "harm" cases as a proportion of total cases removed' (UKBA 2008). Part of the new focus involved redefining 'risk' to reflect the types of political concern raised around the 2006 scandal. In summer 2006, the Home Secretary announced that 'potential harm' was now to become one of the criteria for prioritising removals. As Lin Homer put it in her comments to the Home Affairs Committee in June 2006, the emphasis was now on:

Prioritising cases according to degree of risk; and 'revised interim guidance to reflect his concern that we would exercise our discretion more in favour of the public than the criminal'. (Home Affairs Committee 2006b: Q1052)

The 2007 UK Borders Act further introduced a presumption that foreign national prisoners be deported – a so-called Automatic Deportation provision – which required the Home Secretary to make a Deportation Order against a foreign national prisoner who had received a sentence of imprisonment of twelve months or more.[3]

The new political focus on removals, as codified in these targets, clearly led to a major shift of resources and attention within the new agency. We have already seen that the Home Office set up a unit in late 2005 to deal more effectively with the foreign national prisoner question. This capacity was further augmented in 2006. As an official put it:

there'd been 200 people who'd just been lifted and shifted into foreign national offenders work, into what was called the criminal caseworkers directorate and that left quite an organisational legacy as well, so – it might have been 200 people, it was possibly less, who were literally told on one day, with no notice whatsoever, you are now going to be working on criminal case work. (Interview, August 2014)

The parliamentary committee system also swung behind monitoring the new targets. As a former advisor put it, the new targets became 'a big drive in Home Office behaviour' with senior officials 'dragged in front of the Home Affairs Committee every couple of months to talk about the latest numbers' (Interview, May 2007).

By May 2011, a report of the Independent Chief Inspector gave the Agency a relatively clean bill of health. It found that UK Border Agency:

---

[3] Except where they fall within one of six exceptions, including being a European Economic Area national.

routinely monitored the number of foreign national prisoners deported, the number detained following completion of their sentence and the length of detention. It had assessed the likely numbers and costs of foreign national prisoners remaining in detention or living in the community, and monitored risks at senior Board Level. (UKBA Independent Inspector 2011: 4)

The Agency also appeared to be meeting the 2007 target on deporting foreign national offenders, with 20,360 being deported between 2007 and 2010 (so an average of more than 400 per month). Nonetheless, it found that the new approach to risk assessment was not being fully implemented – there was 'no evidence that a detailed assessment of the risk of reoffending had taken place in each case', prompting a recommendation to carry out a proper risk assessment for each case (UKBA Independent Inspector 2011: 4–5). By and large, though, it appears that the substantial investment of resources had enabled the organisation to adjust its policies and practices in line with political expectations.

Yet this reinforced political scrutiny was, as ever, selective. It focused on quite narrow targets on removals. The Home Office had been lambasted for failing to deal with foreign national prisoners, and by the late 2000s it had largely adjusted its approach to monitor this population in the way the political system demanded. Yet wider problems with immigration enforcement that had surfaced in the debate were not addressed and once more receded from political attention. The Home Office had adjusted its perceptual filter to monitor the new entities that had been singled out for political attention, and especially those that were the object of performance measurement. But its mode of filtering information necessarily remained selective, reflecting new political pressures, but not necessarily in a way that improved operational effectiveness (Painter 2008).

Accountability and Trust

The analysis has shown how organisational filters can screen out social problems, especially where these are not seen as operational or political priorities. Once such problems are identified, the organisation can be exposed as deficient for failing to monitor and gauge their political significance. In the case of foreign national prisoners, the IND and the Home Office more generally were berated for not appreciating the political significance of the problem. But it is entirely comprehensible why officials would have neglected the issue. It had not been identified as an operational priority; indeed, organisational attention was focused on a range of goals that had been formally defined as priorities, and against which its performance was being assessed. Nor was there any political pressure to address the problem. Meanwhile, the 'silo' culture of the organisation militated against the type of initiative-taking or whistle-blowing that might have flagged up a problem to senior management. The case also shows how organisations can adjust once they are exposed to political pressure. A range of new organisational goals and targets, and intensified political and media scrutiny, led the organisation to adjust how it selected and prioritised information. However, this new focus on previously neglected social issues did not imply a new openness to unanticipated information. Rather, it implied a more limited reconfiguration of its perceptual filter to pick up new types of information – those issues that were not included in targets or prioritised for political attention remained the object of neglect.

One of the most interesting aspects of this case is what the scandal reveals about trust. Parliamentary select committees are tasked with holding the executive to account, and an important part of this role is to scrutinise the conduct of organisations in the public administration. Such committees see it as their duty to ascertain whether public agencies are worthy of trust: to vouchsafe how far such agencies deserve to be invested with responsibility to act on behalf of the electorate. Select committee hearings thus become an important venue for a regular ritual of verifying of whether such trust is grounded.

But how is trust grounded in this relationship between parliamentarians and civil servants? It is not based on the type of steering characterising relations between political leaders and the public administration. Select committees have limited scope for adjusting the incentive structures of officials. While such committees have the potential to embarrass officials and expose organisational transgressions, their interventions are not regular enough to exert ongoing or direct influence. Nor do they have sufficiently finessed tools at their disposal to reward or punish behaviour in a way that would reliably steer behaviour. Their influence over resource allocation, organisational structures or career trajectories is too remote. Instead, trust appears to be grounded in truth claims about the motives, conduct and performance of the organisation. Much of this information takes the form of data on organisational inputs and outputs, conduct and procedures. These data offer parliamentarians reassurance that the organisation is making well-founded decisions, that its conduct is correct and that its performance is satisfactory.

This preoccupation with information was evident in the case of the foreign national prisoners scandal. Committee members reacted to concerns about Home Office misdemeanours by demanding ever more granular data. Indeed, it was the incompleteness and inaccuracy of organisational data that proved to be the object of strongest political outrage. Similarly, select committees seemed to consider that the provision of reliable information would be the only reliable means of allaying their concerns about trust. Here it is worth recalling that the scandal was not triggered by any actual instance of harm: no foreign nationals had been identified as committing a crime after their release. It was the fact that the Home Office did not *know* – and that it could not *account* for itself – that was the object of scandal. And the importance of this epistemic omission, this ignorance, reflects the dependence of MPs on immediately obtainable information as their mode of grounding trust. To be sure, there were some exchanges suggesting that MPs might rely on familiarity with the biographies of senior officials to assuage their concerns. But the size and complexity of the Home Office clearly limited the scope for such familiarity to offer any reliable guarantee of organisational conduct. Instead, it was authoritative claims about social problems and organisational action that grounded trust. And presumably in part because of the time and resource constraints on committee members (Geddes 2016), such claims needed to be presented swiftly and in a form that met MPs' expectations about credible management information.

The response to the scandal, as we saw, was to attempt to repair relations of trust by setting clearer goals and performance targets in those areas in which Home Office ignorance had been exposed. For the political leadership, this offered a means of steering the behaviour of officials through adjusting their incentives. For the select committee system, new targets and indicators offered a new focus for their task of scrutinising data on organisational conduct. So targets sought to reground trust between parliamentarians and public administration by generating valid truth claims about organisational conduct.

But we also need to understand this mode of holding to account as to some extent ritualistic. Select committees are keen to signal their influence by exposing government omissions and demonstrating their role in rectifying these. Thus the two committees were happy to embrace a narrative of parliamentary exposure followed up with remedial measures: the imposition of new performance measurement and reporting requirements. As one politician rather cynically described the Home Affairs Committee's quarterly reports from the Independent Chief Inspector, the committee needs 'a steady stream of material to get their teeth into and be on Radio 4 about' (Interview, March 2014). Whether or not such information really grounds trust in the sense of enabling MPs to bracket uncertainty is another question. The new targets provided the committees with a new set of rituals for holding the Home Office to account through scrutinising performance data and exposing deficiencies. This offered a more reliable set of thresholds to enable the committees to decide when, and on what grounds, to withhold their trust. The new information was important for assuaging their anxiety and providing a symbolic form of control.

6 | Political Credit and Public Trust in Targets

Politicians often seek to build public trust through committing themselves to policy promises: pledges, lock-ins, 'cast-iron' guarantees or targets. They adopt robust, often quantitative and outcome-oriented objectives through which their performance can be monitored. Such targets signal a particularly strong commitment on the part of their authors. Setting a specific pledge, and putting in place procedures for monitoring its fulfilment, can be seen as constraining the scope for prevarication or obfuscation. Objectives are codified in the form of precise, quantifiable goals. And progress towards meeting these goals is regularly assessed, usually through publicly available data.

This chapter examines how far targets can succeed in producing public trust. It starts by exploring the relationship between targets, accountability and trust. The setting of targets can be understood as the creation of more specific and rigorous mechanisms of accountability. Targets clarify the precise criteria and procedures through which leaders may be held to account by their electorates. However, unlike most mechanisms of accountability, it is those that are being scrutinised who set the targets and define the procedures for verifying performance against them. This can create a number of problems for those setting targets. Political leaders need to select targets that resonate with public concerns, that are seen as feasible and that have robust and credible reporting mechanisms.

I explore these issues by looking at mass media coverage of two targets: the Labour government's 2003 asylum target and the Conservative Party's 2010 net migration target. This allows us to compare political debate on two targets, one of which was met (the asylum target), the other of which was revealed to be unfeasible. Drawing on opinion polls and analysis of newspaper reporting on the two targets, I consider how far the two governments were rewarded or punished for setting and meeting (or failing to meet) the respective targets.

Targets, Accountability and Trust

The few contributions that have examined the effectiveness of targets as a means of eliciting public support have come to rather pessimistic conclusions. In a review of literature on the uses of performance information by citizens, Pollitt (2006b) found that voters rarely use such data to make political choices. James and John (2007) identified an asymmetry in voters' responses to performance measurement, with incumbents being punished for poor performance but not rewarded for good outcomes. Hood and Dixon (2010) found that Labour targets on education and health care did not produce political payoffs for the government in terms of electoral support or positive media reporting. This was the case both at the stage of announcing the targets, when we might expect the targets to help communicate government commitment, and at the point at which the targets were reported to have been met, when we would expect the targets to have demonstrated improved outcomes.

What explains the apparent failure of targets to produce public support? Hood and Dixon (2010) suggest one explanation is that politicians might be miscalculating the political payoff of targets, overestimating the potential positive effects on public support. Yet on the face of it, it might seem reasonable for politicians to nurture such expectations. By setting targets, political leaders are effectively creating a new mechanism by which their publics can hold them to account. Following Mark Bovens, we can define accountability as 'a relationship between an actor and a forum, in which the actor has an obligation to explain and to justify his or her conduct' (Bovens 2007: 450). By setting targets, political actors are offering to be held to account for certain aspects of their conduct. The target specifies which aspects of their conduct are to be explained or assessed, what information is required to make such an assessment and the procedures through which the conduct in question will be assessed. Prima facie, targets appear to be an ideal tool for tracking and assessing government performance.

Unlike many other accountability mechanisms, however, performance targets tend to be set by those who are being held to account. They constitute an additional, self-imposed layer of scrutiny assumed by politicians, designed to further enhance public trust through creating more specific and robust forms of accountability.

The fact that targets are set by political leaders – those being held to account – creates a number of difficulties. As Patricia Day and Rudolf Klein note, 'accountability is all about the construction of an *agreed* language or currency of discourse about conduct and performance, and the criteria that should be used in assessing them' (1987: 2; italics added). In other words, accountability relationships imply some accord between those being held to account and those assessing them regarding which aspects of conduct should be assessed and how such assessments should be carried out. In setting targets, political leaders therefore need to select areas of government performance that resonate with public concerns (Flinders 2001: 281). This brings us to our first expectation. Targets will be seen as irrelevant or pointless if they are not directed to goals that engage public interest.

A second expectation is that targets need to be seen as sensible and achievable in order to elicit public trust. Where this is not the case, targets may be the object of scepticism, and this can undermine confidence in the government's ability to deliver them. In particular, in cases where the media or political opposition seek to cast doubt on the viability of targets, or on the government's commitment to meeting them, then targets may have limited traction in terms of securing public confidence. Doubt about the feasibility of targets may be articulated as they are set, or may emerge over time, as it becomes clear that the targets in question cannot be met.

Thirdly, the procedures for monitoring performance against targets need to be seen as legitimate. Those assessing government conduct must perceive the information being supplied as relevant and reliable, and they must have confidence in reporting mechanisms. The use of quantitative data for setting and monitoring targets may be expected to lend particular authority to such claims. Statistics are associated with objectivity, precision and rigour (Espeland and Stevens 2008; Hacking 1990). As we shall see, however, in practice they are also frequently the object of mistrust, especially where statistics have been selected and reported by the government.

If we accept the accountability model of public assessment, targets will need to fulfil three conditions in order to elicit public trust: they need to be politically relevant and practically feasible, and their reporting mechanisms need to be credible. In the analysis that follows, we will explore how far these expectations about the conditions for producing trust are met, and how they influence public responses to targets.

In order to explore these points, it is useful to examine how far specific targets have elicited trust. This chapter analyses media coverage of two targets. The first of these is the Labour government's 2003 pledge to halve the number of asylum applications. The second is the Conservative Party's 2010 pledge to reduce net migration from the hundreds of thousands to the tens of thousands. The aim of the analysis is to explore whether their reception was related to one of the difficulties identified, namely the failure of the target to resonate with popular concerns and its perceived unfeasibility, or mistrust at the procedures for monitoring its achievement.

Targets on Asylum Applications and Net Migration

Tony Blair announced the 2003 asylum target as a response to increasingly critical political and media coverage of asylum. As we saw in Chapter 3, in the late 1990s, the number of asylum seekers entering the UK had risen to around 80,000–90,000 per year. The media was portraying the problem in terms of rising numbers of applications, triggered by Labour's reputedly lax approach to border control and asylum support. As a direct response to these concerns, Blair announced a new high-profile goal in February 2003, that of halving asylum applications by September of that year.

Very similar considerations influenced the adoption of the Conservative Party's net migration target in 2010. The level of net migration had risen significantly from 2004 onwards under the Labour government, and from the mid-2000s the media and political opposition were expressing a growing sense that the government had lost control of UK borders. In 2009, the opposition Conservative Party started to moot the idea of a 'cap' on net migration, and in January 2010, the party leader, David Cameron, set a specific objective of reducing net migration 'from the 100s of thousands to the 10s of thousands'. As with Blair's asylum target, the aim was to engender public confidence in the Conservative Party through the goal of reducing overall numbers.

Both targets therefore share a number of key features. They aimed to respond to public concerns by reducing numbers of foreign nationals arriving in the UK. In both cases, the targets also prompted concerns about their feasibility, with politicians, interest groups and media commentators all querying whether they could be met. But while the asylum target was met, by late 2014 it seemed clear that the net migration pledge was unviable. This allows us to compare the evolution of public debate in a case where a target emerges as achievable, and one where it does not. The targets were also set by different administrations. This allows us to observe differences in media reporting based on the ideological affinities of the press. While much of the press was highly critical of Blair's asylum policy, the centre-left press (which enjoys the widest readership) was broadly supportive of Cameron's approach.

The analysis draws on two data sources. The first is IPSOS-Mori polls on public support for different parties. IPSOS-Mori conducts an annual poll of 1,000 people, asking them which is the 'best party' on a range of policy issues, including 'asylum and immigration' (polling in 2003 and 2004 simply asked about the best party on 'asylum', with 'immigration' added in 2005). However, while polling data offer some insight into trends in public support for the two parties, they are far too crude to identify more precise relationships between targets and public trust. The data are limited to one poll per year, which makes it difficult to track changes in public support in response to specific announcements or events. And it fails to tell us anything about respondents' reasons for expressing these preferences.

Given these limitations, I instead drew on an analysis of newspaper coverage of the two targets. Unlike opinion polls and electoral results, newspaper coverage provides more elaborate lines of argument, helping explain the reasoning behind different assessments of government performance. Importantly, it also provides continued coverage over time, allowing us to map shifts in discourse. This can give us considerable insight into the sorts of beliefs and values underpinning responses to targets.

The second consideration relates to the relationship between media reporting and politics. The media has a strong influence on public beliefs about politics and policy. Not only does the media select what information the public receives about party politics and many aspects of policy, it also shapes how this information is narrated. We would therefore expect the public to be influenced by reporting on targets. Just as importantly, politicians tend to treat the mass media as an indicator of public sentiment (Koopmans 2004). So politicians concerned about trust will be keen to pick up signals about public support from media coverage.

This is very clearly the case in the area of immigration and asylum. Time and again, Home Office officials and special advisors describe how intensively the organisation scrutinised media coverage and how sensitive it was to media reporting. The relentless media coverage of immigration was 'impossible to ignore' (Interview, February 2014). A former special advisor under the Blair government describes the atmosphere in the Home Secretary's office:

And so you'd have Sky [News] on. You would, I think at one point we had two televisions, so we had, we had Parliament on. Yeah, I mean we did. We had the Commons [parliamentary channel] on as well. And, you know, and that was, that set the rhythm for the day. (Interview, February 2014)

This sensitivity to media reporting persisted under the 2010 coalition government. As a Home Office official working in private office under the coalition government described it, 'well they have group meetings [with the Press Office] every day, twice a day, three times a day, I think, actually. We all go to at least one of them ... And there's weekly stratcoms meetings, which we will go to. We get the cuts; the press cuts every day. We have email updates every couple of hours or so' (Interview, February 2014). While waiting for a meeting at the Home Office headquarters in Marsham Street, I saw a wedge of photocopies on the coffee table. It turned out to be an eighty-page stapled booklet of press coverage for that day. It was one of multiple copies circulated among Home Office officials to keep track of coverage, covering everything from EU negotiations on asylum to Home Secretary Theresa May's hairstyle. The Home Office was deeply preoccupied with how the media was covering the organisation and its actions. If we are interested in exploring how politicians perceive and respond to the problem of political trust, then media coverage will provide some useful clues as to how political actors interpret public reactions to the problem of public trust.

Of course, there are limitations to the use of newspaper reporting as a proxy for public attitudes. Members of the public may develop beliefs about government policy based on other sources. They may draw on information from their own experiences of public services, or from hearsay about the experiences of others. One good example of this was offered by an interview respondent from the Department of Health, who describes how the Prime Minister came to learn about public views on one of his key health targets. The revelation came in the course of a BBC *Question Time* debate.

The discussion was about GP appointments and access to GPs and the Prime Minister, of course, was kind of saying the usual stuff . . . that we had a target for everybody who can get an appointment with their GP within forty-eight hours ... and that's being met in something like 87 per cent of all appointments. And he declared this, the entire room of the *Question Time* audience just said, 'What?' And it was like, it wasn't just that there was a couple. The entire place just said, 'that's crap!' And he was so kind of shaken by it that he kind of . . . you know, he stumbled on. But immediately there was a sense of, 'hold on a minute, are we saying something here that doesn't quite ring true?' (Interview, May 2014)

In this case, the problem of access to GPs was clearly not being picked up in the media, otherwise the Prime Minister would have been sure to have been apprised of it. Governments can also pick up public concerns through focus groups and through the feedback individual Members of Parliament receive from their constituents. As we shall see in the next chapter, some of these concerns are articulated in parliamentary questions. However, in most cases, we can expect the media to serve as the most important 'sounding board' for politicians (Koopmans 2004).

I analysed coverage in seven daily and four Sunday newspapers. The papers were selected on the basis of popularity, as well as for providing a good balance of positions across the political spectrum. The papers were the *Guardian*, the *Daily Mail* and *Mail on Sunday*, the *Independent* and *Independent on Sunday*, the *Mirror*, the *Sun*, the *Telegraph* and *Sunday Telegraph* and the *Times* and *Sunday Times*. I searched archives through LexisNexis, using a variety of phrases that would capture articles mentioning the target, searching across a specific time frame. For the asylum target, I looked at the period February 2003, when the target was first announced, until August 2004, by which time the target had been met and discussion of it had tapered off. For the net migration target, I looked at the period from July 2010, when the net migration 'cap' was introduced, until September 2014, when it became clear that the target would not be met. I then examined each of the articles to eliminate irrelevant items or duplicates. I included all articles that contained a discussion of the respective targets (even if this was just one sentence), but excluded those that simply listed or referred to the target without any substantive insight or comment. For the asylum target, there were a total of fifty-two articles meeting these criteria; for the net migration target, there were 264. Tables 6.1 and 6.2 summarise the data.

Table 6.1 *Newspaper Articles on Asylum Target*

	2013 (from February)	2014 (until August)	TOTAL
Articles on asylum target	34	18	52

Table 6.2 *Newspaper Articles on Net Migration Target*

	2010 (from July)	2011	2012	2013	2014 (until September)	TOTAL
Articles on net migration target	81	37	33	39	73	264

I then coded the articles according to whether they were: (a) supportive of the target in principle, i.e. the main thrust of the coverage favoured the government's goal; (b) critical in principle, i.e. the coverage was broadly negative about the target on the grounds that it was wrong or inappropriate; (c) supportive of the target but sceptical as to whether it could be delivered; or (d) neutral, i.e. no substantive stance was taken with regard to the target. Many articles involved some combination of these positions. For example, articles might be supportive in principle but consider the target unfeasible. Or they might oppose it on grounds of principle and feasibility. I attributed each article just one value, depending on which of these arguments was predominant (in terms of strength of argument articulated and/or space devoted to this position).

Finally, I carried out a qualitative analysis of the articles to provide a more nuanced interpretation of coverage. For the asylum target, because of the lower volume, I was able to analyse all fifty-two of the articles. For the net migration target, I selected fifty-eight articles that devoted a paragraph or more to the target and were representative of the total sample in terms of temporal distribution and position adopted on the target. I analysed these articles to identify arguments and lines of reasoning adopted to support or critique the targets. I was especially attentive to arguments invoking issues of trust and to the reasons given for trusting or withholding trust in the target, or methods for reporting it.

In the analysis that follows, I start by setting out the background to the two targets, including the political context in which they emerged and the public concerns they sought to address. The following section then analyses how the targets affected public trust.

The Political Context

Until the late 1980s, asylum received very little political attention in the UK. Towards the end of the decade, numbers of asylum applications were beginning to increase across Western Europe, and by the late 1990s, the situation was depicted as an asylum crisis (see Figure 6.1).

I emphasise aggregate numbers not because I think this is the most important or interesting trend. It would be just as revealing to focus on the causes of refugee flows, or countries of origin, or how hosting asylum seekers impacted receiving countries or locales. But this aggregate number was to become the focus of attention in the media and political debate.

As we saw in Chapter 3, the Labour government's initial response in the late 1990s and early 2000s was to fix inefficiencies and loopholes in the asylum system. The initial targets focused on procedural bottle-necks in Home Office operations, with targets adopted to speed up

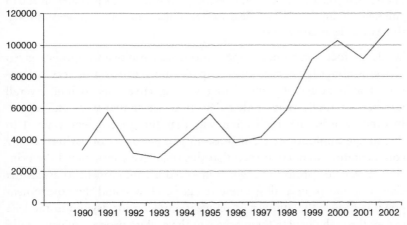

Figure 6.1 Asylum applications (including dependants)
(Source: Home Office)

decision-making and remove rejected applicants. The political priority was to reform the system to reduce 'abusive' claims. Yet Blair and others felt this missed the target of public concern. The media was portraying asylum in terms of a loss of control. Britain was being presented as a soft touch, with Labour's apparently lax approach encouraging so-called bogus applications. In early 2003, with no prior consultation with the Home Office or even Home Secretary David Blunkett, Blair announced on the BBC current affairs programme *Newsnight* that the government would halve asylum applications by September of that year.

It is not difficult to work out why Blair would have opted for this formulation. It offered a simple and succinct goal. It conveyed the government's commitment to a clear goal and offered a seductively simple narrative about the nature of the problem and the appropriate solution. Who could reasonably dispute the goal of reducing numbers, given the constant stream of invective about abuse, bogus applicants and crisis of control? By using a figure – a number – the goal conveyed a clarity and authority that qualitative goals would lack. As one former special advisor put it:

I think the objective was to say to people we have got a grip on this, the numbers have come down and your immigration system is, is being managed effectively. That was the objective ... the Government to show that it could sort it out. You know that was his overriding objective ... If you are on the doorstep, if you are in, you know, in a department, ... the pressure on you to announce things, to have clear policy objectives, is very, very strong. (Interview, February 2014)

While the focus on reducing applications was intuitively appealing given concerns about the rise in asylum applications, it was also very controversial as a target. It implied that the objective was to limit overall numbers of applications, rather than (just) those that were unfounded. In other words, the implication was that the government wanted to discourage applications from those in genuine need of asylum. Many commentators were concerned that this objective contradicted the principle of refugee protection, which involved a commitment to assess the claims of and protect all genuine refugees. How could the government possibly reduce the number of refugees applying for asylum in the UK, except through denying them access to the asylum process, which would contravene its duties under international refugee and European human

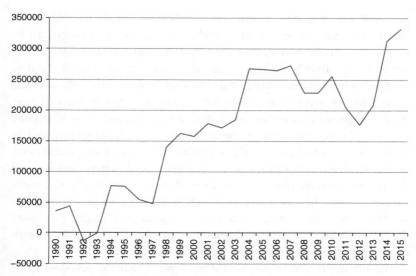

Figure 6.2 Net migration to the UK
(Source: ONS)

rights law? This argument was continually raised in the centre-left news outlets, and by non-governmental organisations and human rights/refugee groups.

Very similar reasoning lay behind the adoption of the net migration target in 2010. Again, it is worth briefly considering the context for the introduction of this target. While the Labour government oversaw a reduction in asylum applications from 2003 onwards, the government was simultaneously liberalising labour migration policy over this period. Labour introduced new routes for high-skilled migrants, and allowed freedom of movement to workers from the eight countries that acceded to EU membership in 2004. Figure 6.2 shows the rise in the level of net migration over the decade.

From around 2005, the media and political opposition were expressing a growing sense of crisis or loss of control. The Labour government had introduced a series of measures to limit immigration from 2007 onwards, including closing off low-skilled routes. However, it shied away from introducing a numerical target. This was left to the Conservative Party, which started mooting the idea of a 'cap' on net migration in 2009. In 2010 it went on to set a specific objective of reducing net migration 'from the 100s of thousands to the 10s of thousands'. Similar to the Blair asylum target, there appeared to be very little consultation behind the target (Hampshire and Bale 2015). And as with Blair's asylum target, the aim was to engender public confidence in the Conservative Party through reducing overall numbers.

As with the asylum target, the net migration target appears to have been a response to a rather crude and unnuanced narrative about the problem. If we think about the sorts of concerns prompting public opposition to immigration, these tended to be issues of pressures on public services, competition between foreign and 'native' workers on the labour market, unfair access to welfare and services and a more general sense that housing and public services were being overwhelmed. So public anxiety tended to focus on what might be termed the 'absorption capacity' of particular communities, faced with particular types of immigration, generally low-skilled.

The net migration target, however, implied that the problem to be addressed was aggregate numbers of immigrants – or even population per se, since the target was to reduce net inflows and outflows, rather than just to reduce immigration. The target might just as well be met through the large-scale emigration of British nationals, as a reduction in the numbers of non-nationals entering the UK. Thus the target appeared to address a more general fear about population growth and overcrowding. The focus on overall numbers was becoming a metaphor for concerns about chaos and loss of control. The target has to be understood as a highly symbolic response to the problem, addressing vague and inchoate anxieties about overcrowding. As one former Home Office official put it:

I think that what the Conservatives and opposition managed to convince themselves was that this was the right measure because it was the kind of purest sense of are the numbers in the country going up or down. And ... therefore being sort of brave, if you want to use that word, enough to say to the public, 'look, that's what we're going to set ourselves a target for because that's actually what is going to make ..., you know, that's actually the number that matters most.' (Interview, February 2014)

Once in place, the target had very similar effects on policy to those described in the asylum case. It galvanised the Home Office to introduce a series of measures to reduce immigration flows. Home Secretary Theresa May rolled out a panoply of reforms, first of all to provisions for high-

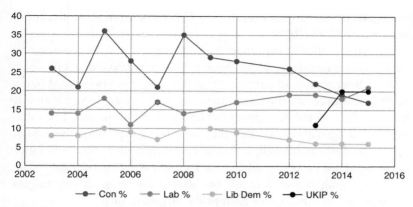

Figure 6.3 Best party on asylum and immigration
(Source: IPSOS-Mori)

skilled immigration, then to those covering foreign students, then to family migration and, notoriously, to tax credits and welfare to non-national workers. But it was clear from the outset that the target was going to be difficult to achieve. As one former Home Office official stated, 'I think there were probably always some misgivings about it as a target because people knew ... there were elements that weren't in control' (Interview, February 2014). A former Labour special advisor put it more strongly:

I nearly fell off my chair when I listened to it, because I thought, 'How could you say that? What would possess you to say that you're going to be able to do that?' Because you cannot, you can't implement that, you can't promise that. (Interview, February 2014)

IPSOS-Mori results suggest that the targets had limited – or negative – impact on public trust (see Figure 6.3). In the case of Labour's asylum target, the setting of the target or its achievement did not appear to translate into an increase in public confidence. Indeed, the proportion of respondents considering Labour the best party on asylum and immigration has remained remarkably steady, hovering at between 14 per cent and 19 per cent.

Data on support for the Conservative Party as the 'best party' in this area are more stark, suggesting that public confidence has actually declined since the introduction of the net migration target. Since the proposal was first publicly mooted in 2009, the proportion of the public who consider the Conservatives the best party on asylum and immigration has steadily declined. The most significant decline is between 2012 and 2014.

As noted earlier in this chapter, however, these data provide only very crude information about how the targets affected public confidence. Other aspects of party performance may have influenced public attitudes. Moreover, the data cannot be temporally disaggregated to identify shifts in public support as targets were announced, and information emerged about whether they were being met. What the data do appear to confirm, though, is that setting targets on asylum and immigration did not yield any substantial gain in public confidence.

More telling is the data on newspaper coverage of the targets. We will look at coverage of each of the targets in turn.

Press Coverage of the Asylum Target

Most coverage of the asylum target supported the broad goal of reducing asylum numbers, so there was no doubt about the target's political relevance. However, overwhelming scepticism about the target's feasibility undermined this potential support. Our qualitative analysis of these articles enabled us to identify four main critiques of the target, revolving around the government's capacity and commitment to delivering the target, dishonest reporting of the target and the means by which the target was achieved.

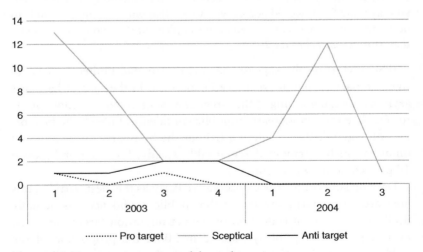

Figure 6.4 Newspaper coverage of the asylum target

First, a number of articles questioned the government's capacity to meet the target. Thus the *Daily Telegraph*, for example, introduced its coverage as follows:

A pledge by Tony Blair to halve the number of asylum seekers coming to Britain within seven months was derided as 'pie in the sky' last night.[1]

Or as the *Daily Mail* put it:

How can he [Blair] possibly hope to succeed when the numbers are already over 100,000 annually and every previous Government promise to take a grip has come to grief?[2]

Much of the coverage suggested that the government had been pressured into making a rash and unfeasible commitment. Indeed, some of the centre-right press were very cynical about the government's reason for adopting the target.

Mr Blair's announcement underlines Government nerves on the issue ... The Premier's spin doctors and poll analysts have been warning for months that the Government's failure to stem the tide of illegal immigrants could hurt Labour at the next election.[3]

In this extract, Blair's motivation for setting the target is questioned, with the implication that he is pandering to electoral concerns.

Media interest was further fuelled by apparent splits between Blair and Home Secretary David Blunkett, as well as contradictory statements emerging from the Home Office.

Tony Blair's credibility took another battering yesterday as his TV promise on asylum seekers was scrapped inside 48 hours ... Downing Street was forced into a humiliating retreat. Officials said the promise was not a target, only 'a signal of the progress we expect to make'.[4]

The usually supportive *Mirror* similarly reported that the government had 'watered down' the target 'in a bid to end four days of confusion'.[5] The *Telegraph* put it in more sober terms:

---

[1] Philip Johnston, 'Pledge to halve asylum seekers derived', *Daily Telegraph*, 8 February 2003.
[2] Paul Eastham, 'Blair: I'll halve the asylum tide by September', *Daily Mail*, 8 February 2003.
[3] Ibid.
[4] Matthew Hickley and David Hughes, 'The asylum somersault: Blair's promise to cut the number of asylum seekers by half lasts 48 hours', *Daily Mail*, 10 February 2003.
[5] Oonagh Blackman, 'Asylum targets rethink', *Daily Mirror*, 11 February 2003.

David Blunkett, the Home Secretary, was caught off guard and does not consider this target to be achievable ... A Government spokesman said Mr Blair was not setting a target but giving an 'indicator of progress'.[6]

Doubts about the government's commitment also revolved around the apparent shift to a more long-term target. Thus the *Independent* reported:

Labour is presiding over 'complete confusion' on asylum, the Tories claimed yesterday ... The Home Office denied reports that David Blunkett, the Home Secretary, had condemned the goal as 'unachievable'. But the department did say that halving the number of asylum-seekers entering the country was a 'longer-term' aim, despite Mr Blair's specific pledge last week.[7]

However, over the next few months, criticism of the target shifted to doubts about the means by which the government was meeting the target. Data suggesting a sharp reduction in the number of asylum applications evoked suspicion that the government was manipulating the data. As the *Daily Mail* suggested, the government was 'attempting to make the asylum problem disappear by burying it in statistics'.[8] Much of the coverage questioned the government's use of the October 2002 baseline figure of 8,900 applications per month, which represented the peak in application numbers. This decision was criticised at the time of its announcement in February 2003, and several newspapers revived this criticism to cast doubt on subsequent government claims that it was meeting its target. For example, a *Times* reporter wrote:

Asylum applications fell by one third in the first three months of this year with figures for February and March hitting a four-year low ... Allegations that the figures are being manipulated result from the fine-tuning by the Home Office of Tony Blair's pledge to halve asylum numbers by September.[9]

Even more common was scepticism about the measures the government adopted to achieve the reduction. In April 2003, the Home Office announced it would admit 20,000 immigrants to work in the food-

---

[6] Philip Johnston, 'Court threat to Blair's asylum vow', *Daily Telegraph*, 10 February 2003.
[7] Ben Russell, 'Blair's target on asylum is a long-term aim, says Home Office', *The Independent*, 10 February 2003.
[8] Eastham, 'Blair: I'll halve the asylum tide by September'.
[9] Richard Ford, 'Tories cry foul as asylum figures fall to 4-year low', *Times*, 23 May 2003.

processing and hospitality industries. The *Daily Mail* suggested that this measure would:

allow many who might otherwise try to come to the UK as asylum seekers to enter legally with work permits ... [T]he Tories accused ministers of trying to solve the asylum crisis by 'fiddling the figures' to give work permits to those who would otherwise try to claim asylum. 'We are beginning to see how the Home Secretary intends to fulfil Tony Blair's pledge to reduce asylum applications by half by September,' said Shadow Home Secretary Oliver Letwin.[10]

The *Independent* picked up on this claim in its coverage of August 2003 statistics suggesting a fall in the number of asylum applications.

A sharp fall in asylum-seekers arriving in Britain has put the Government on course to fulfil Tony Blair's promise to halve the number of applications by September. But the drop was accompanied by an increase in people entering on work permits, prompting accusations that the headline total was being massaged downwards.[11]

In this case, what might have been a story about the government achieving its target swiftly turned to scepticism about how the government had achieved it. Further doubts were cast on the government's commitment when a scandal emerged in April 2004 over the Home Office's apparent decision to waive visa controls on Romanian nationals. The government had made a 'secret deal' with the Romanian government to remove restrictions 'in return for slashing the number of asylum seekers'.[12] The press was quick to suggest that this 'grubby saga' was prompted by the government's commitment to halve asylum applications.

But hasn't his 'success' been achieved largely by rigging the system? Why bother to claim asylum, when he has made it so easy to come here by other means?[13]

A further concern revolved around government measures to deny welfare to asylum seekers who failed to lodge an application soon

---

[10] Author not named, '20,000 migrants offered passport to a job', *Daily Mail*, 10 April 2003.

[11] Nigel Morris, 'Government on track to halve asylum as claims fall', *Independent*, 29 August 2003.

[12] Graeme Wilson, 'Blair's "secret deal on visa controls"', *Daily Mail*, 5 April 2004.

[13] Editorial, 'Grubby saga of a system in chaos', *Daily Mail*, 5 April 2004.

after their arrival. While the centre-right press was generally suppor-tive of this measure, they were keen to point out that this would discourage those illegally resident from applying for asylum. This would have the effect of reducing the number of asylum applicants, but would increase the level of illegal residents. The *Daily Mail* adopted this interpretation, reporting research suggesting that 'a 32 per cent drop in asylum numbers earlier this year was caused by migrants going underground.'[14] Even more seriously, in February 2004 allegations emerged that officials were being dis-couraged from apprehending illegal immigrants out of concern that they would apply for asylum. Again, media coverage suggested that this was motivated by pressure to meet the target.

The *Daily Telegraph* brings together these points in an editorial explaining the decline in asylum applications.

There was a massive, if untrumpeted, increase in work permits. Now, it emerges that the Home Office has ordered staff not to arrest illegal immigrants for fear that they might claim asylum. At the same time, we learn that the Prime Minister has personally reached a deal with his Romanian counterpart ... to admit visitors from that country without visas. Putting these facts together, we can reach only one conclusion. The Government has decided to admit hundreds of thousands of additional migrants, even if this means breaching its own rules ... Why? Because, just over a year ago, the Prime Minister, in order to get himself out of a tight spot, promised to reduce asylum claims by half.[15]

The press was therefore refusing to give the government credit for meeting the targets. This *Daily Mail* article nicely captures the media's reticence.

Credit where credit is due. Tony Blair promised his Government would halve asylum applications. And in headline terms at least, that is what happened ... Yet inevitably there is a 'but'. That dramatic fall in applications, for example, was partly due to a statistical sleight of hand, using last October as the starting point, when asylum numbers blipped to an all-time high. Mr Blair knew the figures were coming down anyway. But there is another and more disturbing explanation. Tough new benefits rules introduced last January

---

[14]   Jo Butler, 'UK migrants policy is a failure, Blunkett warned', *Daily Mail*, 24 June 2003.
[15]   Editorial, 'Immigration policy is built on a fraud', *Daily Telegraph*, 5 April 2004.

mean that people smuggled into Britain in the past no longer have an incentive to claim asylum ... There is a glaring hole in this Government's 'success'.[16]

Even commentators in centre-left outlets agreed that the government had been duplicitous in its means of achieving the reduction, as in the case of this political sketch in the *Guardian*:

So it proves: their success in reducing applications is the result of two initiatives. One, they've stopped arresting illegal workers who then would have claimed asylum, and two, they've quadrupled the number of work permits to 175,000 a year. They've made illegal working legal ... [This] is characteristic of the political class that even when pursuing a benign policy they prefer to defend themselves with a lie.[17]

The *Independent* similarly attributes various dubious measures by the Home Office to the pressure to reduce asylum applications.

To understand how we reached this sorry state of affairs it is necessary to go back to the Prime Minister's pledge in February last year that the number of asylum applications would be halved by the September of that year. This was a panicked response to spurious rants about bogus asylum seekers in the right-wing press. It now seems to have led to a frantic exercise in corner-cutting and sleight of hand by Home Office officials in order to meet an arbitrary target ... it all smacks of desperation.[18]

Just one article, in the *Times*, showed unqualified support for the government's achievement of its target. In August 2003, the *Times* reported that:

The Government is on target to reduce significantly the number of people claiming asylum in Britain after a sharp fall in applications during the first half of the year.[19]

Exceptionally, the article does not caveat its claim by shedding doubt on the data or on the way the government achieved this goal.

---

[16] Editorial, 'Our borders are still wide open', *Daily Mail*, 28 November 2003.
[17] Simon Carr, 'The sketch: When is the truth not the truth? When ministers try to defend it', *Guardian*, 24 February 2004.
[18] Editorial, 'A failure to be honest about immigration is the cause of the government's latest troubles', *Independent*, 5 April 2004.
[19] Richard Ford, 'Tougher action on asylum "is now working"', *Times*, 29 August 2003.

Throughout this period, press coverage was continually raising the wider issue of how the target was contributing to a decline in public trust. When the target was first announced, reporters were keen to point out the political risks involved. The 'pledge threatens to rebound on him if not met'[20]; 'Mr Blair has put his credibility on the line.'[21] Indeed, centre-right newspapers were continually seeking to use the target and various statements around it to question the government's credibility.

Dr Duncan Smith accused Mr Blair of changing his mind from one day to the next. For instance, last Friday, he described his new asylum target as a pledge, on Saturday the Home Office said it was undeliverable and on Monday a Downing Street spokesman said it was an aspiration.[22]

And not surprisingly, the press verdict one year on was that the target had further discredited the government. Unexpectedly, this was not because of the government's inability to meet the target, as the media predicted. Rather, it was because of the supposedly underhanded way in which the target had been achieved. We give the last word to the *Daily Mail*, the government's most virulent critic:

These last few weeks have exposed such depths of dishonesty and deceit that this Government never deserves to be trusted again on anything it says about this issue. We have witnessed barefaced lies from Whitehall and the politicians ... And we now know from leaked emails that officials have been told to avoid arresting illegal immigrants, for fear they will immediately claim asylum thus making nonsense of Tony Blair's promise to halve asylum applications.[23]

The following day, the paper reported: 'Tony Blair finally admitted last night that public trust on immigration has collapsed.'[24]

Press Coverage of the Net Migration Target

We now turn to our second case, to see if the Conservatives received more favourable coverage for their net migration target. A total of 264

[20] Eastham, 'Blair: I'll halve the asylum tide by September'.
[21] Johnston, 'Pledge to halve asylum seekers derived'.
[22] Michael Kallenbach, 'Blair's asylum policy a "complete shambles"', *Daily Telegraph*, 13 February 2003.
[23] Editorial, 'Another crisis, another stunt', *Daily Mail*, 6 April 2004.
[24] Paul Eastham, 'A stunt or will we now get the truth?', *Daily Mail*, 7 April 2004.

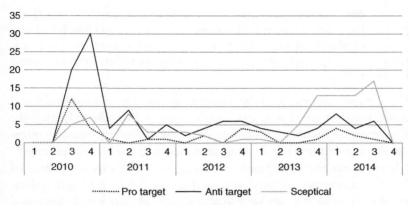

Figure 6.5 Newspaper coverage of the net migration target

articles on the net migration target was published between June 2010 and September 2014. The main themes revolved around concerns that the target undermined business, splits over the target within the coalition government and the feasibility of meeting the target.

Initial reporting on the proposed cap focused on concerns about its impact on business and higher education. Both the *Times* and the *Daily Telegraph* devoted extensive space to business concerns about the effects of the cap on the economy. In its coverage of the June 2010 plans, the *Daily Telegraph* reported that the plan had 'raised concerns about the long-term impact on the economy'.[25] In subsequent reporting, it talked of the cap 'hampering' or 'handicapping' business.[26] The *Times* tempered its acknowledgement of the government's success in reducing net migration by pointing out that the reduction had led to a 'loss of talent'.[27]

Linked to this, there was widespread speculation about whether the government would water down the proposed cap because of the concerns being expressed by businesses. As the *Daily Telegraph* reported:

[25] James Kirkup, 'Business leaders to have say over cap on migrants', *Daily Telegraph*, 25 June 2010.

[26] James Kirkup, 'Minimum salary plans for migrants', *Daily Telegraph*, 6 November 2010; Richard Tyler, 'Migrant cap continues to hamper firms', *Daily Telegraph*, 9 November 2010.

[27] Kaya Burgess, 'Warning of loss of talent as net migration falls by 25%', *Times*, 30 November 2012.

Home Office sources were adamant that even though the Government was prepared to listen to concerns about immigration, the total number of new arrivals would still be capped. 'There will be a cap on immigration. This is what the British people voted for and this is what we will do', said one source last night.[28]

Other papers reported that the government would launch a consultation process to ensure businesses' needs were fully reflected, and the *Guardian* even reported that governing was 'rethinking plans to introduce an immigration cap ... amid fears it could damage the economy'.[29] Claims about the government retreating from the cap in the face of business concerns resurfaced at several points.[30] It is striking that these putative U-turns in policy were almost exclusively attributed to external pressures on the government. As the *Daily Telegraph* reported in November 2010:

Over the past months, Mr Cameron is understood to have been personally lobbied by senior business leaders warning of the economic damage caused by applying too stringent a cap ... One well-placed source said: 'We have listened to the concerns of business and realised that although we need to bring immigration under control, we don't want to damage the economy. We want the best skilled people from around the world to still come here.'[31]

Cameron is depicted as an honest broker trying to juggle conflicting pressures.

Newspaper reporting also focused heavily on tensions within the coalition government. Again, the coalition and other members of the government were consistently perceived as a constraint on the Conservative leadership. The Liberal Democrats were openly critical of the target, as were some of the Conservative members of the government. As the *Guardian* reported:

The home secretary is pressing ahead in the face of concerns among members of the cabinet that an arbitrary cap could deprive the economy of skilled

---

28 Kirkup, 'Business leaders to have say over cap on migrants'.
29 Haroon Siddique, 'Government reconsidering plans to impose immigration cap', *Guardian*, 25 June 2010.
30 James Kirkup and Tom Whitehead, 'Migration cap could be eased to let in best talent, says Cameron', *Daily Telegraph*, 26 October 2010; Robert Winnett, Rosa Prince and Tom Whitehead, 'Cameron will bow to business and relax cap on immigrant workers', *Daily Telegraph*, 15 November 2010.
31 Winnett, Prince and Whitehead, 'Cameron will bow to business and relax cap on immigrant workers'.

labour ... Conservative sources blamed reports of a change of heart on trouble-making by the Lib Dems.[32]

The usually supportive *Daily Mail* suggested that the Liberal Democrats had 'forced a climbdown', implying intra-company transfers would be excluded from the cap. It noted:

The Lib Dems furiously opposed a limit on immigration during the election campaign and a number are deeply uneasy about today's announcement.[33]

Reporting on coalition divisions continued throughout the period. Liberal Democrat Business Secretary Vince Cable was particularly vocal in his criticism of the target, and press reporting was keen to play this up. The *Daily Mail*, for example, reported that:

David Cameron has slapped down his errant business secretary Vince Cable after he reopened the Cabinet rift over immigration.[34]

Sections of the centre-right press were concerned that these divisions would lead the government to abandon what they saw as a necessary cap. Thus the *Telegraph* writes:

Damian Green, the immigration minister, is promising to tighten the system. He should go further. The Tories had a clear policy to fix a cap on immigration, but that is looking worryingly flexible under the Coalition.[35]

Indeed, a theme running was the notion that the Tory leadership's hands were tied by its coalition partner. Any prevarication was attributed to their Lib Dem coalition partners, or pro-business Conservatives. Thus in reporting a rise in net migration in October 2010, the *Daily Mail* suggested that some ministers 'are anxious to stave off the Coalition's promised cap on immigration', the implication being that this would constrain the government in bringing down net migration.[36]

A number of newspapers were also critical of the feasibility of the target from early on. Thus the *Times* wrote in June 2010 that the

---

[32] Nicholas Watt, 'Immigration cap to be put on skilled workers from outside EU', *Guardian*, 26 June 2010.

[33] Kirsty Walker, 'The migrant revolt', *Daily Mail*, 28 June 2010.

[34] Emma Rowley, 'Migration cap a "real headache", warns CBI', *Daily Telegraph*, 1 October 2010.

[35] Editorial, 'The coalition must not wobble on immigration', *Daily Telegraph*, 3 August 2010.

[36] Steve Doughty, 'Foreign worker numbers surge to a record 2.4M', *Daily Mail*, 19 October 2010.

measures introduced 'will not be enough for the Conservatives to meet their election pledge to reduce net migration'.[37] These concerns became more prominent in August 2010 as statistics suggested a rise in net migration.[38] Here is an example of the *Daily Mail* venting its frustration at the government's failure to achieve the target:

These figures show that the Government needs to pull its finger out and get on with it. People are fed up with talk. They want to see significant reductions. People will hold ministers to account for this at the next election. Last week, a Whitehall survey showed four out of five people want to see immigration reduced and more than half the population want to see immigration cut 'a lot'.[39]

However, there was a pronounced tendency to attribute this to external constraints. One factor continually raised was EU provisions on free movement. As the *Daily Mail* reported in December 2010:

Immigration to Britain is 'unlikely' to fall significantly next year because of the parlous state of the Eurozone ... there is nothing the Government can do to stop workers from the EU coming to Britain.[40]

The following year, the paper argued that 'Britain is hamstrung in its ability to influence net migrant numbers because it cannot restrict those coming from inside the EU.'[41] Indeed, the language of the centre-left press continually expresses sympathy with the plight of Cameron. As the *Daily Telegraph* argued:

The Coalition is facing a major headache after figures last week put net immigration at 239,000 for 2010 – a 21 per cent jump on the previous year.[42]

The centre-right press also attributed the rise in net migration to the legacy of the previous Labour government, and suggested the figures strengthened the case for the cap. As the *Daily Mail* reported:

---

[37] Richard Ford and Francis Elliott, 'Number of immigrant workers to be capped; coalition moves swiftly to limit entry to Britain', *Times*, 26 June 2010.

[38] Alan Travis, 'Figures show increase in net migration to UK', *Guardian*, 26 August 2010.

[39] Steve Doughty, 'Britain is migrant magnet of Europe', *Daily Mail*, 20 January 2011.

[40] Gerri Peev, 'Despite cap, numbers will not fall significantly', *Daily Mail*, 30 December 2010.

[41] Jack Doyle, 'Coalition "will miss its migrant targets"', *Daily Mail*, 21 June 2011.

[42] Tom Whitehead, 'Fewer Britons leaving to live abroad as pound slumps', *Daily Telegraph*, 30 August 2011.

Ministers blamed Labour for the latest rise, saying its 'points-based system' for controlling immigration had failed. They repeated their pledge to reduce net migration to the levels of the 1990s.[43]

Similarly, the *Telegraph* explained the government's predicament in the following terms:

In pledging to reduce net immigration to the tens of thousands, the Coalition was always creating a rod for its own back. Labour left the system in such a sorry state that the task of letting in those Britain wants and keeping out those it doesn't is one of almost nightmarish complexity ... reaching that goal will be a gruelling process.[44]

In November 2012, statistics for the first time suggested a significant reduction of net migration, with the implication that the government may be on course to meet the target. The *Daily Mail* was unreservedly upbeat in its reporting:

Migration into Britain has seen the biggest fall in 20 years, official figures revealed yesterday ... Ministers hailed the figures as a major step towards achieving the Government's aim of reducing immigration to the levels of the 1990s ... The figures are a relief to Home Secretary Theresa May and the Prime Minister.[45]

Similar positive reporting followed statistics released in February 2013.[46] However, by November 2013, it was clear that net migration was on the rise again, and that the government would not meet its target. The *Daily Mirror* was especially keen to expose the government's failure, reporting that the pledge was 'in ruins'[47], 'in tatters'[48] and 'in shreds'.[49]

---

[43] Steve Doughty, 'Population grew 200,000 in Labour's last year', *Daily Mail*, 27 August 2010.

[44] Editorial, *Daily Telegraph*, 31 August 2012.

[45] Steve Doughty, 'Biggest fall in immigration for 20 years', *Daily Mail*, 30 November 2012.

[46] Wesley Johnson, 'Migration falls after clampdown on bogus foreign students', *Daily Telegraph*, 1 March 2003.

[47] Tom McTague, 'Tory pledge in tatters as immigration goes up 30%', *Daily Mirror*, 28 February 2014.

[48] Jack Blanchard, 'Immigration pledge is broken as figure rockets to 243,000', *Daily Mirror*, 29 August 2014.

[49] Jack Blanchard, 'Cam immigration pledge in shreds after 20% rise', *Daily Mirror*, 23 May 2014.

Despite the rise in net migration, most newspaper reporting continued to be supportive of Cameron. As the *Daily Mail* reported:

The Prime Minister insisted tough measures to limit the number of incomers
would continue ... 'I'll keep going on this', he said. 'The public want firm
action on immigration and that's exactly what they're getting from me.'[50]

When net migration again rose in February 2014, the *Telegraph*
reported that 'plans to bring down net migration into the "tens of
thousands" are still on track.'[51] The *Daily Mail* used the increase to
demonise the position of the Lib Dem business secretary.

Vince Cable taunted the Prime Minster yesterday by saying the
Government's failure to control immigration was a good thing. The Tories
were dealt a huge blow by new figures showing net migration to Britain had
rocketed by 60,000 to 212,000 in the year to September 2013 ... Rubbing
salt into Tory wounds, he added: 'Any target on migration is totally
impractical, cannot be delivered and would do great damage to the
economy.'[52]

The implication is that Cameron is committed to his target, but is being
obstructed by his Lib Dem coalition partners.

There was surprisingly little reporting on 'gaming' or duplicity in the
way the target was set or monitored. One exception is the *Guardian*,
which queried the way the target had been set, especially the exclusion
of intra-company transferees from the cap on skilled migrants.[53]
The paper was also sceptical about the inclusion of students:

Ministers have included overseas students in the government's net migration
count because they are more interested in playing the numbers game than
with long-term migration, a leading think-tank has claimed.[54]

In the centre-right press, I found just three articles implying some
duplicity in the way the government had set or reported on the target.

[50] James Chapman, 'PM admits migration target may not be met', *Daily Mail*,
      3 December 2013.
[51] Georgia Graham, 'Immigration curbs on track, says Conservative chairman',
      Daily Telegraph, 3 March 2014.
[52] James Slack and James Chapman, 'Migration soars: Good says Cable', *Daily
      Mail*, 28 February 2014.
[53] Alan Travis, 'Immigration cap: Argument within the coalition has only just
      begun', *Guardian*, 23 November 2010.
[54] Alan Travis, 'Ministers "playing immigration numbers game" by including
      students', *Guardian*, 14 May 2012.

One involved a claim that the Home Secretary was 'fiddling' immigration statistics 'by pushing through a change to the visa system':
Home Office officials are considering plans to change the maximum length of visas for some foreign workers by as little as one day to avoid having to describe them as migrants.[55]

Another pointed to 'spin' in the way the government presented the May 2014 figures, which again showed a rise in net migration.

The government put the best gloss it could on the failure to meet a target that it should never have proposed in any case. It pointed to a fall in European Union migrants since 2005, which is true, but this is due to the one-off inflow of migrants from central European countries that acceded to EU membership in 2004.[56]

A third reported on comments by the Public Administration Select Committee that methods for estimating net migration were unreliable.

Ministers were warned that they should not base their controversial immigration target ... on such shaky figures. Some advisers believe that, as a result, the Government should aim to reduce net migration to 50,000 rather than 100,000 in order to achieve its goal.[57]

Yet these are exceptions to the generally respectful and supportive coverage.

Grounding Public Trust

Earlier in this chapter, I suggested that targets need to meet three conditions in order to elicit public trust. They need to address areas of policy that resonate with public concerns. They need to be seen as feasible and credible. And the information and data for verifying them need to be seen as legitimate and reliable. We can now consider how far these conditions were met for the two targets discussed, and how this appeared to affect media coverage of them.

The first point to note is that both targets clearly addressed salient public concerns. And the media reflected this with extensive

---

[55] Peter Dominiczak and Steven Swinford, 'May accused of trying to "fiddle" migrant figures', *Daily Telegraph*, 28 March 2014.

[56] Editorial, *Times*, 23 May 2014.

[57] Martin Beckford, 'UK migration figures rely on counting just 12 people a day', *Mail on Sunday*, 28 July 2013.

reporting on the targets, and – in both cases – an acknowledgement that the targets addressed important policy issues. To be sure, the net migration target was also considered to conflict with other important priorities, namely ensuring a thriving economy. Centre-right and centre-left broadsheets were particularly critical of attempts to reduce numbers of high-skilled migrants and foreign students, measures it believed would have a detrimental effect on business and the higher education sector. However, most newspapers acknowledged the issue was one of the most pressing concerns for large numbers of the electorate.

The question of the feasibility of targets is more complex. Much of the reporting on both targets suggested the goals would be difficult or impossible to meet. In the case of the asylum target, the press initially considered the goal of halving numbers was impossible – 'pie in the sky'. And even when it was met, they attributed this to various forms of gaming and duplicity (more on this in what follows). Thus the media found it very difficult to let go of the idea that the target simply could not be achieved, even when the statistics suggested otherwise. It is interesting to compare this to coverage of the net migration target. In this case, scepticism about the feasibility of the target increased over time, as statistics showed a rise in net migration. However, the media generally attributed this failure to exogenous factors: external constraints on the government's margin of manoeuvre. The centre-right was generally sympathetic to David Cameron's predicament: despite his best efforts, his plans were thwarted by hostile Liberal Democrats, a trenchant business lobby, EU commitments or economic conditions in southern European sending countries.

The contrast between coverage of the two cases is even starker on the question of the credibility of those setting the targets. The authenticity of the Conservatives' commitment to achieving the net migration target was never questioned. The press continually reported statements about Cameron's resolve to achieve the target, and used sympathetic language that implied his concerns were authentic and credible. Yet the press raised persistent doubts about Blair's motives for setting the asylum target, depicting it as a panicked response to opinion polls and media reporting, and as a case of 'spin'. Moreover, there was wide coverage of the supposedly dubious means by which he achieved the reduction – from widening channels for labour migration and easing visa controls, to encouraging officials not to apprehend illegal immigrants. In principle, similar doubts could have been raised about Cameron and May's tactics, for example the inclusion of foreign students in net migration figures, the exclusion of intra-company transferees from the initial cap, the methods used to estimate entry and the apparent loosening of controls on illegal residents. Yet apart from a few exceptions, the media was uncritical of the coalition government's motives, or the measures in place to achieve the target. Indeed, centre-right reporting consistently explained the coalition government's failure to realise the net migration target as arising from external constraints.

The divergent narratives about government credibility and trustworthiness clearly reflect wider media agendas, notably, the centre-right press's scepticism about the Labour administration and its tendency to focus on what it perceived as Blair's excessive 'spin'. Newspapers such as the *Daily Mail*, the *Sun* and the *Telegraph* and, to some extent, the *Times* and the *Independent*, were constantly on the lookout for examples of government duplicity and deceit. Moreover, immigration and asylum are traditionally seen as areas in which Labour is weaker: the party is seen as less firmly committed to restriction and has typically struggled to convince a sceptical media that it will pursue robust control measures. By contrast, it has been easier for Conservative politicians to convince the media that they are committed to restrictive policies. For these reasons, it is perhaps not surprising that the press was much more sceptical of Blair's asylum target than they were of Cameron's net migration target – even if the former was met and the latter failed. We find evidence of similar scepticism about other Labour government targets. As a former Department of Health official put it, a number of key targets were met on health. But:

they were undermined by the idea that this is all just dodgy figures, and playing fast and loose. Which of course, you know, is a real shame because actually the truth is there were massive, enormous improvements in, in all sorts of service standards over that time. (Interview, May 2014)

Yet this contrasting treatment tells us something important about the bases for bestowing political trust. The establishment of a target – even one that resonates with public concerns – may fail to convince the public that political leaders are firmly committed to a goal. Where the decision is depicted as a panicked reaction to opinion polls or focused groups, or an attempt to appeal to the media, then it may lack authenticity. The initial mistrust of motives can then affect subsequent narratives about how the target is achieved and reported. Even the achievement of a popular goal can be questioned where the motives of those setting it are subject to doubt. This scepticism may have little to do with the appropriateness of the measures taken or the robustness of data. Where there is confidence in the integrity of those setting the target, however, the narrative may be quite different. The political leaders in question are seen as genuinely committed to a popular goal. Their failure to achieve it is explained in terms of regrettable constraints, and the audience is encouraged to sympathise with the frustrated authors of the target.

The implication is that public trust may be relatively unaffected by whether a target is met. Far more important is the narrative about their authenticity, or the integrity of those setting the target. On the one hand, this suggests that media coverage may be more understanding of exogenous constraints than might be supposed. They are fully aware that policy-makers face a variety of economic and political impediments to realising immigration policy goals. And where they are sympathetic to those setting targets, they can acknowledge these factors as legitimate constraints on the achievement of their goals. On the other hand, it suggests that press reporting is largely impervious to outcomes. Commentators have made up their minds based on the perceived trustworthiness of the politicians or political party in question. Where information emerges that untrustworthy politicians have achieved their goals, rather than leading to an adjustment of beliefs, such successes are imputed to acts of manipulation or deceit.

Of course, the analysis focused on media reporting rather than public attitudes. It is possible that the media display especially strong ideological biases, and are particularly impervious to information. However, research on public opinion suggests very similar forms of bias, supporting the notion that voters often invest more importance in the perceived trustworthiness of politicians than in their performance (Cheibub and Przeworski 1999; Maravall 1999). Moreover, the media are the main source of information on politics and policy, so their reporting undoubtedly influences public views. Thus it is not unreasonable to suppose similar dynamics in terms of the effect of targets on public trust, though clearly more research would need to be done to support this claim.

The findings have broader implications for theories of political trust. They question the basic assumption of the accountability model set out earlier. Rather than basing trust on information about the conduct of politicians, in the cases we examined, trust appeared to be grounded in far more impressionistic cues. Indeed, the findings support theories of symbolic politics, which see politics as a form of contestation over largely rhetorical claims and symbolic gestures (Edelman 1977; Gusfield 1981). Politicians seek to mobilise support through asserting claims about policy goals and persuading the public of their record in achieving these (Poggi 1990). But the types of judgements underpinning political support and trust are frequently based on more impressionistic beliefs about the values, integrity or authenticity of those asserting these claims. The invocation of performance targets is part of this ritual of claims-making. But the feasibility of the targets and their impact on policy outcomes may in themselves have limited traction in producing public trust.

7 | Targets and Issue Definition

Targets may have a limited or even a negative impact on public trust. Yet tools of performance measurement can have a number of other, often unanticipated effects on political debate. This chapter examines some of the more indirect effects of targets, focusing in particular on how targets can affect the framing of policy problems and responses. A growing body of literature in sociology and law is showing how targets, indicators and rankings can influence how policy problems and responses are constructed (Bhuta 2012; Davis, Kingsbury and Merry 2012c; Espeland 2008; Merry 2011; Rose 1991). These studies argue that the use of such quantitative techniques is performative (Law and Urry 2004), structuring knowledge about policy problems and shifting expectations about appropriate forms of governance.

But how precisely do such quantitative descriptions influence the construction of policy problems? This chapter develops and tests some claims about the effect of quantification on political debate, building on two main bodies of literature. First, it draws on theories of issue definition to develop a number of claims about how changes in the description of policy issues can influence political debate. These contributions can help elucidate how new ways of framing policy problems can shape political debate. However, these political science accounts have not as yet theorised the distinctive effects of *quantitative* descriptions on political attention, venues and actors. For this, we need to draw on sociological literature on the particular effects of quantification. Here, we draw on insights about how quantification can exert an especially strong influence through its scientific authority, its precision and its aptitude for standardisation, comparison and portability across time and space.

This chapter combines these two sets of insights to posit two types of quantification effect. The first is what can be termed a *classification* effect. In order to develop indicators, rankings or targets, different entities need to be conceived of as equivalent units. These processes of categorisation can in turn influence which groups are considered relevant to policy, and how they are depicted in debate. The second can be termed a *measurement* effect. The use of measurement to frame policy issues can influence which venues or actors are considered qualified to deliberate and monitor policy, and – more generally – what are considered normal or appropriate ways of describing problems, setting goals and evaluating policy outcomes. The introduction of quantified descriptions can thus create new expectations about monitoring and accountability.

I explore these ideas through examining the UK government's 2010 target of reducing net migration. As we saw in Chapter 6, the target represented the first attempt to codify immigration policy goals in numerical terms, and so allows us to observe the effects of a new, quantitative framing of the question. It was also a controversial target, so presents a 'least-likely' case (George and Bennett 2005: 121): it shows how a target can reconfigure political debate even when it is not widely accepted as legitimate. If this case reveals the power of classification and measurement effects, then other more widely accepted targets are likely to have a more pronounced impact.

Quantification and Public Policy

As we saw in Chapter 2, statistics have long been associated with objective, scientific techniques of description and evaluation (Espeland and Stevens 2008; Hacking 1990). Yet literature in science and technology studies and sociology is generally critical of the effects of such quantification. Such numerical inscriptions abstract from complexity and context in a number of important ways. They disaggregate and recompress complex phenomena into discrete units, and abstract from difference and context, in order to produce standardised and countable units. As Nikolas Rose argues, these quantitative representations do not reflect 'real' social phenomena in any straightforward way (Rose 1991). Instead, numbers establish a 'plane of reality', one that glosses over nuance, complexity and variation. They privilege one particular category or characteristic, thereby suppressing others. And the framing of social problems or goals in terms of numbers also endows the chosen dimensions with particular influence.

Political sociologists have long recognised the power of quantitative techniques in public debate (Edelman 1977: 31; Gusfield 1981: 28), and some of the classic works on public policy have observed the effectiveness of statistics as a tool of political rhetoric and persuasion (Kingdon 1995; Majone 1989; Stone 2012). More recently, these ideas have been further developed in literature exploring the effects of indicators on governance. Research on performance measurement in national policy has shown how such tools can influence political attention and problem definition (Bevan and Hood 2006). Scholars have also drawn attention to the huge growth in the use of quantitative indicators at the international level. Indicators are increasingly deployed to evaluate the performance or progress of different countries or institutions in areas such as education (Grek 2009), development (St Clair 2006) or governance (Bhuta 2012). Such comparisons also frequently create further demands for regulation, by highlighting discrepancies in performance and raising expectations about 'normal' or 'good' performance. In these ways, indicators can have serious implications for political debate and global governance (Bhuta 2012; Davis et al. 2012a; Hansen and Porter 2012; Merry 2011).

These accounts of the effects of performance measurement offer important insights into how quantification influences political debate and policy interventions. However, such accounts fail to specify the mechanics through which such descriptions are diffused: the political dynamics through which quantitative descriptions come to prevail over other possible descriptions. Quantitative descriptions do not emerge in a vacuum, but are offered as articulations that complement or supersede existing ways of defining social problems or setting policy goals. In order to become influential frames in public political debate, such quantitative descriptions need to be taken up by key actors in the public arena (Hildgartner and Bosk 1988): they need to be mobilised by political elites and feature in mass media coverage. This makes it crucial to specify the processes through which political elites and journalists appropriate and privilege quantitative descriptions over other issue definitions (Kette and Tacke 2015).

Literature on political attention and issue definition can help address these gaps. Indeed, there are important commonalities between sociological analyses of indicators and political science literature on framing and issue definition. Both accounts assume that policy problems are socially constructed: rather than reflecting a given social reality, such constructions involve particular selections that foreground or prioritise certain aspects of social problems. Frank Baumgartner and Bryan Jones (1994) conceptualise this in terms of the multiple components of policy issues. They argue that a single issue 'may be associated with many different, often conflicting, implications' and that, typically, only selected aspects of an issue are salient at any one time (50). The selection of particular aspects of issues may be more or less strategic. Literature on 'framing' focuses on the intentional selection – or manipulation – of policy problems in a way that 'induces preference reversals' on the part of their audience (Sniderman and Theriault 2004: 135–6). However, issue definition accounts are compatible with less rationalist or purposive theories of agency: issue redefinition may occur through more subtle and incremental processes, involving multiple agents, whose behaviour is characterised as 'muddling through' or following a logic of appropriateness rather than as a result of rational reflection or 'strategic' behaviour.

More importantly, both the sociological literature on quantification and theories of issue definition assume that the construction of policy issues influences political debate and policy-making in important ways. As Baumgartner and Jones argue, issue definition 'shifts the terms of the political debate' (1994: 51), influencing both agenda-setting and policy formulation. However, the issue definition literature goes much further in specifying how such shifts occur, setting out a number of mechanisms through which such definitions come to influence political deliberation.

First, Baumgartner and Jones (1994) argue that policy-making takes place in 'policy monopolies' characterised by relatively stable issue definitions and 'policy venues', i.e. the institutions with the authority to make decisions about the issue. Issue redefinition can disrupt existing policy monopolies, through altering which actors and institutions are seen as relevant and authoritative in decision-making. By foregrounding new dimensions of a problem, issue redefinition can engage new actors, for example those operating in different policy sectors, at different levels of government or with different types of specialisations or functions. And such redefinition can imply a change in the venues considered appropriate for policy deliberation, for example privileging venues which enable specialised scrutiny and oversight, or which allow more scope for articulating and representing public concerns. Shifts in the actors and venues engaged in policy deliberation can in turn influence issue definition, stabilising and reinforcing new constructions of policy issues. As Baumgartner and Jones argue, 'where the rhetoric begins to change, venue changes become more likely. Where the venue changes occur, rhetorical changes are facilitated' (1994: 37).

A second type of effect concerns how issue redefinition can reconfigure the linkages between different issues. Where new aspects of an issue are brought to the fore, this can forge connections with other issues previously treated as separate. For example, a new issue definition can imply foregrounding the social or economic consequences of a policy or its ethical or security implications. Equally, redefinition can create new ramifications for other policy sectors, for example it may have implications for education, housing, policing or foreign policy.

Thirdly, issue definition can influence the level and type of political attention bestowed on policy problems. Where new aspects of issues are foregrounded, this can encourage increased political attention, especially where these aspects meet the criteria of newsworthiness: they evoke drama, encourage clear moral judgements and expose scandals. Moreover, such shifts are associated with different evaluations of problems. Positive attention 'may give way to hostile coverage as attention shifts from one component of an issue to another, equally partial, aspect of the same question' (Baumgartner and Jones 1994: 51). Schneider and Ingram's theory of the social construction of target populations takes this point further, suggesting that the construction of different groups in public debate and policy has a profound impact on policy preferences. 'Social constructions become embedded in policy as messages that are absorbed by citizens and affect their orientations and participation patterns' (Schneider and Ingram 1993: 334). Thus issue redefinition can trigger a shift in public attitudes towards target populations.

These contributions offer useful ways of specifying the political dynamics through which issue definition might affect political debate. In particular, they show how issue definition can affect which actors and venues are mobilised, how issues are linked and the level and type of political attention devoted to issues or to the targets of policy. However, they fail to develop specific claims about the influence of *quantitative* descriptions on these dimensions of political debate. In order to elaborate claims about the effects of quantification, we need to return to sociological literature on quantification. Drawing on these latter contributions, we suggest two main features of quantification that are likely to affect these dynamics and show how they might influence the mechanisms identified in the public policy literature.

The first of these is what we term a *classification* effect. This refers to the types of abstractions and regroupings required in order to count entities as equivalent units – what Espeland and Sauders (2007) refer to as 'commensuration' (see also Espeland and Stevens 1998). Classification involves a compression of complexity and nuance, driven by the imperative of creating uniformity and equivalence between different types of events, practices or people. By creating a single category or unit, classification can suppress particular features of the entities being counted. But it can also draw attention to previously neglected groups or entities. Classification can therefore affect which characteristics or entities are considered relevant to policy, and how they are depicted in debate. This implies that classification can influence all three of the mechanisms identified in theories of issues definition. It can affect which venues or actors are considered relevant or appropriate participants in political debate, it can create new connections between different issues and it can reconfigure which groups or entities receive political attention and of what kind.

Of course, the process of classification is not exclusive to quantification. All descriptions involve selecting certain entities and excluding others, and non-quantitative descriptions or goals can have strong classification effects too. Yet the precision and rigidity of quantitatively classified entities implies more limited scope for ambiguity, blurring or adjustment of categories or how these are applied. Moreover, the need to quantify entities imposes a number of technical criteria for selection that further reduce flexibility and nuance. Not everything can be counted, so the choice of a quantitative measure limits the scope of what can be included. Measurement may need to be based on existing data sets or statistical categories, or it may need to exclude a range of variables or entities that cannot be counted. These features of measurement all imply that classification effects may be especially simplifying and distorting.

Second, we identify a *measurement* effect. This refers to the potency of quantification as a particularly authoritative form of description or basis for assessment. The use of such frames can influence what are considered normal or appropriate ways of describing problems, setting goals and evaluating policy outcomes. In this way, the introduction of quantified descriptions can determine which venues or actors are considered qualified to deliberate and monitor policy. It can imply a stronger role for more technical or specialised forms of scrutiny. Because of the authority and objectivity typically associated with quantitative techniques, the use of measurement can also create additional incentives for political actors to invoke such measurement in debating policy. Politicians or journalists may latch on to quantitative descriptions to enhance their credibility or the robustness of their claims. This implies that the depiction of policy problems and outcomes in quantitative terms may increase the overall level of political attention devoted to a policy issue.

By identifying these two effects, we can integrate insights from both the sociological literature on quantification and from political science theories of issue definition. The former offers tools for understanding the particular potency of quantification descriptions, related to their authority, perceived objectivity, standardisation and mobility. Theories of issue definition, meanwhile, allow us to specify how these effects come about, through elaborating the precise mechanisms through which they might shift political debate. Finally, the concepts of classification and measurement effects provide a bridge between these two accounts, enabling us to identify the particular features of quantification that might influence which venues and actors participate in political debate, issue linkages and political attention. Importantly, these concepts help us disentangle those elements of issue definition emanating from the quantitative character of performance measurement. They are therefore useful in helping us to identify the ways in which quantification exerts distinct effects on political debate.

The Net Migration Target

I explore these ideas through examining political debate on the net migration target. As we saw in Chapter 6, in January 2010, David Cameron, the leader of the Conservative Party, announced that a prospective Conservative government would reduce net migration 'from the 100s of thousands to the 10s of thousands'. This was to become known as the net migration target, a pledge that appeared in the party's 2010 election manifesto and became Home Office policy after the election of a Conservative-led coalition government in May 2010.[1]

---

[1]   As Hampshire and Bale note (2015), the target was not agreed by the Conservative's Liberal Democratic partners, so never became formal government policy, but it was adopted by the Home Office and clearly drove immigration policy.

The data analysis attempts to trace how the net migration target produced the two effects outlined earlier. First, I look at how the target affected the classification of entities requiring political intervention, or 'target populations'. Specifically, I explore how this classification effect influenced which groups received political attention, and how it influenced issue linkages. Second, I look at the target's effect on the use of measurement in political debate. I explore how the measurement effect led to an overall increase in political attention towards the issue, and how it influenced expectations about appropriate ways of framing policy problems and goals.

To do this, I analyse two sets of data. The first of these is House of Commons Home Office Questions. These sessions take place around once a month during the parliamentary term (six or seven times a year) and present an opportunity for Members of Parliament (MPs) to pose questions to the Home Secretary or the minister responsible for immigration. Opposition MPs use these sessions to expose flaws or weaknesses in the government's record, while 'backbench' MPs of the incumbent party (those not in ministerial positions) often use them to signal their loyalty to, or occasionally to vent their frustration with, the government. There is also a finite length of time devoted to this session (around one hour), allowing for a relatively consistent number of questions to be posed per session – typically around twenty to twenty-five 'first' questions.[2] Questions are not limited to immigration and asylum issues, but can cover a range of aspects of home affairs. The proportion of those devoted to immigration therefore reflects not just the salience of immigration at the time of the session, but its pecking order in relation to other Home Office issues such as policing, crime, terrorism and drugs.

I collated all Home Office questions between 2009 and March 2015 in NVivo, comprising a total of forty-one sessions, and 547 individual 'first' questions on immigration (see Table 7.1). I then coded data according to: type of immigration, type of impact/concern, focus on technical features of the target and invocation of the target to praise or critique the government/another party. For certain nodes (student migration, high-skilled migration, family migration, EU migration

---

[2] In some cases, questioners ask a follow-up question or offer a rejoinder, but we did not count these as their incidence tends to be associated with individual characteristics of the MP rather than the topicality of the question.

Table 7.1 *Summary of Data on Home Office Questions*

	2009	2010	2011	2012	2013	2014	2015 (first quarter)
Number of sessions	6	6	7	6	7	6	3
Questions on immigration	52	85	78	79	143	66	44

Table 7.2 *Summary of Data on Newspaper Articles*

	2009	2010	2011	2012	2013	2014	2015 (first half)
Articles on net migration target	9	127	33	33	39	107	72

and temporary/permanent migration), I then went on to count the number of initial questions asked on a topic. This allowed us to quantitatively analyse the distribution of political attention across target populations.

Second, in order to examine the measurement effect I also analysed newspaper coverage. This was important for establishing the overall level of political attention the issue attracted. The data include coverage of the target in eleven of the most popular UK newspapers: the *Daily Mail* and *Mail on Sunday*, the *Daily Telegraph* and *Sunday Telegraph*, the *Guardian* and *Observer*, the *Independent* and *Independent on Sunday*, the *Sun* and the *Times* and *Sunday Times*. Articles were found on the LexisNexis database using the keywords 'net migration', 'migration target', 'migration cap' and 'cap on migration', yielding a total of 426 articles (see Table 7.2). I charted the number of articles per year and per quarter. Similarly, to the analysis conducted for Chapter 6, we also analysed articles according to whether they were predominantly supportive of the target in principle, opposed to the target in principle, sceptical of the target's feasibility or neutral (our data here cover a longer time frame than that drawn on in Chapter 6, which only looked at 2010–14). Each article was given a single value. We then selected sixty-eight articles which were primarily about the target and which were representative of the total sample in terms of temporal distribution and attitude towards the target. We analysed these articles qualitatively, focusing on the level and type of attention devoted to the target.

Classification Effects

The classification effect refers to the ways in which quantitative descriptions or goals can influence how entities are categorised. Quantification requires the identification of equivalent units to be counted. The construction of such units implies abstracting from difference, and treating each unit as identical for the purpose of the relevant description or goal. This section explores how the net migration target exerted this type of classification effect, influencing which groups became the focus of political attention, and how.

In applying this concept, we need to be careful to distinguish effects which relate more generally to reclassifications of target populations involved in setting a policy goal; and those reclassifications which are more specifically generated by the use of a quantitative description. As suggested earlier, any term adopted to describe a particular group or entity will necessarily involve selecting some features or entities and excluding others. We are interested more specifically in classifications that deploy (available or established) statistical categories that do not reliably capture the considerations or rationales that motivated the target – in other words, cases in which the choice of category is at least partly driven by technical considerations, such as the ease of procuring data, or the credibility of the statistical category. Once established, the precision of the statistical classification can create rigidity, binding political actors to a very specific form of classification that allows little scope for ambiguity or obfuscation. In this sense, the technical requirements associated with quantification produce especially binding and rigid classification effects.

As we saw, the net migration target was adopted in order to signal the Conservative Party's resolve to reduce levels of immigration to the UK. In specifying the target, the Conservatives chose to use the United Nations definition of long-term immigrant, i.e. 'a person who moves to a country other than that of his or her usual residence for a period of at least a year' (UN 2017). This implied a very broad definition of immigration, including foreign students in the UK for more than twelve months, who would not typically have been depicted as long-term migrants in political debate. It also implied including EU nationals who were entitled to free movement within the EU (indeed, the EU refers to the migration of member state nationals within the EU as 'mobility' rather than 'international migration'). And it implied including categories of migrants who had not been identified in political debate as problematic, such as high-skilled immigrants and intra-company transferees. Finally, it included those who were admitted to the UK based on human rights considerations, including asylum seekers and those entering to join their families. In this sense, the use of an established statistical category to specify the target implied making a number of controversial decisions about classification. By opting for such a precise measurement, and choosing an established UN definition for counting, the government was committing itself to a classificatory scheme that did not neatly fit its policy goals.

The second constricting feature of the net migration target was its focus on net flows, rather than inflows of immigrants. There was a number of reasons for this choice. One was the widespread perception, evident in political debate and media coverage, that immigration was placing a strain on jobs, housing and public services. The implication was that the problem was one of overpopulation. This notion is evident in media concerns about population growth in the UK, and the UK Independence Party's constant evocation of the problem of overcrowding. If the problem was one of population density, then clearly it was relevant to look at overall changes in flows, including how emigration from the UK might help to alleviate such pressures. Moreover, many forms of immigration are relatively short term. The UK typically admits around 200,000 foreign students per year, most of whom leave within four years. It makes sense of data on migration to reflect these outflows. And yet the decision to focus on *net* migration was also misleading in important respects. Much of the concern about immigration revolved around the entry of foreign nationals: their impact on social 'cohesion', their entitlement as non-citizens to access UK jobs, housing, welfare benefits or social services. Thus the problem was not exclusively or even predominantly one of overcrowding – but of extending access of non-nationals to UK resources. The net migration target implied that the government was neutral in terms of how this goal was to be met: whether

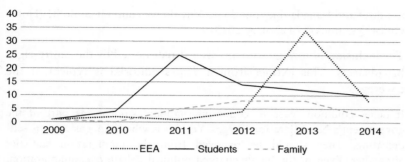

Figure 7.1 Topics of Home Office questions

by increasing emigration (including of UK nationals), or decreasing the immigration of non-nationals.

The first obvious effect of adopting the target was to trigger considerable contestation over the classification exercise itself. David, Kingsbury and Merry (2012b) argue that controversy over indicators is most intensive in the first couple of years after their definition, after which time they become taken for granted. This certainly appears to be borne out in the case of this target. Much of the initial attention to the target focused on the inclusion of foreign students – indeed, this was the dimension of the target that received the most parliamentary attention between 2010 and 2012, receiving twenty-five questions in 2011 and fourteen in 2012 (see Figure 7.1). In some cases, the inclusion of students was queried on the grounds that they were not long-term migrants, as in the following question:

Sheila Gilmore (Edinburgh East) (Lab): Given that the vast majority of international students leave the UK at the end of their courses, why do the Government insist on counting them when calculating net migration figures, which other countries do not do, to the detriment of institutions such as Edinburgh university in my constituency that are competing with other countries for those students? (Home Office Questions, 21 May 2012)

This is echoed in a question by a Liberal Democrat MP:

Greg Mulholland (Leeds North West) (Liberal Democrat): We need a firm, fair and sensible immigration policy, but that is confused by the inclusion of international students in the net migration figures. Those students contribute about £5 billion to the economy. America does not do that, Australia does not do it and Canada does not do it. Why do we continue to do it? (Home Office Questions, 11 February 2013)

The inclusion of foreign students was also criticised by the centre-right broadsheets. This extract from a *Times* editorial is typical of the coverage:

It defies common sense to count international students as part of the government's Net Migration Target. Yet this is what happens ... It is self-defeating. They should be removed from the immigration statistics altogether. Even in the highly-charged political debate over immigration, there is widespread awareness among the public that foreign students benefit Britain.[3]

These arguments of course missed the point that by focusing on *net* migration, the government intended to show how the departure of students largely cancelled out arrivals. But the questions clearly show that this point was lost in coverage of the data, which did not separate out net migration of students from other categories.

Others questioned the decision to focus on net migration, rather than immigration. Thus one Labour Party MP asked:

Diana Johnson (Kingston upon Hull North) (Labour): Can the Home Secretary confirm that net migration of British citizens has fallen by 47,000 under this Government because fewer British citizens are returning home and more are leaving? Does she regard it as a successful immigration policy if two thirds of the reduction in net migration under this Government is down to fewer British citizens in this country? (Home Office Questions, 25 March 2013)

The government itself was clearly in a quandary about the UN definition, and particularly the inclusion of foreign students. Indeed, in 2012 it attempted to separate out data on student migration from that on other categories so it could show that their net migration was low. However, this disaggregated data was not generally taken up in political debate and media coverage, which continued to focus on the aggregate figure. This illustrates the type of 'lock-in' effect of statistical classifications, which allow very little flexibility. Once a statistical measure is established, it becomes difficult to justify modifying it. Moreover, even when the government attempted to disaggregate the

---

[3] Editorial, 'Overseas students benefit Britain and should be exempt from net migration target', *Times*, 24 February 2015.

data, it was unable to control how the statistics were reported. The media tend to prefer simple headline figures, which provide a more sensational story – so the higher the figures, the better.

A second classification effect concerned the influence of the net migration target on the political attention bestowed on particular groups. The target had the effect of bringing various categories of migration into the political limelight, including those that had not previously been seen as significant and certainly not politicised. In some cases, this attention was largely positive. Notably, for foreign students and high-skilled labour migrants, most political discussion and media coverage was focused on criticising the government's decision to include them in the target and on highlighting their importance for the UK economy.

By contrast, the inclusion of other groups of immigrants in this classification attracted more negative attention. One example is that of family migration: provisions to allow spouses or children to join family members already resident in the UK. The number of those entering the UK for the purpose of family migration had remained relatively low, at around 50,000 per year in 2010, up from around 35,000 in the 1990s – a much lower increase than for other categories (Blinder 2015). However, the inclusion of this category of immigration in the net migration target drew attention to a perceived need to reduce this form of immigration. We see a steady rise in questions on the topic after 2010 (see Figure 7.1). Thus, for example, two Conservative MPs asked questions on the issue in September 2011:

JASON MCCARTNEY (CONSERVATIVE): Does the Minister agree that family migration must be based on a real and continuing relationship and not on a marriage of convenience or a forced marriage?

GRAHAM EVANS (CONSERVATIVE): Does the Minister agree that British citizens who cannot support their foreign partners should not expect the British taxpayer to do it for them?

Newspaper coverage also picked up on the issue, as in this *Daily Telegraph* editorial of 24 November 2010.

Regrettably, Mrs May was less forthcoming on the issue of family reunion, particularly from the Indian subcontinent. Since the last government scrapped the Primary Purpose Rule in 1997, it has been possible to enter into a marriage with someone settled here purely for the purpose of immigration. Until this abuse is tackled, these otherwise sound measures to limit immigration will be incomplete.[4]

A similar pattern can be discerned in debates on limiting permanent settlement. This was a goal directly flowing from the target's focus on *net* migration, which implied a concern to encourage the outflow of migrants from the UK. Prior to the introduction of the net migration target, the issue of whether immigrants would reside temporarily in the UK, or whether they would settle permanently, was not generally a focus of debate. If anything, permanent settlement and citizenship acquisition were seen as positive developments, indicating successful integration. But the net migration target implied that encouraging departure was just as significant as discouraging arrivals. New phrases were coined, such as the need to 'break the link between' or 'decouple' temporary and permanent settlement. This is illustrated in questions posed by Conservatives loyal to the government, designed to prompt pre-formulated government statements on policy:

ANDREW SELOUS: The Government's immigration objectives have
   widespread support across the House and across the country. What
   is the Minister doing, however, to tackle the links between
   temporary and permanent migration into this country? (Home
   Office Questions, 12 September 2011)
DR THÉRÈSE COFFEY (SUFFOLK COASTAL) (CON): What steps does she
   [Home Secretary Theresa May] plans to take to decouple temporary
   residence from permanent settlement in the immigration system.
   (Home Office Questions, 7 March 2011)

This is another example of how the decision to use the UN definition created classification effects, shifting the distribution and content of political attention in debates on immigration. It illustrates how the use of a quantitative measure can reconfigure which entities become the focus of debate, in ways that do not appear consistent with the underlying rationale of policy-making.

A third classification effect concerns the emergence of new issue linkages. We saw in Chapter 6 how the inclusion of foreign students and high-skilled workers generated concerns about the negative impact of the target on higher education and business. This implied that actors

---

[4]   Comment: 'The cap on non-European workers is a good start but more limits are
    needed', *Daily Telegraph*, 23 November 2010.

in the business and higher education sectors became more actively engaged in debates on immigration. Even more striking, however, was the issue linkage forged with UK membership in the EU.

EU mobility had already been politicised prior to 2010, in the context of Central and Eastern European immigration after the EU enlargement of 2004. Concerns about EU mobility began to surface more prominently in the run-up to 1 January 2014, the date at which Bulgarian and Romanian nationals would have access to the UK labour market. Politicians and the media articulated concerns about uncontrolled waves of immigrants from these countries. This issue would doubtless have arisen in the absence of the net migration target. But it was given particular focus and prominence by extensive media reporting on the rise in net migration over the period and by the government's patent inability to reach its target. The constant monitoring of net migration, with quarterly publication of detailed statistics, drew attention to the fact that the government was failing to control EU immigration. Moreover, with net migration statistics measuring EU migrants as a category within the overall figures, the issue was widened to one of EU immigration more generally, not just the entry of those from Central and Eastern Europe.

From late 2013 onwards, we see a consensus emerging in political debate that the government's failure to reach the net migration target was attributable to its lack of control over EU migration. In 2013, there were thirty-eight Home Office questions on EU immigration – compared to between one and four for previous years. Frustration about the government's lack of leverage was clearly articulated by Eurosceptic MPs.

PHILIP DAVIES (SHIPLEY) (CON): Is not the fact of the matter that while we remain in the EU with free movement of people we cannot guarantee how many people will come to this country, so we should not be making promises that we are in no position to keep? Is not the fact of the matter that we cannot control the number of people coming to this country while we remain in the EU? (Home Office Questions, 23 March 2015)

MR DAVID NUTTALL (BURY NORTH) (CON): Does the Home Secretary recognise the sense of grievance felt by citizens of Commonwealth countries who for years have abided by the rules when trying to get into this country as immigrants, only to see EU citizens being able simply to walk in and out of the country at will? (Home Office Questions, 23 March 2015)

Concerns about EU immigration became one of the most prominent arguments for the UK leaving the EU. As one MP put it:

MR PETER BONE (WELLINGBOROUGH) (CON): Immigration from the EU is the No. 1 issue in my constituency and across north Northamptonshire. The Prime Minister is the only party leader who will make any attempt to reduce immigration from the EU, and he has given a further guarantee that if he fails to do that the British people will have the chance to vote in a referendum by 2017 to get out of the EU. I am looking forward to that referendum; is the Home Secretary, and might she be voting to come out?

MRS MAY ROSE—

MR SPEAKER: Order. The question relates purely to the likelihood of the next migration target being met, so this is not an occasion for a general dilation on the EU. I am sure that the hon. Gentleman was not hoping for any such thing. (Home Office Questions, 5 January 2015)

This quote is interesting as the Speaker reprimands Mr Bone precisely for attempting to link the issues of migration and EU membership. Indeed, the case for Britain leaving the EU was without doubt strengthened as a result of the net migration target. By including EU immigrants in the target, this group became visible as a component of net migration, and thus viewed as a category to be reduced. And the regular publication of statistics made it more and more patent that the government could not control this element of net migration.

Newspaper coverage was similarly preoccupied with the relationship between migration and EU membership. As the *Daily Mail* reported in February 2014:

The Tories were dealt a huge blow by new figures showing net migration to Britain had rocketed by 60,000 to 212,000 in the year to September 2013. It was driven entirely by a 40 per cent leap in the number of people taking advantage of EU edicts on free movement. The shock increase left Downing Street unable to say if David Cameron would meet his key election promise to slash net migration to the tens of thousands by 2015 ... UKIP and Labour both said Mr Cameron's pledge was 'nothing more than smoke and mirrors' since EU free movement rules rendered Britain powerless to stop workers flooding from the continent.[5]

[5] James Slack and James Chapman, 'Migration soars: Good says Cable', *Daily Mail*, 28 February 2014.

In a similar vein, the *Times* reported in September 2014:

Britain must reclaim control over its borders from Europe and introduce touch immigration controls, a leading Conservative grassroots organisation is demanding. The proposal, outlined in the Conservative Home pre-election manifesto, is supported by YouGov polling, which shows that seven out of ten voters want free movement within the EU scrapped, rising to nine out of ten among Tory voters ... Pressure is growing after Mr Cameron was confronted by high migration figures. Net migration was 243,000 in the year to March, up from 175,000 the year before.[6]

To summarise, any target is likely to shift the focus of political attention, selecting certain categories for attention and overlooking others. However, quantitative targets imply a particular rigidity and precision in their selection, which has strong effects on political debate. Even in a case where the classification involved in the target was controversial, we identified three main classification effects. The target triggered a general increase in political attention, revolving around contestation of the categorisation; it produced a redistribution of attention to particular categories not previously considered important or problematic; and it ushered in new issue linkages, notably concerning the issue of UK membership in the EU.

Measurement Effects

Even while the net migration target was being contested in political debate, it was subtly shifting expectations about the kinds of goals, assessments and descriptions that were appropriate and authoritative. We can identify this measurement effect by looking at the level and content of parliamentary and newspaper coverage.

First, we can chart the level of political attention devoted to the target, and specifically to its statistical features. From late 2010 until the May 2015 election, we see a substantial increase in attention devoted to the target. Over this period, there were fifty-three Home Office questions querying the target, i.e. questions that focused on how it was set and measured, whether it was appropriate and feasible and the government's resolve in achieving it. Meanwhile, there were 427

---

[6] Sam Coates, 'Reclaim our borders from EU, Cameron is urged', *Times*, 1 September 2014.

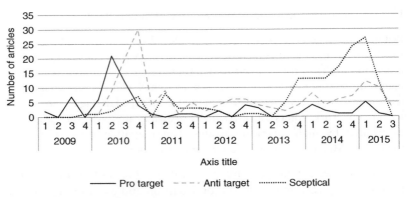

Figure 7.2 Newspaper coverage of the net migration target

newspaper articles on the target over the same period.[7] As we saw in the previous chapter, while initial coverage tended to involve appraisal of the desirability of the target, as time went on, much of the reporting focused on the target's feasibility. Indeed, 161 of these articles were sceptical about whether the government could reach (or was indeed committed to reaching) its target. Most of this more sceptical coverage occurred from late 2013 onwards (see Figure 7.2).

There are a number of reasons why a quantitative target of this kind would attract such strong interest in media and parliamentary debate. First, the nature of the target left the government open to criticism as to whether the aspired goal was feasible and how it was to be counted. Thus for example, there are plenty of cases of opposition politicians questioning the feasibility of achieving the target.

Mr David Hanson (Delyn) (Lab): Given that figures published last week show that net migration rose to 182,000, from 167,000, over the previous year, before the impact of any Romanian and Bulgarian immigration in January, does he think that the target, as set out in the Prime Minister's solemn manifesto pledge, of having a net migration in the 'tens of thousands', to quote the hon. Member for Amber Valley, by May 2015 will be met – yes or no? (Home Office Questions, 2 December 2013)

Other questions simply highlighted figures showing that the government had failed to achieve it. As the same MP put it more bluntly in 2015:

---

[7]   Note that this is a larger sample than the one covered in Chapter 6, spanning a longer time frame.

Could the Home Secretary bring herself to say the words, 'Net migration is 54,000 higher than when Labour left office'? Could she stand at the Dispatch Box and say that today – not tens of thousands, as she promised – and could she say to the House with no ifs and no buts that she has broken her promise made at the election? (Home Office Questions, 23 March 2015)

Another technique was to question how robust the target was. In various speeches and interviews, members of the government had implied that the target might be more aspirational than previously stated. Such statements provided opportunities for opposition politicians to express doubt about the government's commitment to this goal.

STEVE MCCABE (BIRMINGHAM, SELLY OAK) (LABOUR): I know that some members of the coalition have trouble understanding what a pledge means, but after a bit of probing, the Home Secretary gave the House a commitment the other week to reduce immigration to tens of thousands by the end of this Parliament. Does that commitment still hold this week? (Home Office Questions, 6 December 2010)

SHABANA MAHMOOD (BIRMINGHAM, LADYWOOD) (LABOUR): What is the exact reduction that the Secretary of State will achieve in the net migration figures this year and in each year up to 2015 to fulfil the firm pledge, which she appears to have again relegated to the status of an aim, to cut net migration to the tens of thousands by 2015? (Home Office Questions, 24 January 2011)

In these examples, we see how Labour Party politicians who were otherwise opposed to the target nonetheless used it against the government, to expose its supposed lack of consistency or resolve. The target is depicted as vague or weak, and the government as prevaricating on its commitment.

Yet questions interrogating the feasibility of the target, or querying the government's failure to achieve it, imply some acceptance of this way of framing the policy problem. Lambasting the government for failing to meet its target presupposes that achieving this goal might have been a valid endeavour. It thereby helps to consolidate this way of defining the problem. The following question illustrates this tendency well.

Chris Bryant (Rhondda) (Lab): I understand that the main reason why the Minister has introduced these recent changes to the family route provisions on immigration is to cut net migration, as the Prime Minister promised before the general election, to the tens of thousands. Will he confirm, however, that the Office for National Statistics has said that since 2010 there has been no statistically significant difference in the number of migrants to this country? (Home Office Questions, 15 December 2012)

This is an example of a question that implies rejection of the way the target is set (and specifically its inclusion of family migration), while at the same time criticising the government for failing to meet it. The implication is that those opposing the target found it hard to resist using the figures as a means of appraising government success.

We see a similar pattern in media reporting. As we saw, a substantial proportion of newspaper coverage was devoted to questioning the robustness or feasibility of the target, or berating the government for failing to meet it. Thus the *Mirror*, for example, published a succession of articles about how the government's pledge was 'in tatters' (see also Chapter 6). Similarly, the *Telegraph*, which was generally critical of the target, devoted extensive coverage to the government's failure to meet its pledge. Thus, for example:

The target of reducing net migration to below 100,000 a year has been abandoned by the Government after Theresa May admitted that it has been 'blown off course' and was now 'unlikely' ... Mrs May is the first senior minister to admit that the Government is 'unlikely' to hit its net migration target. It will come as a blow to Mr Cameron, who is facing growing pressure to toughen up his rhetoric on immigration and the EU ahead of the general election ... Labour says the net migration target is 'in tatters'.[8]

Newspaper coverage also sought to expose flaws in methods used to measure the target. As the *Daily Mail* reported in July 2013:

Britain is less able to keep track of its visitors than Disney World, it was claimed last night, as a scathing report exposed the failings of official immigration statistics. Crucial estimates of arrivals from overseas rely on random interviews carried out with just 12 people passing through ports and airports each day – and even they may be lying, MPs said. Ministers were warned they should not base their controversial immigration target – to limit population growth to the tens of thousands each year – on such shaky figures. Referring to the International Passenger Survey.[9]

[8] Editorial, 'Coalition abandons target to reduce migration', *Telegraph*, 24 November 2014.
[9] Martin Beckford, 'UK migration figures rely on counting just 12 people a day', *Daily Mail*, 28 July 2013.

Part of the appeal of invoking the target in this way emanated from the rhythm of publication of data on migration. The quarterly publication of net migration statistics by the Office of National Statistics created regular and predictable opportunities for politicians to peg their critique around new information. In this sense, a technical feature of data production created an information environment in which there were regular opportunities for critique (Boswell 2012), with quarterly information releases presenting an ideal cycle of media reporting.

This political and media preoccupation with the target made it highly politically risky for the government to abandon in. In this extract, the *Daily Mail* reports on the Prime Minister's resolve not to abandon the target, even though it may not be met.

David Cameron suggested it would be difficult for the Tories to meet a key immigration target yesterday as he rejected suggestions his Government is losing its grip after a series of U-turns ... 'I'll keep going on this', he said. 'The public want firm action on immigration and that's exactly what they're getting from me'.[10]

The need to persevere with the target comes across clearly in this piece. It may be embarrassing for the government not to meet the target, but now that it has been set, it would be much more politically damaging to appear to be backing down. Again, as the *Daily Mail* reports in March 2015, 'Mrs May is understood to believe that giving up on the target would be a huge error, not least because immigration still ranks in the top two concerns of voters.'[11]

This political risk of abandoning the target is reflected in a more general expectation that government should be held to account through setting a quantitative pledge. Indeed, the government deployed this notion to bait its Labour opponents, as in this response by the immigration minister to a question by Labour MP Chris Bryant:

Mr Harper: I have seen that comment, but with a fall in net migration from 252,000 to 216,000 – a fall of 15% – I will leave it to other Members and the public to judge whether they view that as significant. I know that the hon. Gentleman either tweeted or said at the Labour conference that he

---

[10] James Chapman, 'PM admits migration target may not be met', *Daily Mail*, 3 December 2013.
[11] James Slack, 'Tories split over Cameron's vow to cut net migration', *Daily Mail*, 3 March 2015.

thought having a net migration target was 'ludicrous', but was then forced to unsay it when he was told to do so by his boss. (Home Office Questions, 15 October 2012)

The media, meanwhile, was continually criticising Labour for its failure to adopt a clear position. For example, as this *Daily Mail* article reports:

Mr. Miliband refused to endorse that approach [setting a target] – despite evidence that the huge influx of immigrants in recent years has left health, education and social services stretched. He said: I am not going to do what the Government does. I am not going to make a blanket promise about numbers ... Immigration Minister Damian Green said: Until Ed Miliband supports the Government's measures to cut and control immigration, Labour will have no credibility at all.[12]

Similarly, the *Times* suggested that Miliband's position on addressing the negative impacts of immigration was 'either vague or unconvincing'.

All these possibly laudable objectives will hardly make a dent in immigration. Labour will soon find itself, we predict, playing the numbers game again.[13]

So while the centre-right media was critical of the government's failure to meet the target, it was even more scathing about Labour's reluctance to set a clear target at all.

In sum, once the net migration target had been set, it created incentives for (critical) politicians and media to deploy it as a means of exposing government failings. The appeal of the target partly related to its technical and administrative features. Government transgressions could be exposed by clear and authoritative statistical data. And, moreover, such data were produced on a quarterly basis, allowing regular opportunities to lambast the government. This created strong incentives to hold the government to account. However, in so doing, the media and political opposition contributed to a shift in expectations about how to measure and evaluate performance. Even where actors were opposed to the target, by invoking it they helped normalise the notion that this was an appropriate mechanism of accountability. And once it had been normalised in this way, it became difficult for critics to continue to embrace more nuanced qualitative goals. Compared to the

---

[12] Tim Shipman, 'Miliband: I won't back migration cap', *Daily Mail*, 23 June 2012.
[13] Editorial, *Times*, 23 June 2012.

precise statistical framing ushered in by the net migration target, non-quantitative goals appeared loose and vague. Thus the measurement effect shifted expectations about the way in which governments were to be held to account in the area of immigration policy.

The Paradoxical Appeal of Targets

Political science contributions have suggested that issue redefinition can have important effects on political debate. The redefinition of issues can alter the focus of political attention, who participates in debate and how different issues are linked. However, this body of literature has tended to neglect the particular effects of *quantitative* descriptions on political debate. This chapter drew on sociological literature to develop some expectations about the distinct effects of statistical descriptions on political debate. Such descriptions carry particular authority because of their association with precision, objectivity and neutrality. Moreover, their ability to standardise entities and compress and communicate information in a parsimonious way makes these descriptions especially appealing as a mode of communicating objectives and outcomes, and for holding politicians to account.

Drawing on these two sets of literature, this chapter developed a number of claims about how such quantitative descriptions might affect political debate. It identified two distinct effects of quantification. The first of these was the classification effect. Quantification requires categorising often complex entities as equivalent units, thereby abstracting from difference and creating new binary distinctions between those entities included and those excluded. Such classifications can be especially rigid and constraining where they employ (existing or methodologically viable) statistical definitions or methods, thereby locking their authors in to rigid and simplifying classificatory schema. This chapter suggested that these effects can be gauged by examining how classification generates shifts in which entities or groups receive political attention, as well as the nature of that attention.

The second type of influence is captured in the idea of a measurement effect. The use of quantitative descriptions can create incentives for political and media actors to invoke targets as a mechanism for holding governments to account. The increased political attention to such mechanisms can in turn normalise the use of such statistics as a legitimate means of measuring and assessing performance. These shifts can be identified through examining the level and nature of political attention devoted to quantitative descriptions in political debate.

This chapter examined these claims through analysing the UK government's 2010 net migration target, drawing on House of Commons Home Office questions and newspaper coverage between 2009 and early 2015. This chapter identified three types of classification effect: the target prompted (critical) attention to the statistical category adopted, it led to a rise of negative attention towards previously neglected and unproblematic categories of immigrants and it contributed to issue linkage with EU membership. In terms of the measurement effect, technical and administrative features of target created incentives for both the media and political opponents to use statistics to criticise and hold the government to account, even in cases where protagonists were sceptical about the target. This in turn normalised the use of the target as a tool of accountability, making it difficult for its detractors to justify the retention of less precise and more nuanced qualitative goals.

These points echo observations Nehal Bhuta made in his study of USAID state fragility index. Bhuta shows how there was much disagreement about the index – its theoretical basis and the methods used to measure it. However, as he writes:

Once the concept is pragmatically and provisionally in use – and used in a variety of diagnostic, prescriptive and evaluative ways – its consistency with any 'outer reality' is less significant for its users than its correspondence with a (porous) set of acceptable uses and deployments. (2012)

We could identify a similar dynamic in the case of the net migration target. The use of net migration statistics as a means of measuring, evaluating and setting goals was adopted in a similarly pragmatic and ill-thought-through way. But whatever its haphazard origins, it went on to perform important functions for a variety of political and media actors. For the government, the target signalled its commitment to the goal of reducing migration, in the hopes of eliciting public confidence in its performance. For opposition politicians, the target became a way of holding the government to account, through highlighting its failure to meet the target. And for the media, it became a quarterly ritual for generating news stories based on authoritative statistics that exposed government transgressions. Thus whether or not they accepted the premises or methods through which the target had been constructed, these actors all appropriated this statistical description for different ends. The result was that despite widespread scepticism, the net migration target became the dominant mode of framing and assessing immigration policy.

This points to a striking feature of performance measurement. Once such quantitative descriptions are articulated, it becomes very difficult for participants in political debate to resist being drawn in to this way of framing policy issues. The tenacity of such descriptions partly relates to technical features of statistical definitions and methods of calculation, which, as we saw, limit the scope for flexibility in redefining issues. But the potency of quantification is also derived from its precision and technical authority. Statistics promise to provide a particularly robust mode of holding governments to account. Paradoxically, this authority appears to be at least partially independent of whether participants accept the premises and methods behind the calculation of the relevant statistic. For this reason, even the critics of targets get drawn into this way of framing problems, and find it difficult to resist setting similarly precise and robust pledges.

8 | *After Performance Measurement?*

I have argued in this book that performance measurement emerged as an attempt to reground political trust. The deployment of targets, indicators and rankings can be read as an effort to reconstitute relations of trust through stabilising expectations about behaviour and through establishing authoritative claims about performance. But the attempt to restore trust has created a series of further problems. Targets have undermined relations between politics and public administration, leading to intrusive intervention in government departments, damaging civil service morale and engendering gaming and decoupling. And targets have adversely affected relations between politicians and voters: they have been treated with scepticism in the mass media, while at the same time encouraging the reframing of complex problems in terms of simple and distorting quantitative goals.

In this last chapter, I return to the question of why such tools appear to retain their appeal, despite these acknowledged adverse effects. What features of targets and performance measurement render them so alluring to politicians and public servants? Understanding the appeal of these techniques offers a basis for prognosticating about possible future trends in performance measurement. In particular, I will examine how these techniques are likely to fare given the rise of populist, anti-expert political movements. Does the spectre of populist politics imply that these pre-eminently technocratic tools of governance are becoming less compelling, or even irrelevant?

I begin this chapter by revisiting the conditions that have produced a breakdown of political trust. I suggest that the contemporary crisis of political trust can be usefully conceptualised as a failure of *inference*: a breakdown in the propensity of voters to infer favourable outcomes based on previous experience or reliable motivational structures. I go on to explore the appeal of performance measurement as a mode of underpinning such inference. I explore some of the political risks in deploying such techniques, and ask whether they are likely to retain their appeal when confronted with populist forms of political mobilisation. The third part of this chapter explores how these political dynamics might affect the use of performance measurement in public administration. What conditions have facilitated the appropriation of these techniques in government departments, and how tenacious are they likely to be in the face of populist claims-making?

The chapter argues that scepticism about performance measurement is likely to generate a growing divide between popular political narratives and more technocratic bureaucratic accounts. I consider how politics and public administration may handle this tension, exploring three possible scenarios. The first is a radical decoupling of political rhetoric and organisational practice, characterised by an uneasy tension between populist and technocratic styles. The second is the discrediting of populist incumbents, as unfeasible claims are exposed through botched delivery. The third scenario is a form of crony government, in which a growing drift between political leadership and public administration sees incumbents relying on informal, ad hoc and disjointed arrangements for delivery. I explore what these scenarios imply about the future of performance measurement in public policy.

Political Trust, Inference and Complexity

Our first task is to reconsider the nature of the contemporary crisis in political trust. This crisis appears to be particularly acute at the time of writing: much of this book was written in 2016, the year in which the UK voted to leave the EU and Donald Trump was elected to the White House. But I want to avoid restricting my observations to current political developments. Instead, I will take a step back and start by considering the more general question of how trust in politics is produced. As we saw in Chapter 2, trust involves a form of inference or 'weak induction' from what we know or have experienced. We infer future behaviour or future states based on our experience of relevantly similar entities or episodes. This notion of inference is useful in helping us to understand the nature of the current crisis of trust in politics. In what sense can we say that voters no longer have grounds for inferring trustworthiness based on previous experiences? And what implications does this have for political trust?

Here it is useful to distinguish between two senses in which favourable expectations may be inferred from our experience. The first is the notion that such inference is based on outcomes or states. If we have experience of certain inputs or processes (for example, Labour governments, or citizens' juries) yielding certain outcomes (such as investment in health or political consensus), then trust may be grounded in our confidence that such effects will recur. Where those inputs or processes are in place, we may trust that they will yield the desired outcomes. The second type of inference is based on familiarity with the conduct or behaviour of others. Here, trust is grounded in favourable expectations about the motives and incentive structures of those on whom we bestow trust. We trust them to do the right thing because of their integrity or skills or social background. Of course, these two forms of inference are related in practice. For example, we may lose trust in the conduct of someone who has not been able to produce certain outcomes. But they represent two analytically distinct ways of grounding trust, and it is worth considering how each operates in the sphere of politics.[1]

Much of the literature on political trust has focused on the first type of inference: induction based on observation of chains of causality. On this account, declining political trust is related to disappointment in the *outcomes* of politics. Such accounts have dominated recent analyses of political trust. Thus political commentators have been quick to diagnose the recent backlash against mainstream politics and political elites in the UK, the United States and many European countries as a rejection of the consequences of a set of social and economic practices associated with neoliberalism (Elliott 2017). The ascendance of right-wing anti-establishment populist movements results from the failure of successive governments to protect lower-income groups from the effects of globalisation: deindustrialisation, economic precariousness, uneven development and growing inequality, and the declining capacity of the state in the face of large corporations, international finance and the flow of capital (see for examples Jessop 2017 and Streeck 2016). This failure has been materially manifested in the stagnating incomes of large parts of

---

[1] Note that these two forms of inference should be distinguished from different *objects* of trust (such as procedures or institutions or individuals). What is at stake here is the mechanisms through which people predict future states based on past experience.

the population, especially those in the regional 'backwaters' that have not benefited from economic growth (Jennings and Stoker 2016). Inequality and economic vulnerability are considered conducive to forms of mobilisation that offer in-group solidarity and reject outsiders (Inglehart and Norris 2016: 11). Populist politics represents an attempt to articulate and channel this malaise, promising to reassert various forms of protection from international trade and finance, cultural diversity or security threats.

On this account, the breakdown in trust thus derives from disillusionment at the poor performance of mainstream political parties and governments. Large sections of the public have lost confidence that established political parties and elites are able or willing to achieve the outcomes they promised. This disillusionment with outcomes serves to contaminate attitudes towards politicians themselves: mainstream parties and political leaders have forfeited their trustworthiness. Sections of the public can no longer ground trust in politics and politicians by drawing on favourable experiences of their previous conduct. In this sense, the sources of the current crisis in political trust derive from an inability to infer favourable expectations from past experiences, and this in turn reflects disappointment in the socio-economic outcomes affected by mainstream political institutions.

Yet socio-economic accounts do not capture the full story. Disillusionment with politics and politicians is not solely derived from disappointment at the material outcomes of politics. I would like to suggest that it also has to do with the increasingly complex and opaque relationship between 'inputs' and 'outputs'. In other words, part of the problem is that we simply cannot assess how particular interventions – new governments or policy programmes – lead to particular outcomes. So this first mode of grounding trust, through inferring future states from our experience of past ones, has become problematic. This is not just because the outcomes of politics are disappointing. It is also because the link between the aspirations of voters and the outcomes produced by politics has been rendered opaque.

We can trace this problem in part to a shift in the basis of political contestation from the 1960s onwards. As Giddens observes, the project of rolling out rights and welfare, ongoing in many advanced liberal democracies since the late nineteenth century, had been dominated by a contestation between conservative and labour movements (Giddens

1994). But from the 1970s, two new tendencies emerged. The first was a reconfiguration of ideological cleavages. New social movements and political parties emerged, mobilising around environmental protection, multiculturalism and ethnic minority rights, lesbian and gay rights, human rights and international cooperation (Hooghe, Marks and Wilson 2002). These new values were pitted against conservative, nationalist and protectionist approaches, creating new cleavages that drew attention away from classic issues of economic redistribution (Inglehart and Norris 2016: 29). The new cleavages did not sit easily with established party configurations: the left in particular has struggled to cater for both its green, libertarian, pro-rights constituents and its more traditional, protectionist ones.

The second, related tendency has been the technocratisation of traditionally salient areas of policy: political mobilisation on issues of economy, welfare or social services became increasingly apolitical, revolving around the appropriate means of *steering* society and the economy, rather than rival patterns of socio-economic distribution. Substantial areas of policy debate have become concerned with how best to achieve certain agreed outcomes, rather than the criteria for resource allocation (Fischer 1990). Expertise and evidence have taken on an elevated status in policy-making in these areas, in many instances suturing more ideological debates because of the technical complexity of the issues or the primacy of economic steering (Clarke and Newman 2017: 10).

And yet the shift in the basis of political contestation created a new problem of how to appraise rival political claims. On the traditional view of politics, politicians derive their authority and support from their claims to represent collective interests, values or goals. Their trustworthiness could be inferred from their adherence to a set of coherent and readily identifiable ideological goals. But in new or post-ideological debates, how are voters to evaluate rival claims about performance? Given the complexity of policy-making, publics cannot scrutinise in a straightforward way whether political claims are redeemed in decision-making. Growing specialisation, complexity and functional differentiation confound attempts to observe the effects of policies, and to attribute them to particular interventions. How can voters judge if a government's fiscal austerity policies have been effective? Or if its welfare activation policies have provided the right mix of pressure and support? Or if European countries benefit from participation in the euro or the Single Market? And the messiness of political processes obscures how political claims of representation are translated into actions. A political claim has to pass through innumerable phases of deliberation and scrutiny and is shaped and constrained at many levels – EU law, Whitehall deliberation and local government implementation. Under these conditions, the need for trust becomes greater than ever. Trust becomes increasingly necessary as a way of 'enduring' complexity (Luhmann 1979: 14). But it is precisely this complexity that undermines the possibility of grounding trust in the observation of political outcomes. Chains of causality in politics have become too opaque, with the result that politics continually frustrates and disappoints (Stoker 2006: 10). The path from political pledge to social or economic outcome has never been so convoluted.

One response to the demise of traditional modes of grounding trust is to focus on the motivational structures of politicians. This implies a shift to the second mode of inference, based on the anticipated conduct of others. By understanding the factors motivating behaviour, we can determine when to bestow and withdraw trust. And yet the motives and conduct of politicians have been increasingly cast in doubt over the past four decades or so.

Part of this can be traced to certain structural features of the profession of politics. In other specialised professions – medicine, science, law, education – trust is typically grounded in two features: the certified expertise or qualifications of the practitioner, and expectations that the practitioner will abide by a certain ethos or set of professional codes. Yet professional politicians cannot rely on this form of certified expertise. There is no formal, codified form of expertise required of politicians, just a set of 'soft' skills of communication and leadership. Nor can their behaviour be inferred from clearly recognised professional codes. Indeed, the profession of politics is characterised by a tension between the criteria for advancement (attaining power) and the values and goals of the system (representing and advancing the common good). Politicians and political parties continually struggle to find an appropriate balance between the two. It is hardly surprising that their publics deal with this ambiguity by taking the more cynical view. If someone's motivation remains ambiguous, how can we decide whether to trust them? Such uncertainty exerts a paralysing effect on action. It is more reassuring to ascribe a clear set of motivations and to base decisions on those suppositions, than to deal with ambiguity.

Ascribing self-interested, power-maximising motivations to politicians can help assuage doubt and offset risk.

These more cynical interpretations of the motivations of politicians have been influenced by a second development: the increasing traction of public choice theories. The ascendance of 'new liberal' ideologies in the UK and the United States in the 1980s implied a new understanding of society and the public sphere. Citizens were to be viewed as individual consumers, pursuing their self-interest and seeking competitive advantage. The state and public sector were contracted to maximise their interests through a series of mechanised transactions, informed by consumer research and controlled through monitoring and audit (Clarke and Newman 1997: 123–4). These public choice theories depicted politicians and public servants as self-interested, power-maximising individuals who were not to be trusted. Voters needed to constrain the transgressions of their political leaders through monitoring and scrutiny, including establishing clearer chains of representation and accountability. This in turn encouraged a shift in modes of political mobilisation. Electoral competition was reimagined as a quest to appeal to the individual interests of 'consumer' voters. And the techniques of mobilisation were increasingly characterised by professionalised market research, branding and product placement (Hay 2007: 57; Stoker 2006: 10). In this sense, theories of public choice have been performative, engendering the types of behaviour they sought to describe (Law and Urry 2004). Politics appears to lack the equipment to narrate its own interventions: to make sense of the complexity, compromise and deliberation involved in translating broad preferences into specific policies and outcomes. This has left the door open to simplistic and distorting accounts, which have further contributed to the decline of trust in politicians.

In short, the lack of trust in politics cannot be solely attributed to the problem of disappointed outcomes. This is not to say that outcome-based accounts of political disenchantment do not play their part. But the crisis of political trust can also be traced to a distinct set of developments: the increasing complexity of policy, the shift from ideological to technocratic modes of contestation and the opacity of political processes – all of which have made it hugely challenging to infer political outcomes from particular inputs or processes. It has become almost impossible for voters to make inferences about trust, because the political processes that convert inputs into outputs are so opaque.

At the same time, the ascendance of simplistic and self-interested theories of political agency engender cynicism and a reluctance to ground trust in favourable expectations about the conduct of politicians. Voters are thus unable to find compelling grounds for bestowing their trust in politics and politicians.

Attempts to Reground Political Trust

Disillusionment with politics generates a range of attempts to modify or supplement existing processes for grounding trust. As I have argued in this book, one favoured strategy is to establish ever more robust mechanisms to hold decision-makers to account. There is an understandable impulse to reduce uncertainty about the conduct of politicians through closer monitoring. This has spawned a huge number of bodies and procedures dedicated to scrutinising the conduct of politicians and public agencies – ushering in an era of 'monitory democracy' (Keane 2009). Monitoring promises to enable voters to keep tabs on their political leaders and public servants through obtaining regular information about their conduct. In this way, it is designed to address the problem of the opacity of political processes and conduct. It aspires to make politics transparent, observable and – of course – accountable.

Yet as I argued in Chapter 2, the raison d'être of these bodies is to expose such transgressions. Their survival and legitimacy is contingent on reinforcing the very anxieties that led to their creation. So while they are designed to obviate the need for trust through constant observation of trustees, in actual fact they serve to further erode the bases of trust. They question outcomes and augment doubts about the motivation and conduct of politicians, thus contributing to voters' reluctance to develop favourable expectations based on past observations and narratives. And they perpetuate narratives about individual transgressions and oversights, insisting that some person or group of persons must be held to account for their personal failings. It is rarely 'the system' – the set of interactions or structural conditions shaping behaviour – that is to blame. At the same time, trust is a very precarious state. Individual transgressions tend to take on inordinate significance for the whole: 'one falsehood and misrepresentation can unmask the "true character" of somebody or something, often with unrelenting rigour' (Luhmann 1979: 28). The compulsion to generalise from individual and unusual cases to produce sweeping pronouncements means that exposure through scrutiny can have a disproportionate effect on relations of trust. These types of monitoring again reinforce assumptions about self-interested behaviour: their activities yield evidence that vindicates the sceptical premises that brought them into being.

Given the patent problems with traditional modes of grounding political trust, it is little wonder that politics looks to other templates for justifying its decisions. With the discrediting or perceived irrelevance of traditional tools of political accountability, politics has sought to import other models from science, business and law. One favoured strategy has been to introduce performance measurement as a mode of establishing trust. As I have argued in this book, performance measurement, and especially targets, offer the prospect of stabilising expectations about behaviour, through locking politicians into particular courses of action and creating incentives for them to adhere to their pledges. Such techniques are also intended to create reliable modes of establishing valid claims about political interventions. In doing so, performance measurement borrows authority from two domains. It draws on business narratives about performance: the promise of importing techniques that guarantee efficiency, effectiveness, value for money and customer satisfaction. And it draws on scientific notions of validity: the rigour, objectivity and precision of statistical methods.

How do these narratives or models come to be appropriated by politics? Much of the literature on the spread of performance measurement assumes a seamless translation of techniques and practices from science to politics (Davis, Kingsbury and Merry 2011; Hansen and Porter 2012; Merry 2011). I have suggested that take-up of such ideas in politics is in fact highly selective. Moreover, such techniques or models are given meaning according to the particular logic and concerns of the political system. Politics will appropriate such ideas only where they promise to solve political problems. Thus many instances of the take-up of ideas from business or science are likely to be tactical. Politics may adopt the trappings of successful organisational models from business, or rigorous auditing methodologies from economics, in the belief these are relevant to advocating political goals (DiMaggio and Powell 1983). For example, civil servants deploy management tools and rhetoric to establish their credibility vis-à-vis the core executive or select committees; governments reel off statistics in response to parliamentary scrutiny; politicians capitalise on former roles in business to enhance voter confidence; and politicians use business practices as a benchmark for assessing performance of public services.

Over time, such ideas may become normalised, taken for granted as credible and appropriate techniques or models for doing politics. In this sense, they become absorbed as part of the background ideas (Schmidt 2008) shaping communication in the political system. It has become expected, even required, that a minister explain her department's performance through invoking business concepts and models, or that a civil servant chart his division's performance through elaborate statistics.

Yet the tactical use of performance measurement to shore up credibility runs the risk of being viewed with cynicism. Political communication in democratic systems (and others to some extent) is geared towards the mobilisation of an audience: the political system needs to continually generate justifications for its collectively binding decisions (Luhmann 1981). Party political contestation is a ritual in which participants need to be seen to be marshalling arguments based on their factual validity, practical viability or ethical soundness (Edelman 1977; Gusfield 1981), but the criteria for selection are based on what promises to resonate with the 'public' via mass media reporting. This implies that the mobilisation of authority from business or science may be largely disingenuous. Such resources are deployed with a view to signalling the competence or integrity of politicians. Sophisticated statistical techniques are marshalled to signal improved performance, but in reality, those who deploy them may not themselves feel convinced of their validity. Parliamentary scrutiny or audits of such statistics can become largely ritualistic. Similarly, politicians may follow the latest management fad to demonstrate the rationality and progressiveness of their administration, but the reforms involved are largely cosmetic. In this sense, politics marshals these authority resources from other systems in an ironic way: not itself committed to the validity of such claims or techniques, but hoping to transmit such validity to its audience.

The risk of such tactical deployment is that politics is exposed as deploying such resources cynically, to bolster support. Insofar as politics borrows scientific or business techniques to seek authority, such moves can easily be exposed as lacking authenticity. Politics is not inherently interested in scientific truth, or in maximising organisational productivity – and why should we expect it to be? These goals are instrumental to the more fundamental preoccupation with politics, i.e. contestation over the shaping and implementation of collectively binding decisions. So the rhetorical commitment to such tools can appear hollow to their audience. This realisation may have the effect of contaminating the tools themselves. Performance measurement becomes discredited. Such cynicism may be reinforced by theories of politics absorbed from social science or business, which further pare down such a model to one of self-interested actors seeking to maximise egoistic interests.

Disillusionment may be especially strong where performance measurement jars with people's day-to-day experience. People may be sceptical about performance data because they do not feel that they are better off or that public services have been improved. This may in some cases reflect the inadequacy of the measurements put in place – they do not capture those elements that matter most to people (Stiglitz 2009), or they have been achieved through forms of decoupling or gaming that undermine their original rationale (see Chapter 4 for examples of such decoupling). So indicators end up measuring the wrong things, or doing so in the wrong ways. However, public cynicism may also derive from the authorship of such measurements: the fact that they were generated by a discredited political elite, whom the public do not trust. Indeed, Chapter 7 showed how instead of relying on abstract statistics, in practice more symbolic cues about authenticity based on personal characteristics appear to exert a huge influence over media and public perceptions of trustworthiness in politics. This is more than just a trend towards the personalisation of politics. It seems to reflect the unsuitability of scientific or business modes of shoring up relations of trust to the sphere of politics.

The implication is a gap between the types of assurance or certainty created by these modes of accountability and validation, which derive their appeal from deeply engrained beliefs about accountability and validity, and the informal modes of grounding trust that still prevail in politics. Rhetorically, politics may set store by rigorous statistical techniques for measuring performance, and the various bodies monitoring political conduct – including the mass media – typically buy into the ritual of techno-scientific techniques of appraising performance. But when it comes to bestowing trust on politicians, parties or governments, the media still tend to rely inordinately on more symbolic cues: authenticity, integrity, ability to 'connect' and, increasingly, positioning oneself as outside of a political elite, so paradoxically rejecting these markers of rationality or technocracy. At one level, or in certain fora, we expect our politics to conform to scientific or business standards, but in practice, such criteria are often treated with scepticism or disdain. We have a deep-seated attachment to more impressionistic modes of grounding trust in politics.

Nonetheless, through constantly deploying these techniques, politics gradually normalises them as modes for framing and assessing politics. This has the result of reinforcing simplistic theories of politics and unrealistic expectations about political performance and delivery. We still cling to the idea that our decisions are more rationally grounded – and this notion of rationalistic grounds for political support continues to guide (at least mainstream) politics in its quest for trust. This implies a basic confusion about how we are grounding trust in politics. We do not have just one scale for evaluating politics. We operate with multiple, and often incompatible beliefs about accountability and trust in politics. And we appear to be capable of a form of ironic detachment: formally adhering to rationalist, information-based modes of vouchsafing conduct and outcomes, whilst informally relying on more impressionistic cues about the character and values of political leaders.

Organisations, Trust and Accountability

I turn my attention now to the second set of trust relations dealt with in this book: those between politicians and public administration. Here, it would be misplaced to talk about the same type of crisis or breakdown in trust. There is a long and well-documented history of scepticism and mistrust between politicians and civil servants; indeed, the problem has spawned extensive theorising of principal–agent relations over the past few decades. But we cannot chart any major deterioration in these relations, at least not on the scale of the crisis of public trust in politics. To be sure, the decentralising or 'hollowing out' of government has in some ways exacerbated problems of trust, creating new challenges for politicians in monitoring and controlling the wide range of actors involved in policy-making and implementation. And indeed, I have argued that performance measurement becomes an important mode of assuaging anxiety and signalling credibility in this context of outsourcing and decentralisation. But this problem of trust does not approximate to the level of disillusionment characterising perceptions of politics.

Instead, the more pressing problem of trust between politicians and civil servants arises as a repercussion of the crisis of public trust. Indeed, one of the main focuses of this book has been the effects of this broader crisis in political trust on public administration. I have argued that one response to the problem of political trust is to set precise outcome-oriented targets as a mode of generating political support, and that in doing so, government becomes more reliant on its civil servants to deliver on its pledges. This dynamic – which I have termed the chain of dependency – places particular strain on trust relations between politics and the administration. It engenders forms of intrusive intervention in organisational practice, and encourages the decoupling of formal compliance and informal deviation in organisations. I have explored these dynamics in some detail in this book (Chapters 3–5).

But we also saw how performance measurement was taken up by organisations to solve their own internal problems. It is this dynamic that I want to probe in this section. What is the utility or appeal of performance measurement from the perspective of organisations in the public administration? How and why do organisations become attached to such techniques? This will help us to explain the persistence of performance measurement not just as a tool of politics imposed on organisations, but as a set of techniques and practices that appear to have become indispensable to public sector organisations.

One of the claims I have developed in this book is that the political environment of organisations profoundly affects their behaviour. Organisations in the public administration embrace performance measurement not merely because it is more efficient or improves performance, nor simply because it is imposed on them by their political leaders. Just as important is the organisation's need to meet environmental expectations about appropriate governance arrangements. Performance measurement has become standardised as part of the expected management repertoire of large, modern organisations. And this in turn shapes organisations' perceptions about how they can elicit support from key actors in their environments – from their political leaders and the various bodies involved in scrutinising and appraising their performance.

We saw an example of this in Chapter 5, in the analysis of select committee scrutiny of the Home Office. Parliamentary select committees were keen to hold public servants to account through requesting performance data. To be sure, they were not always confident about the performance measures proffered by the Home Office. This supports research findings that identify a reluctance of parliamentary committees to accept government targets and indicators as a reliable gauge of performance (Johnson and Talbot 2007). Quite apart from the issue of their credibility, they may not find such data particularly relevant to their line of enquiry. After all, as we saw in Chapter 5, political constructions of policy problems are likely to differ from those produced by operational organisations. But we should not be too hasty in dismissing the relevance of performance measurement to parliamentary scrutiny. Indeed, we saw that select committees are only too keen to request performance data and to use it to scrutinise government action. Select committees are likely to look askance at an organisation that is unable to supply such information or that does not use tools of performance measurement. Statistical data are one of the few tools for monitoring government performance – and one that conforms to engrained expectations about rigour and objectivity.

As with public trust in politics, the deployment of such tools may be largely ritualistic. Politicians may infer the trustworthiness of public servants through other means – and indeed, we saw in Chapter 5 how one committee sought reassurance in the familiar biography of a senior civil servant. The very practice of inviting public servants to attend in person and to give an oral account of themselves and their department also shows how inadequate performance data alone are for the job of holding government to account. But this in no way lessens the expectation that senior mandarins and their organisations should be able to produce extensive performance data, to enable effective scrutiny. It is part of the reassuring ritual of select committee scrutiny. Select committee oversight is just one example of external pressure to produce performance data. Other bodies may exact similar data – audit commissions, the core executive, independent inspectorates or international organisations.

The pressure to deploy tools of performance measurement does not emanate solely from those bodies holding the executive to account. Such pressures can also derive from more general processes of standardisation across organisations (Brunsson and Jacobsson 2000). John Meyer and his colleagues have shown how such governance practices can become standardised as part of the expected repertoire of modern, progressive or rational organisations. Certain models of governance become constructed as rational and modern, influencing how national authorities seek to build credibility (Meyer et al. 1997; Strang and Meyer 1993). Claims about standardisation build on the notion of isomorphism: the idea that organisations and other actors approximate their behaviour and structures to relevantly similar organisations in their environment (Scott and Meyer 1991). Mimetic isomorphism is particularly relevant here: the tendency to imitate the structures and rhetoric of relevantly similar units (DiMaggio and Powell 1983). Organisations adopt the trappings of rationalistic and accountable decision-making styles in order to enhance their credibility and status. They conform to models of good practice that are associated with appropriate management, with a view to garnering support from key actors in their environment. Such forms of diffusion and standardisation can be especially strong amongst countries participating in regional groupings, such as the EU or the OECD (Radaelli 2000). Here, strong expectations about 'good governance' or 'smart regulation' may emerge, and government departments will be under considerable pressure to adopt the requisite management philosophies and governance techniques.

Yet organisations are not just concerned about meeting external expectations; they are also preoccupied with sustaining internal legitimacy. In order to sustain loyalty and motivation, members of the organisation need to feel their organisation and its leaders are managing tasks in a credible way, one that gains recognition from its environment. This will typically imply embracing techniques and practices that correspond to sector-wide norms.

Here it is useful to bring in the views of some of the senior managers I interviewed for this project. My respondents generally shared the view that good management required some sort of performance goals and indicators. As a Home Office official commented:

Obviously it's such a huge organisation. You've got to have some kind of control. You can't just say, 'go and reduce immigration' and be told week upon week upon week, 'yeah, it's, it's reducing, it's reducing'. You need to understand why it's reducing. Is it sustainable and is it a blip and all that kind of stuff. (Interview, February 2014)

Here, we see how targets are seen as a way of underpinning a compelling narrative about organisational performance. A former Home Office official made a similar observation:

I think at some level, a demonstrable commitment to making progress was, is always very important for whatever you're doing. And for us, targets became a way of doing that and filling that gap. (Interview, February 2014)

The need to draw on performance measurement tools is unlikely to decline, even if such techniques fall out of favour in political discourse. As an official in the Department of Work and Pensions put it:

Big public sector, customer-facing operational businesses still need, for internal purposes, to know how they are performing. And to monitor how they are doing to some of those things. (Interview, February 2014)

But we also saw in Chapter 4 how targets became embraced as a means for individuals and teams to set goals and assess how they were doing. Performance targets gave officials a sense of purpose. As a former special advisor observed:

They needed a sense that, that there was a sort of purpose and there was, they were moving towards some goals and when they'd achieved those goals something decent would have happened that they had improved. Because there is this, it is a very demoralising thing to work in an immigration asylum ... organisations need to know what their basic purposes are. They need to have kind of goals that they're all working to. (Interview, February 2014)

Or in the words of the official cited in Chapter 2, who was describing life without targets:

It was completely disorienting for everyone, they just didn't know what good looked like. What their rate of productivity should be. And they felt that lots of people were getting away with it and they didn't know how to manage each other without that kind of benchmark. (Interview, August 2014)

Organisations have multiple ways of avoiding the crude imposition of simplistic targets from politics. But they will still be called upon to account for their actions to various audiences. Many of the bodies scrutinising government performance have come to rely on performance measurement as a particularly adept tool for holding government agencies and departments to account. International and cross-sectoral processes of isomorphism produce strong pressures of standardisation, again leading organisations to appropriate similar management tools. And these techniques have proved useful to organisations in clarifying goals and tasks, and giving members a sense of purpose. Thus we are far from seeing the demise of performance measurement in public administration. A range of organisational pressures and interests would imply the continued use, even necessity, of such techniques to sustain internal and external legitimacy.

Complexity and Populism

It is difficult to end this book without considering the future of performance measurement in an age of populist politics. At the time of writing, the growth of populist political movements appears to be challenging the authority of expertise and evidence in underpinning political claims. This raises the question of whether the rise of populist political claims-making will prompt a rejection of targets and performance measurement as a mode of producing political trust.

Populist movements may be understood as those that mobilise support through claiming to articulate the interests of 'the people' as against established institutions and elites (Canovan 1999; Mudde 2004; Taggart 1996). Frequently, their claims are targeted at a discredited ruling elite and their values: not just those seen as part of the political and economic establishment but also the media, academics and other experts (Canovan 1999). While populism does not necessarily imply the rejection of technocratic measures (Mudde 2004: 547), populist styles of mobilisation tend to reject complex, technical arguments in favour of simple claims and spontaneous action. Where this style of political claims-making gains influence, it is reasonable to suppose that targets and performance measurement may lose their traction. Such techniques may be seen as overly technocratic and suffer from their association with a discredited elite and their failed pledges. Thus targets may become a casualty of the disappointment in political outcomes referred to earlier in this chapter, or of scepticism about political motivation.

Yet in many ways, the use of targets is eminently suited to populist styles of claims-making. Populist movements tend to be keen to articulate in clear and simple terms what sorts of changes they want to bring about, and to offer various promises and pledges that these will be achieved. Indeed, populist movements may be especially susceptible to committing themselves to ambitious, outcome-oriented targets, and indeed to framing these in simple numerical terms. As a former special advisor put it, targets 'gives them [the voters] something to get their teeth into ... You need a set of simple messages which are touch points and you need to repeat them until you're blue in the face' (Interview, February 2014). Recent populist movements in the UK and the United States have also set store by business models of management. Leaders emanating from business are seen as more competent and trustworthy than career politicians, bringing with them a direct, can-do style that cuts through the perceived prevarication and dissembling of elite political discourse. Simple numerical pledges with a corporate flavour may appeal to voters dissatisfied with vaguer or more convoluted formulations. So the rise of populism does not imply that targets will become any less ubiquitous as a form of political communication.

The difference, however, is likely to lie in how far these claims are grounded in technical or scientific knowledge. One reason for this is that populist movements tend to reject established narratives about social problems. Part of their distinctiveness resides in their eschewal of a mainstream, 'elite' consensus, which is bolstered by various forms of discredited expertise: the expertise or specialist knowledge of public officials, economists, journalists, researchers and other professionals who are seen as complicit in perpetuating the status quo. Populist narratives do not derive credibility from being backed up by such experts – indeed, such narratives are often premised on a rejection of their methods and claims. This implies that populist targets may well be set without a solid grounding in 'evidence' or specialised experience. Part of their appeal may derive precisely from their defiance of such expertise. As Michael Freeden puts it, populist claims are characterised by their simplicity and urgency, and should not be 'adulterated by reflection and deliberation' (2017: 6). Moreover, the audience of such targets may not set store by the technocratic trappings of such tools. Claims about the technical precision and mathematical rigour of targets may not instil the same degree of reverence.

This is not to say that supporters of populist movements have no interest in how political claims or promises are grounded. They may reject established elite sources of expertise, but this is not the same as eschewing any type of knowledge base for informing policy. Indeed, part of the appeal of populist leaders is likely to reside in their claim to tap into alternative forms of knowledge or experience: their acumen as business leaders, or their ability to empathise with voters, or their more realistic appraisal of international politics. It is not that they lack knowledge; indeed, they may be seen as having access to superior or more relevant forms of knowledge. It is more that their claims are not derived from the conventional sources of expert knowledge, including from specialists and professionals within the public administration. Part of this is what Clarke and Newman describe as a different 'sense of time', evident in the campaign on the UK's membership in the EU. While the knowledge claims underpinning conventional mainstream politics rely on expert analysis and economic forecasts, acknowledge complexity and some degree of uncertainty about the future and factor in temporal delays to implementation, populist claims effectively efface time. They promise immediate fulfilment – a capacity to dispense with planning and negotiation, to achieve instantaneous results. And the knowledge they appeal to is often experiential, harking back to a 'celebrated and imaginary past' (Clarke and Newman 2017: 12).

The populist rejection of expertise creates an awkward gap between the types of knowledge claims grounding pledges and prevalent modes of knowledge use within the administration. Populist politics invokes different causal stories about policy problems and responses, drawing on quite distinct sources of knowledge. The gap is likely to be especially pronounced where populist movements offer up specific pledges or commit themselves to precise outcomes. Incumbents seeking to mobilise support through signalling commitment to populist targets will face substantial challenges when it comes to implementing them. As we saw in Chapter 3, where such targets commit the government to specific outputs or outcomes, this will create immense strains in relations between politics and public administration. Government bureaucracies cannot be expected to abandon their commitment to rational modes of deliberation and justification. In this respect, we need to acknowledge an importance difference. Political claims-making oriented towards the mobilisation of public support displays great variety and fluidity in the types of narratives that appear viable. Bureaucratic modes of reasoning, by contrast, show no such flexibility. They are firmly grounded in technocratic modes of settlement, which employ well-established repertoires of rationales, method and modes of appraisal. The implication is that their internal modes of constructing and responding to problems will be starkly out of kilter with the narratives emanating from populist politics (Boswell and Rodrigues 2016). Where this happens, the target may simply be ineffective as a mode of disciplining the organisation. The legal or operational assumptions on which it is based may not be translatable into a meaningful course of action for the organisation.

How can the political system handle this tension? One possible scenario is a more radical decoupling of political rhetoric and organisational practice. Organisations in the public administration respond to unfeasible demands through a strategy of separating talk from action: attempting to mollify the political leadership by going through the motions of implementing the policy, whilst simultaneously shielding its operations from what are seen as damaging adjustments. Where faced with intrusive pressures to adjust, there may of course be a full-scale breakdown in relations, with civil servants using the channels available to them to undermine or discredit the political leadership (leaks, resignations or public contradiction of government claims). Another variant of this 'decoupling' scenario is that political leaders themselves shoulder the tension between rhetoric and practice. Rather than foisting unfeasible demands on their civil servants, politicians take on a brokering role between two sets of narratives – outward-facing populist ones, which tap into intuitive narratives of social problems, and more technical ones, which reflect beliefs within specialised executive departments. This implies that rather than obliging the organisation to decouple talk from action, politicians instead decouple their populist rhetoric from their more technically informed communications with experts and officials.

Under the second scenario, a failure to implement promises means that populist incumbents become discredited and lose their popular appeal. As I have shown in this book, mobilising support through popular pledges and targets that are not grounded in specialised appraisals of policy is highly risky as a political strategy. Where such pledges are not redeemed, voters are likely to be more disappointed than ever at the failure of governments to deliver. The problem is especially acute for areas of policy in which the outcomes of interventions are tracked and monitored, as is the case with areas subject to performance measurement. Where this occurs, we may see a rejection of populist styles of politics, insofar as they have been exposed as incapable of redeeming their pledges.

The third scenario involves a growing drift between political leadership and public administration. Political claims remain highly populist, and populist leaders eschew expertise and advice from their civil servants. Pledges and targets are largely symbolic or aspirational, and incumbents avoid putting in place mechanisms to measure performance to targets. On this scenario, we would see a widening gap between popular claims-making, and the types of data and knowledge mobilised in public administration. Politics and the administration would be pulled apart by divergent pressures: politics moving more and more towards popular narratives and symbolic gestures, with public administration remaining guided by more technical rationalities. Trust between politics and public administration would break down, with political leaders instead relying on crony government: politically appointed advisors and informal, ad hoc arrangements for policy formulation and delivery. Again, one wonders how sustainable such an approach would be, given the huge potential for botched delivery.

Reflecting on these scenarios, it might seem in order to temper some of the more critical claims of this book. Much of the argument, after all, has focused on the negative effects of performance measurement, and targets in particular. It has analysed the tension between performance measurement as a means of addressing the problem of political trust, and as a means of steering public administration. It has suggested that attempts to combine the two functions in one target are highly problematic: they trigger political intrusion in organisations, encourage decoupling of rhetoric and practice and damage morale. Moreover, ambitious public-facing targets create political risks, setting up unfeasible goals and potentially exacerbating the problem of political trust. Even when they are met, such targets tend to be ignored or mistrusted. And even when they are not trusted, they nonetheless influence political debate in important ways, encouraging simplistic and distorting framing of policy problems.

And yet, performance measurement and targets represent the ultimate instantiation of rationalistic ideas of accountability. They offer a clear and compelling model for holding policy-makers to account. For all their clunkiness, they sustain a ritual of holding to account which may be highly symbolic, and which may have numerous adverse effects. But performance measurement at least preserves a link between political claims-making and policy outcomes. And it similarly sustains an expectation that claims are grounded in an appraisal of what is politically feasible. This form of accountability may be clumsy and distorting in contexts where democratic processes are functioning well (or well enough). But they become more appealing where serious abuses of authority or reckless policy decisions are a real possibility. In an era during which populist movements are on the rise, the importance of performance measurement in preserving a link between political claims and outcomes should not to be dismissed lightly, however flawed it is in practice.

Bibliography

Bacon, R. & Hope, C. (2013). *Conundrum: Why Every Government Gets It Wrong – And What We Can Do about It*. London: Biteback Books.

Barber, M. (2007). *Instruction to Deliver: Tony Blair, Public Services and the Challenge of Achieving Targets*. London: Politico's Publishing Ltd.

Basu, O. N., Dirsmith, M. W. & Gupta, P. P. (1999). The Coupling of the Symbolic and the Technical in an Institutionalized Context: The Negotiated Order of the GAO's Audit Reporting Process. *American Sociological Review*, 64(4), 506–26.

Baumgartner, F. R. & Jones, B. D. (1994a). *Agendas and Instability in American Politics*. Chicago, IL: Chicago University Press.

(1994b). Attention, Boundary Effects, and Large-Scale Policy Change in Air Transportation Policy. In D. A. Rochefort & R. W. Cobb (Eds.), *The Politics of Problem Definition: Shaping the Policy Agenda* (pp. 50–66). Lawrence: University Press of Kansas.

BBC Online (2006). Immigration System Unfit – Reid, *BBC News Online*. http://news.bbc.co.uk/1/hi/uk_politics/5007148.stm. Accessed 4 June 2015.

Beck, U. (1992). *Risk Society: Towards a New Modernity*. London: Sage Publishing.

Bevan, G. & Hood, C. (2006). What's Measured Is What Matters: Targets and Gaming in the English Public Health Care System. *Public Administration*, 84(3), 517–38.

Bhuta, N. (2012). Governmentalizing Sovereignty: Indexes of State Fragility and the Calculability of Political Order. In K. E. Davis, A. Fisher, B. Kingsbury & S. E. Merry (Eds.), *Governance by Indicators: Global Power through Quantification and Rankings* (pp. 132–64). Oxford: Oxford University Press.

Blair, T. (2010). *A Journey*. London: Arrow Books.

Blinder, S. (Ed.). (2015). *Non-European Migration to the UK: Family Unification and Dependents*. Oxford: Migration Observatory.

Boswell, C. (2009). *The Political Uses of Expert Knowledge: Immigration Policy and Social Research*. Cambridge: Cambridge University Press.

(2012). How Information Scarcity Affects the Policy Agenda: Evidence from Immigration Policy. *Governance*, 25(3), 367–89.

Boswell, C. & Rodrigues, E. (2016). Policies, Politics and Organisational Problems: Multiple Streams and the Implementation of Targets in UK Government. *Policy & Politics*, 44(4), 507–24.

Boswell, C., Yearley, S., Fleming, C., Rodrigues, E. & Spinardi, G. (2015). The Effects of Targets and Indicators on Policy Formulation: Narrowing Down, Crowding Out and Locking In. In A. J. Jordan & J. R. Turnpenny (Eds.), *The Tools of Policy Formulation: Actors, Capacities, Venues and Effects* (pp. 225–44). Cheltenham: Elgar Publishing.

Bovens, M. (2007). Analysing and Assessing Accountability: A Conceptual Framework. *European Law Journal*, 13(4), 447–68.

Bovens, M. & Hart, P.'t (1996). *Understanding Policy Fiascoes*. New Brunswick, NJ: Transaction Publishers.

Boyne, G. A. & Chen, A. A. (2007). Performance Targets and Public Service Improvement. *Journal of Public Administration Research and Theory*, 17(3), 455–77.

Boyne, G. A. & Law, J. (2005). Setting Public Service Outcome Targets: Lessons from Local Public Service Agreements. *Public Money & Management*, 25(4), 253–60.

Bromley, P. & Powell, W. W. (2012). From Smoke and Mirrors to Walking the Talk: Decoupling in the Contemporary World. *The Academy of Management Annals*, 6(1), 483–530.

Brunsson, N. (1993). Ideas and Actions: Justification and Hypocrisy as Alternatives to Control. *Accounting, Organizations and Society*, 18 (6), 489–506.

(2002). *The Organization of Hypocrisy: Talk, Decisions and Actions in Organizations*. Copenhagen: Abstrakt and Liber.

(2009). *Reform as Routine: Organizational Change and Stability in the Modern World*. Oxford: Oxford University Press.

Brunsson, N. & Jacobsson, B. (2000). *A World of Standards*. Oxford: Oxford University Press.

Brunsson, N. & Olsen, J. P. (1993). *The Reforming Organization*. London: Routledge.

Callahan, J. (1983). Cumber and Variableness. In *The Home Office: Perspective on Policy and Administration* (pp. 19–22). London: Royal Institute of Public Administration.

Campbell, A. (2008). *The Blair Years: Extracts from the Alistair Campbell Diaries*. London: Arrow Books.

Canovan, M. (1999). Trust the People! Populism and the Two Faces of Democracy. *Political Studies*, 47(1), 2–16.

Carter, N. (1988). Measuring Government Performance. *The Political Quarterly, 59*(3), 369–75.

(1991). Learning to Measure Performance: The Use of Indicators in Organizations. *Public Administration, 69*(1), 85–101.

Carter, N., Klein, R. & Day, P. (1992). *How Organisations Measure Success: The Use of Performance Indicators in Government.* London: Routledge.

Cheibub, J. A. & Przeworski, A. (1999). Democracy, Elections, and Accountability for Economic Outcomes. In A. Przeworski, S. C. Stokes & B. Manin (Eds.), *Democracy, Accountability, and Representation* (pp. 131–53). Cambridge: Cambridge University Press.

Christensen, T. & Lægreid, P. (2006). Agencification and Regulatory Reforms. In T. Christensen & P. Lægreid (Eds.), *Autonomy and Regulation: Coping with Agencies in the Modern State* (pp. 9–46). Cheltenham: Elgar Publishing.

Cini, M. (1996). *The European Commission: Leadership, Organisation and Culture in the European Union Administration.* Manchester: Manchester University Press.

Clark, J. & Newman, J. (1997). *The Managerial State: Power, Politics and Ideology in the Remaking of Social Welfare.* London: Sage Publishing.

(2017). 'People in This Country Have Had Enough of Experts': Brexit and the Paradoxes of Populism. *Critical Policy Studies,* early online, 1–15.

Committee of Public Accounts (2005). Oral Evidence Taken before the Committee of Public Accounts, 26 October 2005. Ev 1. London: House of Commons.

(2006a). Oral Evidence Taken before the Committee of Public Accounts, 26 April 2006. Ev 1. London: House of Commons.

(2006b). *Home Office Resource Accounts 2004–05 and Follow-up on Returning Failed Asylum Applicants.* Sixtieth Report of Session 2005–6. Report, together with formal minutes, oral and written evidence. House of Commons 1079.

Copeland, G. & Johnson-Cartee, K. S. (1997). *Inside Political Campaigns: Theory and Practice.* London: Praeger Publishers.

Cram, L. (1997). *Policy-Making in the European Union: Conceptual Lenses and the Integration Process.* London: Routledge.

Crozier, M. J., Huntingdon, S. P. & Watanuki, J. (1975). The Crisis of Democracy: Report on the Governability of Democracies to the Trilateral Commission. New York: Trilateral Commission.

Davis, K. E., Fisher, A., Kingsbury, B. & Merry, S. E. (2012a). *Governance by Indicators: Global Power through Quantification and Rankings.* Oxford: Oxford University Press.

Davis, K. E., Kingsbury, B. & Merry, S. E. (2012b). Indicators as a Technology of Global Governance. *Law & Society Review, 46*(1), 71–104.

(2012c). Introduction: Global Governance by Indicators. In K. E. Davis, A. Fisher, B. Kingsbury & S. E. Merry (Eds.), *Governance by Indicators: Global Power through Quantification and Rankings* (pp. 3–28). Oxford: Oxford University Press.

Day, P. & Klein, R. (1987). *Accountabilities: Five Public Services*. London: Tavistock Publications.

Dickinson, H. T. (1994). *The Politics of the People in Eighteenth-Century Britain*. Basingstoke: Palgrave Macmillan.

Diefenbach, T. (2009). New Public Management in Public Sector Organizations: The Dark Sides of Managerialistic 'Enlightenment'. *Public Administration, 87*(4), 892–909.

DiMaggio, P. J. & Powell, W. W. (1983). The Iron Cage Revisited: Institutional Isomorphism and Collective Rationality in Organizational Fields. *American Sociological Review, 48*(2), 147–60.

(1991). Introduction. In W. W. Powell & P. J. DiMaggio (Eds.), *The New Institutionalism in Organizational Analysis* (pp. 1–38). Chicago, IL: University of Chicago Press.

Downs, A. (1957). *An Economic Theory of Democracy*. New York: Harper.

Dunleavy, P. & Rhodes, R. A. (1990). Core Executive Studies in Britain. *Public Administration, 68*(1), 3–28.

Easton, D. (1965). *A Systems Analysis of Political Life*. New York: Wiley.

Edelman, M. (1977). *Political Language: Words that Succeed and Policies that Fail*. Orlando, FL: Academic Press.

(1999). *The Politics of Misinformation*. Cambridge: Cambridge University Press.

Eisenhardt, K. M. (1989). Agency Theory: An Assessment and Review. *Academy of Management Review, 14*(1), 57–74.

Elliott, Larry (2017). 'Populism Is the Result of Global Economic Failure', *The Guardian*, 26 March.

Espeland, W. N. (1998). *The Struggle for Water: Politics, Rationality and Identity in the American Southwest*. Chicago, IL: Chicago University Press.

Espeland, W. N. & Sauder, M. (2007). Rankings and Reactivity: How Public Measures Recreate Social Worlds. *American Journal of Sociology*, 113 (1), 1–40.

Espeland, W. N. & Stevens, M. L. (1998). Commensuration as a Social Process. *Annual Review of Sociology, 24*(1), 313–43.

(2008). A Sociology of Quantification. *European Journal of Sociology, 49* (3), 401–36.

Feldman, M. S. & March, J. G. (1981). Information in Organizations as Signal and Symbol. *Administrative Science Quarterly, 26*(2), 171–86.

Finnemore, M. & Sikkink, K. (1998). International Norm Dynamics and Political Change. *International Organization, 52*(4), 887–917.

Fischer, F. (1990). *Technocracy and the Politics of Expertise*. Newbury Park, CA: Sage Publishing.

Flinders, M. (2001). *The Politics of Accountability in the Modern State*. Aldgate: Ashgate.

(2009). *Democratic Drift: Majoritarian Modification and Democratic Anomie in the United Kingdom*. Oxford: Oxford University Press.

Freeden, M. (2017). After the Brexit Referendum: Revisiting Populism as an Ideology. *Journal of Political Ideologies*, 22(1), 1–11.

Gansler, J. (1980). *The Defense Industry*. Boston, MA: MIT Press.

Geddes, M. (2016). Interpreting Parliamentary Scrutiny: An Enquiry Concerning Everyday Practices of Parliamentary Actors in Select Committees of the House of Commons. PhD, University of Sheffield.

George, A. L. & Bennett, A. (2005). *Case Studies and Theory Development in the Social Sciences*. Boston, MA: MIT Press.

Giddens, A. (1990). *The Consequences of Modernity*. Cambridge: Polity Press.

(1991). *Modernity and Self-identity: Self and Society in the Late Modern Age*. Cambridge: Polity Press.

(1994). *Beyond Left and Right: The Future of Radical Politics*. Cambridge: Polity Press.

Gray, B. (2009). *Review of Acquisition for the Secretary of State for Defence*. London: Ministry of Defence.

Greening, D. W. & Gray, B. (1994). Testing a Model of Organizational Response to Social and Political Issues. *Academy of Management Journal*, 37(3), 467–96.

Grek, S. (2009). Governing by Numbers: The PISA 'Effect' in Europe. *Journal of Education Policy*, 24(1), 23–37.

Gupta, P. P., Dirsmith, M. W. & Fogarty, T. J. (1994). Coordination and Control in a Government Agency: Contingency and Institutional Theory Perspectives on GAO Audits. *Administrative Science Quarterly*, 39(2), 264–84.

Gusfield, J. R. (1981). *The Culture of Public Problems: Drinking, Driving and the Symbolic Order*. Chicago, IL: University of Chicago Press.

Haas, P. (1990). Obtaining International Environmental Protection through Epistemic Consensus. *Millennium*, 19(3), 347–63.

(1992). Epistemic Communities and International Policy Coordination. *International Organization*, 46(1), 1–35.

Habermas, J. (1976). *Legitimation Crisis*, tr. T. McCarthy. Boston, MA: Beacon Press.

Hacking, I. (1990). *The Taming of Chance*. Cambridge: Cambridge University Press.

Hallett, T. (2010). The Myth Incarnate: Recoupling Processes, Turmoil, and Inhabited Institutions in an Urban Elementary School. *American Sociological Review*, *75*(1), 52–74.

Halpen, C. (2010). Governing Despite Its Instruments? Instrumentation in EU Environmental Policy. *West European Politics*, *33*(1), 39–57.

Hampshire, J. & Bale, T. (2015). New Administration, New Immigration Regime: Do Parties Matter after All? A UK Case Study. *West European Politics*, *38*(1), 145–66.

Hansen, H. K. & Porter, T. (2012). What Do Numbers Do in Transnational Governance? *International Political Sociology*, *6*(4), 409–26.

Hatton, T. J. (2009). The Rise and Fall of Asylum: What Happened and Why? *The Economic Journal*, *199*(535), 183–213.

Hay, C. (1996). Narrating Crisis: The Discursive Construction of the Winter of Discontent. *Sociology*, *30*(2), 253–77.

(2007). *Why We Hate Politics*. Cambridge: Polity Press.

Heinrich, C. J. (2002). Outcomes-Based Performance Management in the Public Sector: Implications for Government Accountability and Effectiveness. *Public Administration Review*, *62*(6), 712–25.

(2012). Measuring Public Sector Performance and Effectiveness. In B. G. Peters & J. Pierre (Eds.), *The SAGE Handbook of Public Administration* (pp. 32–49). London: Sage Publishing.

Hildgartner, S. & Bosk, C. L. (1988). The Rise and Fall of Social Problems: A Public Arenas Model. *American Journal of Sociology*, *94*(1), 53–78.

Hoffman, A. M. (2002). A Conceptualization of Trust in International Relations. *European Journal of International Relations*, *8*(3), 375–401.

Hoggett, P. (1996). New Modes of Control in the Public Service. *Public Administration*, *74*(1), 9–32.

Home Affairs Committee (2003). Fourth Report of Session 2002–03, Asylum Removals (HC 654-I). London: House of Commons.

(2004). Home Office Target-Setting 2004, Third Report of Session 2004–2005. London: House of Commons.

(2006a). Home Affairs Committee: Evidence. 16 May 2006. Ev 148. London: House of Commons.

(2006b). Home Affairs Committee: Evidence. 6 June 2006, Ev 170. London: House of Commons.

(2006c). Home Affairs Committee: Evidence. 12 June 2006, Ev 189. London: House of Commons.

(2013). The Work of the UKBA (January–March 2013), Eighth Report of Session 2013–14. London: House of Commons.

Home Office (2001a). *Bridging the Information Gaps: A Conference of Research on Asylum and Immigration in the UK*. London: Home Office.

(2001b). *Home Office Departmental Report*. London: Home Office.

(2003). *Home Office Departmental Report*. London: Home Office.

(2005). *Home Office Departmental Report*. London: Home Office.

(2006). *Fair, Effective, Transparent and Trusted: Rebuilding Confidence in Our Immigration System*, London: Home Office.

Hood, C. (1991). A Public Management for All Seasons? *Public Administration*, 69(1), 3–19.

(2006). Gaming in Targetworld: The Targets Approach to Managing British Public Services. *Public Administration Review*, 66(4), 515–21.

Hood, C. & Dixon, R. (2010). The Political Payoff from Performance Target Systems: No-Brainer or No-Gainer? *Journal of Public Administration Research and Theory*, 20(2), 281–98.

Hood, C. & Peters, B. G. (2004). The Middle Aging of New Public Management: Into the Age of Paradox? *Journal of Public Administration Research and Theory*, 14(3), 267–82.

Hooghe, L., Marks, G. & Wilson, C. J. (2002). Does Left/Right Structure Party Positions on European Integration? *Comparative Political Studies*, 35(8), 965–89.

Hosmer, L. (1995). Trust: The Connecting Link between Organizational Theory and Philosophical Ethics. *The Academy of Management Review*, 20(2), 379.

Inglehart, R. & Norris, P. (2016). Trump, Brexit, and the Rise of Populism: Economic Have-Nots and Cultural Backlash. Harvard Kennedy School Working Paper No. RWP16–026.

James, O. (2004). The UK Core Executive's Use of Public Service Agreements as a Tool of Governance. *Public Administration*, 82(2), 397–419.

James, O. & John, P. (2007). Public Management at the Ballot Box: Performance Information and Electoral Support for Incumbent English Local Governments. *Journal of Public Administration Research and Theory*, 17(4), 567–80.

Jennings, W. (2009). The Public Thermostat, Political Responsiveness and Error-Correction: Border Control and Asylum in Britain, 1994–2007. *British Journal of Political Science*, 39(4), 847–70.

Jennings, W. & Stoker, G. (2016). The Bifurcation of Politics: Two Englands. *The Political Quarterly*, 87(3), 372–82.

Jessop, B. (2017). The Organic Crisis of the British State: Putting Brexit in Its Place. *Globalizations*, 14(1), 133–41.

Johnson, C. & Talbot, C. (2007). The UK Parliament and Performance Challenging or Challenged? *International Review of Administrative Sciences*, 73(1), 113–31.

Jordan, A. J., Wurzel, R. K. W. & Zito, A. R. (2005). The Rise of 'New' Policy Instruments in Comparative Perspective: Has Governance Eclipsed Government? *Political Studies*, 53(3), 477–96.

(2013). Still the Century of 'New' Environmental Policy Instruments? Exploring Patterns of Innovation and Continuity. *Environmental Politics*, 22(1), 155–73.

Keane, J. (2009). *The Life and Death of Democracy*. London: Pocket Books.

Kette, S. & Tacke, V. (2015). University Rankings: Between Organization and Society. In B. Holzer, F. Kastner & T. Werron (Eds.), *From Globalization to World Society: Neo-institutional and Systems-Theoretical Perspectives* (pp. 215–36). London: Routledge.

King, A. (1975). Overload: Problems of Governing in the 1970s. *Political Studies*, 23(2–3), 284–96.

Kingdon, J. (1995). *Agendas, Alternatives and Public Policy*. New York: Longman.

Koopmans, R. (2004). Movements and the Media: Selection Processes and Evolutionary Dynamics in the Public Sphere. *Theory and Society*, 33(3), 367–91.

Kydd, A. H. (2005). *Trust and Mistrust in International Relations*. Princeton, NJ: Princeton University Press.

Latour, B. (1993). *The Pasteurization of France*. Boston, MA: Harvard University Press.

Latour, B. & Woolgar, S. (2013). *Laboratory Life: The Construction of Scientific Facts*. Princeton, NJ: Princeton University Press.

Law, J. & Urry, J. (2004). Enacting the Social. *Economy and Society*, 33(3), 390–410.

Lazear, E. P. (2000). Economic Imperialism. *The Quarterly Journal of Economics*, 115(1), 99–146.

Lewis, J. D. & Weigert, A. (1985). Trust as a Social Reality. *Social Forces*, 63 (4), 967–85.

Luhmann, N. (1964). *Funktionen und folgen formaler organisation*. Berlin: Duncker & Humblot.

(1979). *Trust and Power: Two Works by Niklas Luhmann*. Chichester: Wiley.

(1981). *Political Theory in the Welfare State*, tr. J. Bednarz Jr. Berlin: Walter de Gruyter.

(1991). *Soziologie des Risikos*. Berlin: Walter de Gruyter.

(1997). Limits of Steering. *Theory, Culture and Society*, 14(1), 41–57.

Majone, G. (1989). *Evidence, Argument and Persuasion in the Policy Process*. New Haven, CT: Yale University Press.

Maravall, J. M. (1999). Accountability and Manipulation. In A. Przeworski, S. C. Stokes & B. Manin (Eds.), *Democracy, Accountability, and Representation* (pp. 154–96). Cambridge: Cambridge University Press.

March, J. G. & Olsen, J. P. (1976). *Ambiguity and Choice in Organizations.* Oslo: Scandinavian University Press.

   (1983). The New Institutionalism: Organizational Factors in Political Life. *American Political Science Review, 78*(3), 734–49.

McGoey, L. (2012). Strategic Unknowns: Towards a Sociology of Ignorance. *Economy and society, 41*(1), 1–16.

Merry, S. E. (2011). Measuring the World. *Current Anthropology, 52*(S3), S83–S95.

Meyer, J. W., Boli, J., Thomas, G. M. & Ramirez, F. O. (1997). World Society and the Nation-State. *American Journal of Sociology, 103*(1), 144–81.

Meyer, J. W. & Jepperson, R. L. (2000). The 'Actors' of Modern Society: The Cultural Construction of Social Agency. *Sociological Theory, 18* (1), 100–20.

Meyer, J. W. & Rowan, B. (1991). Institutionalized Organizations: Formal Structure as Myth and Ceremony. In W. W. Powell & P. J. DiMaggio (Eds.), *The New Institutionalism in Organizational Analysis* (pp. 41–62). Chicago, IL: University of Chicago Press.

Micheli, P. & Neely, A. (2010). Performance Measurement in the Public Sector in England: Searching for the Golden Thread. *Public Administration Review, 70*(4), 591–600.

Miller, G. J. & Moe, T. M. (1983). Bureaucrats, Legislators, and the Size of Government. *The American Political Science Review, 77*(2), 297–322.

Ministry of Defence (2004). *Annual Report and Accounts 2003 and 2004.* London: Ministry of Defence.

Mitnick, B. M. (1980). *The Political Economy of Regulation: Creating, Designing, and Removing Regulatory Forms.* New York: Columbia University Press.

Modell, S. (2001). Performance Measurement and Institutional Processes: A Study of Managerial Reponses to Public Sector Reform. *Management Accounting Research, 12*(4), 437–64.

Möllering, G. (2001). The Nature of Trust: From Georg Simmel to a Theory of Expectation, Interpretation and Suspension. *Sociology, 35*(2), 403–20.

Moran, M. (2001). The Rise of the Regulatory State in Britain. *Parliamentary Affairs, 5*(1), 19–34.

Morgenthau, H. (1948). *Politics among Nations: The Struggle for Power and Peace.* New York: Alfred Kopf.

Mudde, C. (2004). The Populist Zeitgeist. *Government and Opposition, 39* (4), 541–63.

National Audit Office (1997). Ministry of Defence: The Defence Evaluation and Research Agency: Review of Performance (HC 411).

(2001). Measuring the Performance of Government Departments. Report by the Comptroller and Auditor General, House of Commons 301 Session 2000–1: 22 March.

(2004). Ministry of Defence: The Rapid Procurement of Capability to Support Operations. Report by the Comptroller and Auditor General. House of Commons 1161 Session 2003–4, 19 November.

(2009). Performance of the Ministry of Defence 2008-09. Briefing for the House of Commons Defence Committee, October 2009. Available at www.nao.org.uk/wp-content/uploads/2010/02/0910_M oD_Performance_200809.pdf. Accessed 4 April 2015.

Nayyar, D. (2013). The Millennium Development Goals beyond 2015: Old Frameworks and New Constructs. *Journal of Human Development and Capabilities, 14*(3), 371–92.

Noël, A. (2006). The New Global Politics of Poverty. *Global Social Policy, 6* (3), 304–33.

Norris, P. (2011). *Democratic Deficit: Critical Citizens Revisited.* Cambridge: Cambridge University Press.

(Ed.). (1999). *Critical Citizens: Global Support for Democratic Government.* Oxford: Oxford University Press.

Offe, C. (1972). *Strukturprobleme des kapitalistischen Staates.* Frankfurt: Suhrkamp.

Oliver, C. (1991). Strategic Responses to Institutional Processes. *Academy of Management Review, 16*(1), 145–79.

Orlikowski, W. J. (1992). The Duality of Technology: Rethinking the Concept of Technology in Organizations. *Organization Science, 3*(3), 398–427.

Orton, J. D. & Weick, K. E. (1990). Loosely Coupled Systems: A Reconceptualization. *The Academy of Management Review, 15*(2), 203–23.

Page, L. (2006). *Lions, Donkeys and Dinosaurs: Waste and Blundering in the Military.* London: Arrow Books.

Painter, C. (2008). A Government Department in Meltdown: Crisis at the Home Office. *Public Money and Management, 28*(5), 275–82.

(2012). The UK Coalition Government: Constructing Public Service Reform Narratives. *Public Policy and Administration, 28*(1), 3–20.

Panchamia, N. & Thomas, P. (2014). Public Service Agreements and the Prime Minister's Delivery Unit. London: Institute for Government.

Pederson, L. H. (2007). Ideas Are Transformed as They Transfer: A Comparative Study of Eco-taxation in Scandinavia. *Journal of European Public Policy*, 14(1), 59–77.

Perrow, C. (1986). *Complex Organizations: A Critical Essay* (3rd edn.). New York: McGraw Hill.

Pfeffer, J. & Salancik, G. R. (1978). *The External Control of Organizations: A Resource Dependence Approach*. New York: Harper and Row Publishers.

Pidd, M. (2005). Perversity in Public Service Performance Measurement. *International Journal of Productivity and Performance Management*, 54(5/6), 482–93.

Poggi, G. (1990). *The State: Its Nature, Development and Prospects*. Cambridge: Polity Press.

Pollard, S. (2004). *David Blunkett*. London: Hodder and Stoughton.

Pollitt, C. (1990). *Managerialism and the Public Services: The Anglo-American Experience*. Oxford: Basil Blackwell.

(2006a). Performance Indicators for Democracy – The Missing Link? *Evaluation*, 12(1), 38–55.

(2006b). Performance Management in Practice: A Comparative Study of Executive Agencies. *Journal of Public Administration Research and Theory*, 16(1), 25–44.

(2013). The Logics of Performance Management. *Evaluation*, 19(4), 346–63.

Pollitt, C. & Bouckaert, G. (2011). *Public Management Reform: A Comparative Analysis – New Public Management, Governance, and the Neo-Weberian State*. Oxford: Oxford University Press.

Porter, T. M. (1992). Quantification and the Accounting Ideal in Science. *Social Studies of Science*, 22(4), 633–51.

(1996). *Trust in Numbers: The Pursuit of Objectivity in Science and Public Life*. Princeton, NJ: Princeton University Press.

Power, M. (1996). *The Audit Explosion*. London: Demos.

(1997). *The Audit Society: Rituals of Verification*. Oxford: Oxford University Press.

(2000). The Audit Society – Second Thoughts. *International Journal of Auditing*, 4(1), 111–19.

(2003). Auditing and the Production of Legitimacy. *Accounting, Organizations and Society*, 28(4), 379–94.

(2004). Counting, Control and Calculation: Reflections on Measuring and Management. *Human Relations*, 57(6), 765–83.

Radaelli, C. (2000). Policy Transfer in the European Union: Institutional Isomorphism as a Source of Legitimacy. *Governance*, 13(1), 25–43.

Rhodes, R. A. (1994). The Hollowing Out of the State: The Changing Nature of the Public Service in Britain. *The Political Quarterly, 65* (2), 138–51.

(1997). *Understanding Governance*. Buckingham: Open University Press.

Richards, D. (2014). A Crisis of Expectation. In M. Smith & C. Hay (Eds.), *Institutional Crisis in 21st-Century Britain* (pp. 15–38). Basingstoke: Palgrave Macmillan UK.

Richards, D., Talbot, C. & Munro, E. (2015). Targets? More Targets! Even Less Change and More Continuity in the Performance Regime in Whitehall. Retrieved from http://blog.policy.manchester.ac.uk/posts/ 2015/08/targets-more-targets-even-less-change-and-more-continuity-in -the-performance-regime-in-whitehall/.

Richardson, J. J. (1982). *Policy Styles in Western Europe*. London: Allen and Unwin.

Rose, N. (1991). Governing by Numbers: Figuring out Democracy. *Accounting, Organizations and Society, 16*(7), 673–92.

Rose, N. & Miller, P. (1992). Political Power beyond the State: Problematics of Government. *The British Journal of Sociology, 43* (2), 173–205.

Russell, M. (2005). *Must Politics Disappoint?* London: Fabian Society.

Sauder, M. & Espeland, W. N. (2009). The Discipline of Rankings: Tight Coupling and Organizational Change. *American Sociological Review*, 74(1), 63–82.

Schmidt, V. A. (2008). Discursive Institutionalism: The Explanatory Power of Ideas and Discourse. *Annual Review of Political Science* 11.

Schneider, A. & Ingram, H. (1993). Social Construction of Target Populations: Implications for Politics and Policy. *American Political Science Review*, 87(2), 334–47.

Scott, R. W. (1995). *Institutes and Organizations*. London: Sage Publishing.

Scott, R. W. & Meyer, J. W. (1991). The Organization of Societal Sectors. In W. W. Powell & P. J. DiMaggio (Eds.), *The New Institutionalism in Organizational Analysis* (pp. 108–40). Thousand Oaks, CA: Sage Publishing.

Seyd, B. (2016). Exploring Political Disappointment. *Parliamentary Affairs*, 69(2), 327–47.

Shapiro, S. P. (1987). The Social Control of Impersonal Trust. *American Journal of Sociology*, 93(3), 623–58.

(2005). Agency Theory. *Annual Review of Sociology, 31*(1), 263–84.

Simmel, G. (1950). *The Sociology of Georg Simmel*, tr. K. H. Wolff. New York: The Free Press.

Sitkin, S. B. & Roth, N. L. (1993). Explaining the Limited Effectiveness of Legalistic 'Remedies' for Trust/Distrust. *Organization Science, 4*(3), 367–92.

Smith, P. (1990). The Use of Performance Indicators in the Public Sector. *Journal of the Royal Statistical Society: Series A, 153*(1), 53–72.

(1995). On the Unintended Consequences of Publishing Performance Data in the Public Sector. *International Journal of Public Administration, 18* (2/3), 277–310.

Sniderman, P. M. & Theriault, S. M. (2004). The Structure of Political Argument and the Logic of Issue Framing. In W. E. Saris & P. M. Sniderman (Eds.), *Studies in Public Opinion: Attitudes, Nonattitudes, Measurement Error, and Change* (pp. 133–65). Princeton, NJ: Princeton University Press.

Star, S. L. & Griesemer, J. R. (1989). Institutional Ecology, Translations and Boundary Objects: Amateurs and Professionals in Berkeley's Museum of Vertebrate Zoology, 1907–39. *Social Studies of Science, 19*(3), 387–420.

St Clair, A. L. (2006). Global Poverty: The Co-production of Knowledge and Politics. *Global Social Policy, 6*(1), 57–77.

Stiglitz, J. (2009). The Great GDP Swindle. *The Guardian*, 13 September 2009. www.theguardian.com/commentisfree/2009/sep/1 3/economics-economic-growth-and-recession-global-economy.

Stoker, G. (2006). *Why Politics Matters: Making Democracy Work*. Basingstoke: Palgrave Macmillan.

Stone, D. A. (2012). *Policy Paradox: The Art of Political Decision Making*. New York: W. W. Norton and Co.

Strang, D. & Meyer, J. W. (1993). Institutional Conditions for Diffusion. *Theory and Society, 22*(4), 487–511.

Strathern, M. (Ed.). (2000). *Audit Cultures: Anthropological Studies in Accountability, Ethics, and the Academy*. Oxford: Routledge.

Streeck, W. (2016). *How Will Capitalism End?: Essays on a Failing System*. London: Verso Books.

Suchman, M. C. (1995). Managing Legitimacy: Strategic and Institutional Approaches. *Academy of Management Review, 20*(3), 571–610.

Taggart, P. A. (1996). *The New Populism and the New Politics: New Protest Parties in Sweden in a Comparative Perspective*. Basingstoke: Palgrave Macmillan.

Talbot, C. (1999). Public Performance – Towards a New Model? *Public Policy and Administration, 14*(3), 15–34.

(2010). *Theories of Performance: Organizational and Service Improvement in the Public Domain*. Oxford: Oxford University Press.

Taylor, J. (2009). Strengthening the Link between Performance Measurement and Decision Making. *Public Administration, 87*(4), 853–71.

Torres, L. (2004). Trajectories in Public Administration Reforms in European Continental Countries. *Australian Journal of Public Administration, 63*(3), 99–112.

Treasury, HM (1998). *Public Services for the Future: Modernisation, Reform, Accountability*, Comprehensive Spending Review: Public Service Agreements 1999–2002 (December), Cm 4181.

(2000). *Spending Review: Public Service Agreements* (July), Cm 4808.

(2002). *Outcome Focused Management in the United Kingdom*. Working document. London: HM Treasury.

Treasury Committee (1999). Seventh Report, Session 1998–99. London: House of Commons.

Turnhout, E. (2009). The Effectiveness of Boundary Objects: The Case of Ecological Indicators. *Science and Public Policy, 36*(5), 403–12.

UKBA (2008). UK Border Agency Business Plan, 2008–11. London: Home Office.

UKBA Independent Inspector (2009). *Asylum: Getting the Balance Right? A Thematic Inspection: July–November 2009*.

(2011). A Thematic Inspection of How the UK Border Agency Manages Foreign National Prisoners. Independent Chief Inspector of the UK Border Agency. London.

United Nations (2017). International Migration: Concepts and Definitions, Statistics Division. Available at: https://unstats.un.org/unsd/demo graphic/sconcerns/migration/migrmethods.htm. Accessed January 2017.

Van Dooren, W., Bouckaert, G. & Halligan, J. (2015). *Performance Management in the Public Sector*. London: Routledge.

Walshe, K., Harvey, G. & Jas, P. (Eds.). (2010). *Connecting Knowledge and Performance in Public Services*. Cambridge: Cambridge University Press.

Waterman, R. W. & Meier, K. J. (1998). Principal-Agent Models: An Expansion? *Journal of Public Administration Research and Theory, 8*(2), 173–202.

Waterman, R. W. & Wood, B. D. (1993). Policy Monitoring and Policy Analysis. *Journal of Policy Analysis and Management, 12*(4), 685–99.

Weaver, G. R., Trevino, L. K. & Cochran, P. L. (1999). Integrated and Decoupled Corporate Social Performance: Management Commitments, External Pressures, and Corporate Ethics Practices. *Academy of Management Journal, 42*(5), 539–52.

Weick, K. E. (1976). Educational Organizations as Loosely Coupled Systems. *Administrative Science Quarterly, 21*(1), 1–10.

Wendt, A. (1992). Anarchy Is What States Make of It: The Social Construction of Power Politics. *International Organization, 46*(2), 391–425.

Werron, T. (2015). What Do Nation-States Compete For: A World-Societal Perspective on Competition for 'Soft' Global Goods. In B. Holzer, F. Kastner & T. Werron (Eds.), *From Globalization to World Society: Neo-institutional and Systems-Theoretical Perspectives* (pp. 85–106). London: Routledge.

Woelert, P. (2015). The 'Logic of Escalation' in Performance Measurement: An Analysis of the Dynamics of a Research Evaluation System. *Policy and Society, 34*(1), 75–85.

Zucker, L. G. (1986). Production of Trust: Institutional Sources of Economic Structure 1840–1920. *Research in Organizational Behaviour, 8*(1), 53–111.

Index